CW00820133

Coping with Stress and Adversity: Inspirational Stories

By Raj Soren

Published by Studio 3 Publishing

Printed by Book Printing UK www.bookprintinguk.com

Remus House, Coltsfoot Drive, Peterborough, PE2 9BF

Printed in Great Britain

ISBN 978-1-9160981-2-1

ACKNOWLEDGEMENTS

I would like to thank my family and friends who have shared their stories, and those who have remained anonymous. Your support has been amazing, and I really appreciate your kindness and generosity.

I am very grateful to Andy McDonell and Studio 3 for believing in me and supporting the editing, promotion and production of this book. I would also like to say a big thank you to Rachel McDermott for her patience and professionalism in editing and proof reading this book.

Special thanks go to: Jyoti Soren, Dr Dhuni Soren, Suraj Soren, Chandni Soren, Lukhi Soren, Professor Andrew McDonnell, Rachel McDermott, Denise McDonnell, Dr Swati Chapman, Kevin Eugene, Kevin Grant, Brian Efediyi, Claire Rogers, Natalie Lockyer, Yuki Yamaguchi, Lily Hart, Chris Teague, Tony Sargeant, Adam Jenkins, Steve Bander, Josh Netherwood, Adrian Trench, Gordon Milward, Karen Lambert, Peter Hinkley, Hazel Shumaker, Ted Brandon, Kathryn Atkinson, Terence Whitcomb, Vladamir Ambramov, Rachel Gue, James Owen, Derek Cayton Jones, Richard Robinson, Jim Bass, Frank Birkenstein, Tim Sorsky, Edwin Gupta, Denis Aubert, Phil Redhouse, Tony Gill, Simon Toy, Princeton Walker, Tom Ive, Hannah Stacey, Antoinette Adams, Trevor Badridge, Sarensen Peters, Jaime Morrish, Adam MacQueen, Tom Dugmore, Rhianna Gately, Iszi Lawrence, Andreas Lerch, Karen Johnson, Kim Burton, Ian Lambert, Catherine Montgomery, Bhavina Rahani, Tomkin Allinson, Terence Barkistend, Nick Hofstead, Simon Zimmer, Edward Henry Kruger, Evgenia Markova, Gillian Friarsdale, Patrick Waagner, Amanda Plumb, Joe Pritchard, Dave Gardner, Kent Splawn, Christy Bischoff, Terry Chittock, Sue Duncombe, Radhia Tarafder, Katy Deacon, Ingrid Walker, Sara Jackson, Tina Masson, Dr Reena Murmu Nielsen, Daniel Fahy, Muhammad Mustaqeem-Shah, Anna Gorst, Gordon Gibb, Subhash Jogia, Earl Lynch, Carys Weed, Colin, Steven, Helen, Kristie Seddik, Mike, Simon, A Smile, David, Jon, Chris, Thomas, Kia, Dave, Keith, Kalpna, Harris, Nick, Rita, and all my friends who have helped me or submitted a story.

CONTENTS

FOREWORD
by Professor Andrew McDonnell

I have been fortunate enough to know Raj personally for over thirty years. Initially, I knew him through our collaboration in the martial art of Jiu Jitsu. I have long been aware of Raj's work as a life coach and his interest in stress management, which happens to be a mutual interest of ours. My work as a practicing Clinical Psychologist specialises in stress reduction and stress management. Much of this work has focused both nationally and internationally on the development of non-confrontational approaches to supporting vulnerable individuals to manage their stress and well-being. I have authored over fifty research articles on this topic, and my book *The Reflective Journey* (2019) outlines an approach to crisis management that has stress reduction at its core. I have learned a great deal from colleagues from a variety of academic disciplines over the years. For my own part, I also specialise in the field of autism, which led to me being awarded the title of Visiting Professor of Autism Studies at Birmingham City University.

It is very important to understand the role that literature on stress from people with authentic lived experiences can have for many individuals. Accounts of real people's coping strategies are profound learning opportunities for all. These types of books face the challenge of conveying complex information in a manner that is simple to understand and relate to. In my view, this is an excellent example of a reflective piece of work, in which I am sure many individuals will find specific elements that they can relate to in their experiences of stress. At the time of writing, the profound uncertainties and unpredictability of the COVID-19 pandemic is still ever-present in our lives. This is an important time for us to be regulated and reflective. If there is a positive and optimistic message that has come from the recent pandemic, it is that human beings can be remarkably resilient and overcome adversity. However, for some individuals, the lack of control and unpredictability can have a profound negative impact on their psychological well-being. Whether people use everyday coping strategies such as physical exercise, mindfulness, or even just being with family and friends, we can always do more.

The first section of this book outlines some of the knowledge we have developed collectively in the area of stress and stress management. Although there are many academically nuanced models of stress, the author presents an easy-to-understand overview of the stress response in the context of modern-day challenges and triggers. Nearly all models of stress and anxiety focus on not only the experience of stress, but also the coping strategies that are necessary to respond to stressful situations. In essence, developing positive coping strategies is an effective approach to managing stress, as it helps individuals to develop physical and emotional resilience.

The first time I remember this type of model being presented was by Richard Lazarus and Susan Folkman (1994). An eminent colleague of mine once said to me that there are three important responses to stress; good coping strategies, more coping strategies, and even more coping strategies. Everyone has to develop their own personal coping strategies for stress. If your primary strategy is using physical exercise to thought block or purge your body of cortisol, then do so. Alternatively, if you are an individual who finds the use of relaxation or mindfulness techniques helpful, then that is what you should apply. Not every coping strategy will work for every person, and it's important to experiment with different stress reduction techniques to find what works for you.

Applied research in this field is beginning to reflect this long-held belief of mine. In 2020, I published an article with my colleagues from the University of Northumbria's Stress Research Group which examined the experiences of frontline care staff supporting individuals who could be described as having 'behaviours of concern' (Rippon et al., 2020). These staff members identified what they thought was most stressful about their work through an interview process. Conducting research in this way avoids the menu-driven approach which is becoming increasingly popular in psychology. Menu-driven approaches ask people to select from a set of pre-generated items what they find to be stressful. In our study, there were some very surprising results that we could not have predicted in this manner. Most importantly, we found that staff in these highly stressful and difficult situations reported that the behaviour of their colleagues was often a highly stressful factor. Even the simple act of whether a plan is followed or adhered to could cause disputes amongst colleagues. This book focuses in a large part on the accounts of individuals from different occupations and their reactions to stressful home and work situations. The commonality and diversity of these responses is intriguing, and again I believe that sharing real life accounts in this manner is the best way to learn new coping strategies to tackle stress.

The examples range from specific professional experiences of stress to the wider world stresses of interpersonal relationships, dealing with life events such as bereavement, and even disputes with neighbours. This sets the scene for the reader to understand the universality of the stress response. It is also important to understand how social context determines our responses. For example, there are rules about what a therapist can say to an individual in their specific context. There are different rules for a dispute with a stranger as opposed to someone you're familiar with. Situations such as these can lead to an experience of profound stress for some individuals, and a desperate desire to either avoid or take control of the situation. Paradoxically, the answer can often be to neither fight nor run away, but to regulate yourself and reflect on the situation.

However, we should also avoid being overly judgemental of our own behaviour. We are, in essence, 'fallible human beings.' Whilst it may be better not to make mistakes in the first place, it is worse to fail to learn from experience. Take the accounts of the people within these pages and learn from their experiences. Proactively take steps to reduce your own stress levels and identify your stress triggers before it is too late. Failing to act can lead to a profound sense of helplessness and hopelessness. It is always better to implement stress reduction into your daily routine than to wait for an explosive build-up of stress, frustration and exhaustion.

Raj Soren has achieved an end product which is easy to read, and I am very confident that there are numerous examples here that will help any reader struggling to manage their own stress levels. This is a helpful guide for any member of society, young or old, to look to for sound advice and representation.

PREFACE

"The greatest weapon against stress is our ability to choose one thought over another."

- William James

I have written this book especially for you, collating real-life stress stories from around the world to help you manage your stress levels by relating to the stories of others. It is written in such a way that you can learn from others who, just like you, have faced stressful times in their lives. Any stress you experience is unique to you; however, this book gives you the chance to walk in someone else's shoes and experience their unique journey. By reading the stories of others, you will start to relate to, understand, and feel some of their emotions which, in turn, will help you to find your own solutions. These solutions and strategies will be ones that you can implement into your life, and that suit your personality and the current challenges that you are facing. This book also provides plenty of practical tips and background theory to help you on your journey to a calmer and more relaxed way of living. If you are already a calm person, that's fantastic, but maybe you can pick up some useful tips to help and support others more stressed than yourself.

The different stress stories I will be sharing will give you a flavour of what others have gone through. There is also an accompanying step-by-step approach on how to look and feel more relaxed in many aspects of your life, be it at work, with family or friends, or when on your own.

It is good to have some stress, as this can incentivise us to reach our goals and aspirations. However, excessive levels of stress can negatively impact our well-being and performance. Managing stress is an integral part of our lives, and the inability to deal with it can have a devastating impact on how we perform across our work and personal lives.

Having an appropriate level of knowledge to tackle stress in all aspects of your life is vital to handling it with greater confidence and ease. One of the most stressful situations I experienced in my life was suffering with COVID-19 for four weeks and not knowing if I was going to wake up each morning, which I will touch upon later on in this book. I also grew up being the only person of colour (as a boy of Indian descent) in a school of 1200 students. Needless to say, this presented its own levels of stress and anxiety for me. I had a good upbringing and strong family support network, was an attentive and hard worker, and even had private tutors, but I still struggled at school and was a slow learner. I failed exams on a yearly basis and had to retake English three times at age 16 and 18. I found exam periods incredibly stressful, and I failed Biology and Chemistry which really knocked my confidence. After retaking my exams, I managed to get accepted on an Applied Biology Diploma at University, and then later completed a degree in Biology and Chemistry. I failed more job interviews than I passed, but later succeeded in a sales, training, and management career. Some 15 years later, I successfully completed my Master's degree in Business and Social Entrepreneurship, whilst still working full time.

Throughout my life, public speaking was also very stressful for me. I would sweat profusely, my legs would feel like jelly, and my vocal cords would tighten so much that I could not speak. I am now, however, able to speak to hundreds of people at any one time. In sports, I was one of the worst in my Jiu Jitsu martial arts class when I first started in 1984. I could not remember the Japanese technology, would be stressed before taking part in gradings, and would suffer from dizziness when I was asked to do rolls in class. Nevertheless, I persisted and became a national champion over several years and then a senior black belt, teaching nationally and internationally as part of The Jiu Jitsu Foundation. I also gained a second black belt in Aikido in my mid-50s. My three children (all now adults) have also gained Jiu Jitsu black belts, which I am immensely proud of. I am privileged to run one of the most successful Jiu Jitsu clubs in The Jiu Jitsu Foundation, with the support of my wife, Jyoti, and my co-instructors. Finally, I gained a Life Coaching Diploma in order to help others improve their confidence and goal-setting, as well as deal with stress. This Diploma also afforded me the opportunity to provide supporting work for the charity Mind in their Bradford location.

I share my background with you in order to highlight that I too had lots of stressors in my life, including ones that really knocked my confidence and lowered my self-esteem. I overcame bullying and racism in my early years, as well as experiencing a lot of anxiety and panic attacks. I had to learn how to be a father, a husband, a sales manager, and a martial arts instructor. You may relate to some of the same stress and lack of confidence that I have experienced, and so I hope that I can offer you some help and advice.

I have written this book to help you recognise and manage your stress and all of its potential triggers, as well as give you the opportunity to learn from other likeminded individuals. I am confident that you will take some of the advice and apply the steps in this book to improve your own life circumstances, as well as open your world to more possibilities.

CHAPTER 1: Understanding Stress

"Life can be found only in the present moment. The past is gone, the future is not yet here, and if we do not go back to ourselves in the present moment, we cannot be in touch with life."

\- Thich Nhat Hanh

The Monk and the Tourists

Let me start with a story about Jane and Bob, who each travelled to Tibet to meet a Monk.

Jane was in her mid-30s and ran her own marketing consultancy business, all whilst being a wife and mother. Bob, meanwhile, was in his mid-50s and working as a manager in the retail sector, not leaving much time for his family, friends, or even himself. These individuals did not know each other yet; however, their paths were soon to cross. They were both suffering from stress due to their respective work and home lives. They both sought a solution, and felt that they had to travel in order to do so. They found themselves searching the internet, each identifying that Tibet may have the answers for them. So, they booked their flights.

Jane and Bob landed in Kathmandu and then took a connecting flight to Lhasa Gonggar international airport in Tibet. Jane and Bob later bumped into each other on a train and, as they were in the same carriage, they struck up a conversation. They talked for hours about how they had both lived stressful lives and how they were hoping that Tibet could provide some answers and peace for them. They realised that they were both staying at the same hotel but on different floors. Jane and Bob met early for breakfast the next day and realised that they had the same habit of leaving their mobile phone on the table just in case an important call, text or email came in. They began to realise that they were quite similar.

They decided to explore the sights, and along the way they came across an elderly woman at the local bazaar who held a handwritten sign that read, "The answer you seek is closer than you think. He is waiting for you."

An arrow was pointing from the woman's sign in the direction of a mountain some miles away. "Who is waiting for us?" Jane and Bob both asked. "The monk that you seek is waiting for you," the woman replied, beckoning them to climb the mountain with her warm, broad smile.

Jane and Bob looked at each other with surprise and excitement, realising that this was the reason they had come all this way. This could be the same wise monk that they had read about in the tourist books and stories of old. This monk must be close to 100 years old by now!

As they gazed up at the mountain, Jane and Bob noticed a temple perched near the top with some smoke billowing out of its chimney. The temple was pulling them towards it like a magnet. Later that day they travelled by jeep to where the temple was situated. They were keen to meet this wise monk, so they made haste to the temple with the help of some local guides. They were excited to meet the monk who was reputed to be the wisest in Tibet; maybe he could provide the answers they sought.

Jane and Bob climbed the 3000 steps to the temple with anticipation, not knowing what to expect. Maybe the monk sat on a golden throne surrounded by many worshipers. They soon found the monk, sitting silently with his prayer beads in his hands and meditating under a tree. Jane and Bob slowly approached the tree, trying not to disturb the monk. The monk noticed their presence and asked them to join him for tea.

"Why have you travelled so far and abandoned your families?" the monk asked. Jane and Bob paused for a few seconds, rather shocked by this monk's directness. They both replied that they had come to seek peace and enlightenment so that they could reduce the stress and worries they were both facing. The monk then started to pour tea to the top of their cups, asking them if that was enough. They both replied "Yes," but the monk kept pouring until the tea was overflowing. "Stop! It's overflowing! It's too much!" Jane and Bob exclaimed. "Yes," the monk replied, "They are overflowing, just like your lives, which are full of stress. You must empty the cup and allow knowledge and peace to enter your heart and mind."

"What do you mean?" Jane and Bob asked, to which the monk replied with the following: "When is enough, enough? The reason you are so stressed is because you are trying to fill too much into this cup. If you keep adding more problems and more stress, how will you find the time to rest your mind, be calm and give back to your family and friends? Your cup is full of feelings and emotions which are raging like a storm. You must learn to calm this storm and take care of this cup before it breaks. Did you not notice the beauty on your journey here? Did you not notice the deer giving birth to its young? Did you not notice the young children begging outside the hotel as you rushed into the bazaar? Did you not notice the beautiful blue lake and the rivers that ran down the side of the mountain? Did you smell the flowers and listen to the sound of nature along the way? You missed most of these sights because you were too eager to achieve your next task and meet me. Just like you are rushing to do all your jobs in your to-do list, you forget to enjoy the journey. Be more like the majestic eagle that soars in the sky above us. The eagle flies with ease by using the fast-flowing currents in the air that Mother Nature provides to keep it above all its troubles."

Jane and Bob felt that they had been struck by lightning after hearing these profound words. They soon began to realise that the monk's teacup represented their lives, and by continually filling them up with stress, they were doing their health and minds a great deal of harm. Stress was affecting their families and they were spending less and less time with them. Even when they did spend time with family, it was not quality time as arguments (for example, about money) would arise, and they would still be thinking about work. Even after vacations, the stress and problems soon came back, with things returning to how they were before. Jane and Bob realised that they were both reaching burnout points within their lives.

Jane and Bob decided that things had to change. They both spent a few more days with the monk and started to appreciate the good things in their lives, which in turn made them calmer. They both travelled back home and kept in touch to see how each was coping with reducing their respective stresses. Could they create new habits and change their lives for the better before the storm broke their teacup?

You may identify with some of the same stresses and worries that Jane and Bob had. The stories in this book will help you and all the Janes and Bobs out there in learning new ways to cope with stress. All that it requires of you is to stay open minded.

1.1: What is Stress?

"Give your stress wings and let it fly away."

- Terri Guillemets

You have picked this book for a reason. Perhaps the title simply caught your eye, or you were looking for some help and advice to overcome the stresses currently present within your life. You may be one of those individuals who says that they do not get stressed, or you may alternatively feel that you are always stressed. I believe most of us probably sit somewhere in the middle.

This book is about sharing tangible stress stories that you can relate to. The experiences described are also supplemented by scientific inputs from doctors, psychologists, and life coaches. Additionally, I have also included some tried and tested methods to help you better manage your stress levels.

You have a choice whilst reading this book: either you can sit as a spectator at the sidelines, or you can live and experience life through the eyes of my book's brave story tellers. Their motivations and intentions come from a good place, and all the contributors wanted to share their stories in order to help others learn from their experiences. Each of their stories is a gift to help you in your own lives.

While reading, please take the time to reflect on your life and see how these stories and coping strategies fit into your own personal playbook when dealing with stress. You may have assimilated coping strategies from your family, friends and work colleagues, or attended courses and read other books on the subject. Providing that your ways of coping already work for you then this is a great start, but if they do not, then perhaps what is within these pages may suggest some alternative methods for you. Ultimately, it is important to have your own tailor-made approach that you have developed, and this can be achieved by applying your learning.

It may take you some time to find strategies that work for you. Some of the new methods you try out may feel like trying on a new pair of shoes. They may feel uncomfortable at first, but over time they mould to fit your feet and their comfort increases. The alternative is to keep trying on different pairs of shoes until you find the one that fits you straight away. In the past, you may have even bought shoes that did not fit you, but you liked how they looked. Over a period of weeks, you began to realise that you made the wrong decision, but could not admit this to your friends and family as they had told you that the shoes looked great on you. Each time you wore them, your feet would hurt and start to form blisters, meaning that you had to apply cream and plasters in order to heal them.

Why have I used this metaphor about shoes? Well, sometimes we have been presented with a method of coping with stress and, despite perseverance, it has not really worked. The poor coping strategy may have had a negative impact on your health and well-being, but you kept going because you did not know any better. It is like treating a bleeding, broken leg with a plaster and paracetamol; a short-term, superficial 'fix' that does not really solve the problem. Sometimes, we need to pause, reflect, and re-evaluate in order to realise that plasters will not fix everything in life.

Personally, I have certainly used the wrong methods to handle stress in the past. I would not invest enough time in myself, instead getting busier and busier and taking on more and more responsibilities until I, at one point, ended up in hospital. I had heart palpitations, hot flushes, an irregular heart rate, clammy hands and feet, and what seemed like pain in my left arm. I honestly felt like I was having a heart attack. The doctors did several blood tests and a treadmill test, and I wore a chest monitor for a week to check my heart rate and rhythm. I was glad to be told that I was not having a heart attack, but I was informed that I most likely had too much stress and anxiety. I was also informed that I had high cholesterol, and began a course of tablets to reduce it. Additionally, I was borderline diabetic, and I had a high liver function test even though I did not drink alcohol. These are all worrying health concerns, and were most likely brought on by stress, diet and lifestyle.

This was a big wakeup call and turning point in my life. I had to reassess how I would change my daily habits. Both my mind and body could not continue to take on consistently high levels of daily stress and possible burn-out. This was a very worrying and stressful time for me, my wife, and my family. I have always been a go-getter and deeply passionate about creating and running non-profit organisations, in addition to leading and training teams both in my career and within martial arts. I would work 40–50 hours per week as a Sales Manager, plus another 20 teaching or organising martial arts classes. Jiu Jitsu and Aikido combined could occupy me seven times a week, plus I also took part in medieval sword fighting classes. I could also be away for multiple weekends at a time to either teach martial arts seminars or learn from others. This was on top of being a husband and father.

Having to deal with the demands of an extremely active lifestyle made me rethink my strategies for dealing with stress. I decided to reduce my responsibilities at work, and stood down from being a Director of The Jiu Jitsu Foundation (which I had done for 17 years). I reduced my teaching sessions and dropped some of my committee appointments, making way for others to lead.

Having such a wakeup call was ultimately my motivation for writing this book: I could improve my mental health and well-being, whilst helping others in the process. As I was halfway through writing, the world was hit by COVID-19, and the game-changer of lockdown came along. Unfortunately, my wife, daughter and I were all later diagnosed with

COVID-19 in November 2020. It was an extremely stressful time for all of us, which will be covered later in this book.

Below is a story written by my father about stress from his experience as a doctor. He also gives a helpful summary about what stress is. Further details about the types of stress, their triggers, and coping methods are given throughout the book.

Dr Dhuni Soren's Story - Retired General Practitioner, England

'As a GP, psychological problems were one of the most common ailments that I treated. This fact is backed up by the General Practice 'Health of the Nation 2018' survey of more than 1500 GPs. The report also shows that stress experienced by doctors when compared to the general population is disproportionately high. Research has shown that stress levels are 25-28% for doctors compared to around 15-18% for the general working population. Doctors tend to work long hours and must deal with many patients who are ill or need routine medical check-ups. This is in addition to dealing with the death of patients, mountains of paperwork, staff management, scrutiny from medical bodies, litigation, and many other stressors. Many Doctors do not have good, regular sleep patterns due to long hours, shift work, and over-exhaustion. Stress can be both physical and psychological reaction to a person's daily activities, and can be harmful to health and well-being if prolonged and frequent. It affects virtually everyone at some time in their life, and is becoming increasingly common in the modern world.

What Causes Stress?

Stress is an in-built physical response of the body to stressful situations, like the pressure of work, challenges or danger of any kind. When faced with such situations, the body reacts quickly by releasing hormones called Cortisol and Adrenaline to help respond to threats. Many things in life, or the anticipation of these things, can lead to stress. These include:
- Worrying about reaching somewhere on time
- Pressure to perform well at school/sports/work etc

- Moving to a new house
- Arguments
- Family conflicts and misunderstanding
- Relationship problems (including divorce)
- Unemployment
- Financial troubles/concerns
- Threats of physical and/or psychological violence
- Sickness and poor health
- Bereavement
- Alcohol and drug abuse

Sometimes, stress arises out of a series of minor episodes, or without any reason at all.

Symptoms of Stress

It is important to recognise stress early in order to take steps to deal with it or avoid stressful situations in future. Everyone reacts to stress differently, and some people are better able to cope than others. There are some common effects of stress that can help people to recognise it. In times of extreme stress, some people may shake uncontrollably, breathe faster and deeper than normal, or even vomit. For those suffering from chronic illness (e.g., Asthma), stress can trigger an attack.

Other symptoms are:
- Periods of irritability or anger
- Loss of interest in day-to-day activities
- Loss of appetite
- Comfort eating
- Lack of concentration
- Loss of libido
- Anxiety
- Excessive smoking, drinking or recreational drug taking
- Depression

Physical symptoms of stress may include the following:
- Tiredness
- Aches and pains due to tense muscles (e.g., neck and back pain and tension headaches)
- Worsening of pain from arthritis and other conditions
- Heart palpitations
- Skin problems
- Irregular or missed periods
- Post-traumatic stress

Stress can affect anyone who has been through an extremely difficult or violent experience, for instance being mugged, witnessing an armed robbery, a violent death or disaster, being involved in a serious car crash, or surviving a fire.

People suffering from Post-Traumatic Stress can experience any of the above symptoms of stress. They may also feel a mixture of emotions including fear, a sense of shame or guilt, depression, and anger. They can also have recurrent memories or images haunting them that can lead to nightmares. These symptoms can last for a short period, or may persist for years and require specialist advice and therapy.

Who Gets Stressed?

Everyone is at risk of being stressed, and everyone will have different mental responses following the body's natural reaction to a stressful situation. For some, it can be a stimulus which motivates them to achieve more. In others, it can have adverse and harmful effects, creating feelings of being unable to cope as well as failure.

How to Cope with Stress

First and foremost, it is important to differentiate between temporary stress that you know will go away when a situation is resolved, and long-term/chronic stress:

- Short-term stress can often be relieved by relaxing, taking a walk, talking/discussing issues of concern to family and friends, and having a good night's sleep

–   Chronic or long-term stress is much harder to deal with and can be psychologically and emotionally damaging to the individual, their family and friends

Managing Possible Causes of Stress

Try to identify the aspects of your life that are causing stress. Sometimes, simple lifestyle changes can make all the difference. For other aspects, you can try different ways and means to cope with stress, such as:

*   Talking to friends or family and sharing your thoughts and fears
*   Organising your time to maximize your opportunities
*   Delegating or sharing your responsibilities at work
*   Avoiding confrontation with difficult colleagues and others
*   Learn to be more assertive
*   Regular exercise
*   Practice yoga or any other relaxing meditation
*   Do not use alcohol or drugs to cope
*   Eat a healthy and balanced diet, rich in fruits and vegetables
*   Find humour or absurdity in stressful situations
*   Never take on more than you think you can cope with
*   Tensing and then relaxing your muscles (starting at the toes and working up to the head)
*   Listening to music or relaxing tapes

When to See a Doctor or Therapist

You should seek advice from your family doctor or any member of your Primary Health Care Team sooner rather than later if the following applies to you:

*   You are unable to identify the condition of stress
*   You are unable to cope with the stress even if identified

- You have symptoms associated with your condition
- You already have pre-existing medical conditions
- You have a family history of stress

Do not ignore the symptoms of stress, and seek help and advice as early as possible as it can harm your health and well-being.'

Dr Swati Chapman's Story – Consultant Clinical Neuropsychologist, England

'I have heard these words often: "I don't understand why I feel like this… I have coped with much worse and never needed help."

In my experience, people who seek out therapy at difficult times in their lives fall broadly into two camps. The first are those who have had struggles with their mental health and, as burdensome as this is, have developed some understanding of what this means for them. The others are those who have displayed lifelong resilience to stressors big and small; individuals who live by the mantra that if they got through those things that they endured in their past, they can get through this too. These individuals often find it difficult to accept help and can feel uneasy about the idea of therapy.

Often, their words are tinged with a sense of bewilderment and even failure. Many times, there is an air of anxiety that tried and tested solutions have not yielded relief from these feelings. Yet, they remain so stuck in the pragmatics of the situation that they lose touch with how they feel or the emotions that may underlie these.

As a Psychologist, I introduce the possibility that surviving the past by problem-solving stress does not offer immunity to its effect on the person. The notion that 'what doesn't kill you makes you stronger' is a popular war-cry for those battling their newfound sense of vulnerability.

I have asked individuals to consider if those things that did not kill them at least felt frightening or difficult at the time, and to consider how it may feel if this happened again and again. One may feel stronger for getting through it; however, one may inevitably come to believe that the world is a dangerous place. This idea of unpredictability and lack of control is indeed the psychological cornerstone for stress and how we deal with it. People very often find it difficult to identify triggers to their presenting difficulties.

People often ask, "Why now? Things are going well, there's no reason for me to feel this way... It can't be stress - it must be something else." The aim of therapy is to create a connection between it all: the present, the past and the things that connect them. It allows exploration of what can be done to break the negative cycle of descent into avoidance, loss of control and hopelessness.

A good start is to allow individuals to 'get to know their stress;' to give it a name and recognise what it looks like; to understand when it arrives and, most importantly, to recognise the feelings it evokes. The first realisation for many individuals is that they had spent so long ignoring and avoiding the things that caused them stress that they had no real sense of managing it effectively, or a plan for how to manage future stress.

Through therapy, one client identified his relationship with stress as 'avoiding the school bully all my life.' He identified that this is where his stress had originated at the age of nine years old: feelings of dread and powerlessness in the school playground which quickly developed into a strategy of avoidance, with his mum asking teachers to keep him away from the bully. These 'strategies' formed dysfunctional patterns of behaviour, including avoidance of stress and ignoring any thoughts or sensations that triggered those past feelings of powerlessness. Most significantly, he was able to identify the trigger for the current episode of low mood as being difficulties with an employee at work. These together formed the basis for a powerful reclaiming of control and moving forward.

How many of us would suggest that ignoring a broken leg and hobbling along regardless would make them a stronger athlete? And yet, we somehow feel that we can carry on past grief and rejection, abuse and hopelessness, stress and anxiety, and that in doing so we become 'stronger' people for handling future stresses. This is not resilience; this is the art of ignoring our pain. Eventually we will tire and struggle to stand.

An emerging approach in psychology is moving away from previous models that emphasised reducing the symptoms of stress, and focusing instead on learning to recognise uncomfortable feelings, and to accept and be present with them. This results in a positive spiral of feelings whereby individuals can better contextualise physiological symptoms, and diffuse the sense of powerlessness over those symptoms.

One thing I have taken away from working with others that I try to apply to my own life is the value of acceptance and self-compassion; acceptance that, when I feel anxious or overwhelmed or sad, no matter how insignificant the current stress may appear to me, my mind and body are experiencing them differently. Forgiveness and self-compassion allow me to take the time and space to forgive myself for perceived responsibility, and to sit with my feelings and wait for them to pass. I have learnt not to try and run with my broken bones, but rather to pay attention when it hurts and allow myself to sit and heal.'

1.2: Types and Causes of Stress

"In times of stress, the best thing we can do for each other is to listen with our ears and our hearts, and to be assured that our questions are just as important as our answers."

- Fred Rogers

Stress affects most people during their lifetime as it has become part of our day-to-day lives. Stress can be harmful to your health and well-being if it persists over a long period of time (WebMD, 2020).

Stress can be a physical and psychological response to stressful stimuli, such as the pressure of work, life's challenges, or facing danger of any kind. The body releases two hormones while under stress - adrenaline and cortisol. Stress is the result of internal or external stimuli, which can then lead to a state of mental or emotional tension resulting from seemingly adverse or demanding circumstances. Stress can happen to all of us and can take many forms. As summarised by Selye (1965), stress is 'the non-specific responses of the body to any demand for change.'

Stress is the body's response to certain situations that we face on a daily basis. Stress can also be subjective, as what may be stressful for you can have little-to-no effect on another person. Stress helps us survive our daily lives and it can improve our performance with a given task. At the same time, stress can also pull us down and be our Achilles' heel, making us less productive if not handled in the right way. It is important to note the difference between short-term or temporary stress that you know will go away when a situation is resolved, and long-term or chronic stress. We will be visiting the different types of stress in this chapter.

The 'Fight-or-Flight' Response

Stress originates from our early reactions in human behaviour, known as the 'fight-or-flight' response (Cherry, 2019). Our body's natural reaction is to sense and avoid danger. If we go back to the Paleolithic Era, we were hunter-gatherers living in caves and forest dwellings where we would have faced danger daily. When searching for food and shelter, the caveman would come across ferocious animals or other cavemen. They would either fight or run to a safe place. Their heart would have been pounding in order to help circulate blood to the muscles for them to run away or fight. The vast majority of us no longer live in caves or have to run away from ferocious animals, but we still experience 'fight-or-flight' responses. Our coping strategies, stress load-carrying ability, and attitudes inform how we respond to the levels of stress we face.

The Nervous System

Stress can impact on the nervous system, specifically the sympathetic nervous system. The Greek physician Hippocrates defined stress as 'that which involves suffering' (Lanese & Dutfield, 2021).

The parasympathetic nervous system, which involves coping mechanisams and the ability to relax, can also be negatively impacted by stress. The surge in hormones from the sympathetic nervous system can lead to aggression, anger and anxiety. This concoction of stimuli, hormones and emotions can either be harnessed, or overwhelm us like a tsunami.

Types of Stress

There are many types of stress, some of which are discussed below (Dias, 2012):

Acute - Acute stress comes on quickly and is typically short-lived. This type of stress can be experienced several times a day. Acute stress is often in response to immediate perceived threats, for example arguments, traffic jams or criticism from others.

Episodic - Episodic stress occurs when someone experiences one stressful acute event on top of another. This often occurs in individuals who have trouble saying no, and those who take on too much. They may be restless and show signs of frustration. This leads to exhaustion and irritable behaviour.

Chronic - Chronic stress is the result of repeated, consistent, and long-term exposure to situations that lead to the release of stress hormones (Scott, 2020). Chronic stress is long term, and can be brought on by many things, for instance a job redundancy, the loss of loved one, or caring for an unwell family member. On many occasions, this can lead to self-neglect and poor coping mechanisms, such as eating junk food, little exercise, taking drugs or drinking excessive alcohol. Chronic stress can lead to other a decline in others areas of health, such as mental illness, depression, increased blood pressure and heart disease.

Eustress - The term originates from the Greek language, 'eu-' (meaning 'good') stress. This type of stress is usually experienced by those who take part in exhilarating sports (such as skiing) or competitions. The levels of stress within the body in these circumstances is sometimes referred to as an 'adrenaline rush.' This stress improves our awareness and muscular strength in order to complete the race or competition. Our heart function improves, our stamina increases, and our thinking is also sharpened. Some experts say eustress even helps our bodies resist infection!

Eustress has both physical and emotional health benefits, and differs from distress according to following characteristics (Mills, Reiss & Dombeck, 2018):

Distress	Eustress
Lasting for the short as well as the long term	Adds energy to your body and mind
Beyond our coping abilities	Only lasts in the short term
Generates unpleasant and unhealthy feelings	Motivational and exciting
Triggers anxiety, concern and other health problems	Perceived as something within our coping ability
Poorer focus and performance	Better focus and performance

Burnout - Burnout is both a physical and mental reaction to long-term stress. The term was first coined in 1974 by Herbert Freudenberger in his book *Burnout: The High Cost of High Achievement.*

Signs of burnout (Volodina, 2010):
- Reduced motivation
- Over-exhaustion, feeling drained and low energy
- Headaches, upset stomach and irritable bowels
- Reduced focus, productivity and creativity
- Emotionally distancing oneself and feeling numb about relationships and work

Other Types of Stress - There are many other types of stress, such as those based on time pressures. There is also situational stress, which is based around life events such as births, marriages, divorce, moving home or taking exams. Another form of stress can be anticipation-related, whereby the mere fact of over-thinking about what may happen before the actual event takes place can cause us stress (ACO Staff Writers, 2021).

Symptoms of Stress

The symptoms of stress can be divided into four areas, as summarised in the following table:

Physical	Behavioural	Mental	Emotional
Tiredness	Trouble sleeping	Indecision	Irritability
Shortness of breath	Changed eating habits	Concentration issues	Anger
Dizziness	Smoking & drinking more	Memory loss	Anxiety/Panic
High blood pressure	Avoiding others	Feelings of inadequacy and low self-esteem	Numbness
Chest Pain	Avoiding activities	Racing thoughts	Hypersensitive
Indigestion	Sexual problems	Low confidence	Feeling drained
Headaches			Feeling Overwhelmed
Aching Muscles			

Many of us tend to replay memories of stress in our minds. This does not help the situation but instead exacerbates it, causing you to simply relive the stress. This and more are covered by Dr Kuathy Gruver in her book *Conquer your Stress with Mind Body Techniques* (2016).

When to See a Doctor or Therapist

You should seek medical advice sooner rather than later if the following applies to you:

- Unable to find the cause of stress
- Unable to cope with the stress
- Have physical signs and symptoms associated with your condition
- Already have other medical conditions

- Have a family history of stress
- A history of mental illness

Buckets and Funnels

Work carried out by Brabban and Turkington in 2002 led to the development of a term known as the 'Stress Bucket.' As human beings, we take on several different stresses simultaneously and keep on filling our 'bucket' with them. If we keep taking on more responsibility without releasing some of these existing stresses, then our bucket becomes full and overflows. Once you start to do things you enjoy, rest and relax, talk to trusted people, and plan your time more effectively, the body and mind can release some of this stress, tension and anxiety that has built up.

Another term is the 'Stress Funnel.' If you have a wide 'funnel' then you are likely to be able to handle more stress. However, this funnel too can overflow if you do not let go and release the pressure at its bottom. If the bucket or funnel overflows, that is when we show signs of stress which, if not managed appropriately, will drastically and negatively affect our behaviour. Therefore, we need to look at helpful coping strategies that help our health and well-being.

We all have a certain ability to manage stresses, also known as our 'stress load.' If you keep taking on more responsibility and not offloading some of the load then, as the expression goes, the last straw will break the camel's back. Unless you can adapt to and control the stressors around you, stress will control you.

Stress and Physics

Stress can also be explained in terms of Physics, with the stretching of an elastic band used as a simple analogy for human stress. If an elastic band is stretched, it will soon return to its original shape; however, over-stretching it will break it. This is also true of our bodies and mind, and we should not over-stretch ourselves with excess stress.

In regard to linking with stress with extension and compression, this can be explained by Dr Robert Hooke's Law (Hooke, 1678). Extension happens when an object increases in length, and compression happens when it decreases in length. This is related to a person's ability to deal with stress and how long they experience this level of stress for. This can be related to the stretching of an elastic band. For the scientifically minded, the section below explains this in more detail: The extension of an elastic object, such as a spring, is described as:

Force = Spring constant × extension
This is when: Force (F) is measured in Newtons (N)
Spring constant (k) is measured in Newtons per Metre (N/m)
Extension (e), or increase in length, is measured in Metres (m)
In terms of stress, this could therefore be:
Stress = Person's ability deal with stress x the period of stress applied

1.3: Performance and Stress

"I promise you nothing is as chaotic as it seems. Nothing is worth diminishing your health. Nothing is worth poisoning yourself into stress, anxiety, and fear."

— Steve Maraboli

Too little stress can lead to unproductivity, being less engaged and motivated at work, and being too laid back. There is arguably a 'Goldilocks Zone' (also known as Eustress) which allows the optimum level of stress and maximum amount of productivity. This stress level will vary from person to person. There is equally a tipping point in each person, whereby too much stress starts to have a negative impact on productivity. The body becomes tired, fatigued, and exhausted, leading to anxiety, anger, and irritability. If this level of stress is consistently high over a long period of time, it can lead to sickness, burnout, panic attacks, and low levels of productivity. This can lead to other physical and mental health problems.

Companies and organisations are becoming more aware of the link between stress and productivity. This is the main driver for companies developing and introducing courses on topics such as well-being, resilience, relaxation techniques, and mindfulness. Managers are also learning to identify the signs and symptoms of stress, as well having more empathy, listening to concerns, and identifying triggers. Employers are also beginning to understand the importance of compassionate leadership, and taking a more caring and understanding approach at work, including encouraging their employees to take regular breaks and holidays.

All this work in stress awareness is being driven by Human Resources and company value statements. The impact of COVID-19 and lockdown has accelerated this training and support due to the negative impact of isolation, having to work from home, and the possible downsizing of organisations. This level of support is admittedly more difficult if you are a sole trader and work for yourself, or you run a small to medium size enterprise (SME). It is therefore important to seek help and advice from HR departments, occupational health, or external organisations such as private healthcare or charities. Many organisations have had to downsize, and jobs previously done by two or three people are now expected to be done by one person. This adds additional stress and pressure for employees, who are also expected to show more flexibility, agility, and adaptability in these ever-changing times.

The test of a good company, manager or organisation is whether or not they can recognise the increased demands on their staff. This means putting plans in place to provide the right level of help and support, and have well-being at the core of their working practices (Aldana, 2021). They must also allow for open and honest conversations without judgement, and listen to employees' concerns about their work and home lives. They should have the right change management process in place with HR and occupational health. Healthy, happy, motivated staff members will always be more loyal and productive than over-stressed individuals.

1.4: Stress Triggers

It is important to know what contributes to an increase in your stress levels, as this is different for each person. The first step towards conquering your personal stressors or stress inducers is to identify them. Triggers or stressors fall into several categories:

Work triggers: Caused by the pressures of performing in the workplace or working from home. These may include trying to meet tight deadlines, an unpredictable boss, or trying to cope with endless demands.

Emotional triggers or internal stressors: Typically fears and anxieties. These may include, for example, concerns about getting married or finding a job. This creates a sense of helplessness or lack of control over one's life

Family triggers: These may include changes in a relationship, financial problems, and teenage and parental relationships.

Change triggers: Such as new employment, moving homes, a new relationship, or having a baby.

Physical triggers: This may be due to over-working, or little rest or sleep. This may also include pregnancy, premenstrual syndrome, or even too much exercise.

Decision triggers: These may be caused by making important decisions, like getting married or divorced, or a career change.

Environmental triggers: These may include pollution, noise, temperature, or a lack of space.

Social triggers: These include public speaking, attending parties, dating, and meeting new people.

Chemical triggers: These include alcohol, drugs, caffeine, nicotine etc.

Phobia triggers: For example, claustrophobia (fear of enclosed spaces), fear of flying, arachnophobia (fear of spiders), or having to speak in public.

Disease triggers: These may be due to stress arising from health problems or concerns.

Pain triggers: These can include acute or chronic pain from a previous injury or illness

Uncertainty

Post-World War II, a study was conducted regarding the bombings in London, England and the surrounding areas. It was found that, for those who lived within the areas bombed in London, the number of people with ulcers present increased by 50% (Miller, 2010). More interestingly, it was also found that the number of people with ulcers in the areas *surrounding* London (i.e., where bombings were less likely to take place) increased by 500% (Jones, 2012).

The rationale for this was that for residents outside London, there was more irregularity and less predictability surrounding whether bombings would occur, contributing to the body responding in this way.

If this uncertainty during war times can lead to ulcers and the body reacting in such a manner, then it is plausible to say that the uncertainty in recent times around COVID-19 and lockdown could also impact on our stress and well-being in a physical manner. You may have asked many questions during these uncertain times, such as:

- When will things get back to normal, if at all?
- When will my health get better?
- When can I start meeting people and hugging again?
- Will I be able to find a new job?

You have control over certain situations in your life, but not all. You may not be able to change external factors outside of your control, but you can change how you deal with and respond to them (Robinson & Smith, 2021). In many situations, we feel we cannot change the situation, but it is important to note that it is you who is making the decisions!

Triggers Exercise

Within the below table, put a tick in the box(es) for those triggers that currently cause you stress, thus giving you a good idea of what presently impacts you. The rest of the table (explained further in the next section) can then help you to formulate and track your progress, as well as log how you could manage those triggers and thoughts. There is no time limit to do this, and you can go beyond 30 days.

Trigger	Currently experiencing	Reduction/ Elimination Tactics	30 Day Coping Strategy	Outcome
Work				
Emotional				
Family				
Change				
Physical				
Decision				
Environment				
Social				
Chemical				
Phobia				
Disease				
Pain				
Total				

Reducing Triggers

Rather than try to eliminate your triggers entirely, aim at reducing their number and intensity. For example, if your morning work commute forces you to drive two hours in heavy traffic every day, try another option such as public transport or carpooling. You can even bring along an activity to pass the time on the commute, such as reading the morning paper, a good book or listening to music.

Go back to the above table and add an 'R' or 'E' for each item to column three (R for reduce or E for eliminate), as well as a 'C' against each item you want to learn a coping strategy for. Now that you have identified and organised your triggers and stressors, you are in a better place to make genuine positive steps to improve and reduce your stress levels.

1.5: Stress Statistics

You may be familiar with some of the levels of stress across different industries. Here are some useful statistics to allow you to understand how big an impact stress plays on the lives of people across the globe.

A Labour Force Survey found that the UK alone had just over half a million workers who suffered from work-related stress, depression, or anxiety between 2018-2019 (LFS, 2020). Each year, millions of workdays are lost due to stress across the globe.

This same survey also found that stress, depression or anxiety accounted for 44% of all work-related ill health cases, and 54% of all working days lost due to ill health. The survey also found that public services such as education, administration, defence and education employees had more depression, stress and anxiety than other sectors.

The study identified that the main factors causing work-related stress, depression or anxiety were workload pressures, including tight deadlines, too much responsibility, and a lack of managerial support.

A Gallup poll in 2019 showed that Americans appear to be among the most stressed out populations in the world, with stress rates being 20% higher than other countries (2019). From this survey, 65% of the 30-49 age group experiences stress. 64% of Americans aged between 15-29 also reported feeling stressed, while 44% of people older than 50 felt the same.

In a study comparing incidences of burnout between US physicians and a population control sample, Shanafelt and colleagues observed symptoms of burnout in 37.9% of physicians, compared to 27.8% of the control population which was statistically significant (2012). Burnout prevalence is between 5% and 45% of the working population depending on the sector and profession (Li, Li & Castaño, 2019).

The levels of stress shown by these surveys can look quite worrying, however it's good to be aware of these figures so we can do something to improve our situation and working environment.

CHAPTER 2: Work-Related Stress

"Remember that stress doesn't come from what's going on in your life. It comes from your thoughts about what's going on in your life."

- Andrew Bernstein

Work-related stress is defined as a negative and harmful reaction to undue pressures and demands placed on people at work (CIPD, 2021). Dealing with stress at work can be very challenging as individuals may be dealing with things that their knowledge and abilities have not prepared them for, and which can challenge their ability to cope.

Stress can occur in a wide range of work circumstances, but is often made worse when employees feel that their company or colleagues offer little support. Employee stress levels can spiral if they feel that they have little control over the situation. This can lead to staff sickness, which costs billions of dollars each year to businesses and the economy (Daff, 2021).

2.1: Work Stress

"It's not stress that kills us, it's our reaction to it."

- Hans Selye

What are stress-related hazards at work?

Stress-related hazards at work can be divided into two parts; work content and work context:

31

Work Content	Work Context
• Monotonous tasks • Meaningless tasks • Lack of variety • Workload and work pace (too much or too little to do, work under time pressure, etc.) • Working hours (strict or inflexible, unsocial, unpredictable, badly designed shift systems) • Lack of participation in decision-making, lack of control over work processes, pace, hours, methods, and the work environment)	• Career development (job insecurity, lack of promotion opportunities, under or over promotion) • Status (work of 'low social value,' over or under qualified for a job, unclear or unfair performance evaluation) • Pay (rate payment schemes, inequality) • Role in the organisation (unclear roles and responsibilities) • Interpersonal relationships (inadequate or unsupportive supervision, poor relationships with colleagues, bullying/harassment, violence, isolated or solitary work) • Organisational problems (poor leadership and communication, lack of strategy, unclear rules) • Work-life balance (lack of support for home problems, poor governance and policies)

Work Stress Statistics

A survey by Cartridge People (2019) produced some shocking statistics about work stress in the UK. They found that 48% of the British population are stressed at least once a week. For 12% of the population, that is every single day. Men feel more stressed at home than at work, while more women feel stressed at work than at home. More than half of women are stressed at work at least once a week - for 23% of women, at least once a day.

Workload was reported as a stressor for 43% of men compared to 53% of women. 30% of women reported that they go on social media at least once a day due to stress. More than 1 in 10 women have left their job due to stress in the last 12 months, and more than 1 in 10 people are thinking about leaving their job due to stress. 16% of women are stressed by their boss, whilst one in three women will escape to the toilet at least once a week when stressed. Almost half (39%) of the British population is stressed at least once a week at work. For 15%, it's every single day.

The Health and Safety Executive (HSE) England report on 'Work-related stress, anxiety or depression statistics in Great Britain' (2020) showed that from 2019-2020, there were an estimated 828,000 workers affected by work-related stress, depression or anxiety. This represents 2,440 per 100,000 workers, and results in an estimated 17.9 million working days lost. In 2019-2020, work-related stress, depression or anxiety accounted for 51% of all work-related ill health and 55% of all days lost due to work-related ill-health.

Over recent years, the rate of self-reported work-related stress, anxiety or depression has increased. However, there is no clear trend in the rate of working days lost per worker for work-related stress, anxiety, or depression. Days lost per worker is a combination of the overall case rate and the days lost per case.

Kevin Eugene's Story – Imaging Informatics Technologist, Canada

'The best piece of advice I received about how to manage and deal with stress was from an article I read in Men's Health as a young man. It described how there are many types of stress, such as mental, physical, or logistical. The important thing to note overall is to try and move past the stress and deal with the item at hand. It is also important to reflect on what about those instances put us in that stressed state. The article concluded that many of the feelings we describe about our experience of stress are very similar to fear. It concluded that if any one person was to say they were stressed about a specific thing, the best resolution was to detail what scared them about that stressful thing, and create a plan to deal with that instead.

From my own personal journey, I found myself in what I would describe as a highly stressful scenario several years ago when I started a new job. The new position entailed more money and more responsibilities, but I would later find out that two of my new colleagues were not fond of me. In the beginning, it seemed like I was being micromanaged. I was scrutinised for every action I took, and overall felt that these two individuals were not trying to build me to their level of expertise but instead using their energy to demonstrate as often as they could that I was not on their level. Communication was often one way in direction, and if I asked for assistance the answer was always noticeably short and vague. Feedback about areas of lacking knowledge often went straight to our supervisor instead of being communicated to me first.

In an attempt to mitigate this contempt, I would often take extra reading materials home about some of the IT that was in use and would often show up, in my own time, to try and learn about the workflow and infrastructure of information for which I was responsible. This effort never seemed to be acknowledged by my peers and was never part of the feedback given to the supervisor.

Given that I was new to the position, I didn't know many other peers in the field, and had difficulty troubleshooting this tense situation. I also suspected that, even if I were to have the favour of someone else in the field, they may not necessarily be willing to confront these individuals.

My supervisor had made attempts to intervene and make the environment more constructive, but ultimately, they concluded that I did not satisfy the requirements of the probationary period and needed to return to my old job (in public healthcare). While this came as a blow to my ego, when I asked myself what stressed me out about the job, I could immediately identify what it was I was afraid of. Ultimately, I was afraid of dealing with two toxic personalities who did not create a healthy working environment. Thus, for my own well-being, I conceded that it was worth giving up a little extra money to not be around those individuals and their negative attitude.

Overall, this approach to stress has made it such that the feeling of impending doom never consumes me. It is OK to be sad, frightened or fearful, as these uncomfortable feelings often pave the way to creating solutions.'

Kevin Grant's Story – Employee Benefits Consultant, England

'I've always been a natural worrier. I used to worry about anything and everything, whether it was within my control or not. Add being a perfectionist on top of that, and you can see how being stressed (a lot) was just a part of my life. Having said that, I didn't really believe stress had a negative impact on me - I saw it as just a part of my character.

In the early part of my career, I was able to progress relatively quickly, and excelled due to my conscientious, pragmatic approach. I progressed through the ranks, from administrator, to senior administrator, to team leader. Looking back on first 10 years of my career, these were relatively stress-free times. Although I was good at my job, I didn't feel I was being challenged enough and started to lose interest.

There came a point where the company I was working for had been acquired by a larger organisation, and I decided that this was an opportune time to change career and do something more challenging. I saw being a consultant as glamorous, well respected, well-paid, but most of all, interesting job. I've never been much of a salesperson, and knew the role involved selling to an extent, but believed I could eventually acquire the necessary skills and be good at it if I just worked hard.

I took the plunge and landed my first full consultancy role shortly after the acquisition at another company. It was a fresh start, and things went relatively well in the first year. Then my troubles started. In the second year, I was introduced to sales targets, and quickly realised I needed a whole different skill set to be successful. These sales skills weren't particularly aligned with my character and personality. My line manager, who I didn't get on with, reminded me in no uncertain terms that I was in a sales job, and that if I didn't step up, I would be gone. All of a sudden, I found myself in a very uncomfortable place: my performance was under real scrutiny, and all my client meetings were being supervised and graded. I felt a real sense of dread just getting up to go to work, and this was reflected in my demeanour, to the point that people would make comments like, 'You look like you really don't want to be here.' The pressure mounted, and I started to make fundamental mistakes which finally resulted in the loss of a major client and some significant income. This was the ammunition needed to put me on a 'performance review' and potentially get rid of me. I was encouraged to resign, and so I did. This experience destroyed my confidence.

I took the safe option (or so I thought) and returned to operational roles for a while. However, things didn't go to plan, and I was made redundant not once but twice. The only thing that kept me going was knowing that my family depended on me, and I needed to support them no matter what. I wasn't a happy person though, and every mistake, no matter how small, made me anxious.

My kids were growing up fast and money was getting tight: operational roles were not going to pay the mounting bills and childcare costs. I had no choice but to return to a consultancy role, which was the only realistic way to maintain our lifestyle. Again, things didn't go well, and in 2016 I was signed off with work related stress and anxiety for two weeks.

It was during this time that I knew things had to change. I sought counselling, which really helped me to resolve my anxiety and confidence issues. The counsellor listened, evaluated, and taught me a few simple skills to help manage my anxiety. Fortunately, I had a really supportive manager who saw my potential and gave me the space I needed to reset myself. Soon, I was back on track and performing well. I had regained my confidence and started to thrive in a role I had originally thought that I was unsuited for.

So, what did I learn from my discussions with a counsellor? There were lots of lessons, a few of which I will summarise:

- Everyone makes mistakes - accept it. No one is perfect, because there's no such thing as perfection
- Don't be afraid to ask for help; it's not a weakness, human beings are interdependent
- You need to acknowledge when you're feeling stressed or anxious. Don't try to ignore or suppress it
- There will always be times when you feel stressed or anxious. This a temporary state which will come and go, and can be managed
- Dispel irrational thoughts and feelings by asking yourself, 'What's the worst that can happen? What is actually likely to happen based on evidence?'
- Only worry about the things you can control, then take steps to control them
- Use deep breathing exercises to overcome immediate feelings of stress or anxiety
- Remember to take time out for yourself and do something that you love. It's important to value yourself, and you absolutely deserve it
- Get a decent amount of sleep
- Exercise regularly. You don't have to spend hours in a gym or running, just 20-30 minutes daily and you'll be surprised how much of a difference it makes
- Make a list of 10 things you're grateful for daily. This helps to put life into perspective

I hope there is a least one thing you can take away from my experience. If only a single person benefits from it, I will be delighted.'

Brian Efediyi's Story - Biotech Engineering Manager, England

'2020 is a year that many would soon forget, for obvious reasons. It brought with it many, varied challenges to individuals and businesses alike. When unprecedented situations presented themselves during the global pandemic, the world had to adapt. Many businesses had to adapt to the new normal of remote working, which for many was a novelty. In my job working for a biotechnology organisation, we too embraced measures from senior leadership on how to protect our employees, as well as keep our commitments to our customers. Having the entire business work remotely became and still is a new norm. In my role as the manager of an engineering team, the question became 'How do I ensure the well-being of my team (remotely) and keep them engaged with work?' I am certain many leaders pondered questions along the same vein as mine. One of the key measures taken was to ensure my team had the necessary office equipment to be productive while working remotely. Firstly, a homeworking risk assessment was prepared to ensure my team had a conducive environment to work in. When this was confirmed, they were allowed to have access to equipment from the office such as monitors, docking stations, and even office chairs which provided better lumbar support.

Receiving progress reports on the various engineer-to-order projects and new product introductions is a crucial part of ensuring commitment to defined timelines. Bi-weekly face-to-face team meetings were replaced with weekly online meetings. It was important to increase the frequency of the progress report meetings to accommodate the fact that we rarely saw each other personally. During online team meetings, the first item on the agenda was Team Well-being. This time was dedicated to speaking to each member of the team to ask how they were individually, and how their family was adapting. Any issues that required further attention were escalated but otherwise closely monitored. It was also important to setup one-to-one time with each team member, where subjects that could not be discussed during the team meeting were discussed, as well as to provide feedback on performance, and to gain understanding of any further support that could be provided to the employee. Instant messaging and calls on Microsoft Teams replaced walking over to a colleague's desk in the office. Although this could not replace the richness of meeting face-to-face, it allowed for consistent contact, considering the circumstances.

Remote working provided its fair share of challenges. Team members with families had to juggle interruptions to daily work. As a manager, it was necessary for me to understand these dynamics, and allow for their impact on my team's performance. To reduce this impact, I set even clearer goals, expectations, and encouraged earlier escalation of issues, to ensure that there was sufficient time to take mitigative steps.

Although 2020 was challenging in many ways, I observed growth in myself and my team. I have seen that it is people who make a business successful. People really are its greatest assets. We have grown to appreciate one another on a deeper level, knowing that life can be fleeting. We value even more what each team member contributes to the business, and the impact of their personal interactions with us. Quite oddly, the challenges of 2020 have brought us closer together, which I believe will contribute to a stronger team effort to face whatever challenges the New Year has in store for us all.'

Lukhi Soren's Story – Fashion Designer and Founder of UnLukhi, England

'I was extremely excited to start my part-time job as a student in a vintage store, which I had set my heart on for some time. The first few months seemed to start off well and the people seemed friendly enough. However, I soon began to realise that I was being treated unprofessionally and with extreme prejudice. I had two different managers who did shift work, and one of them had extremely poor management and people skills. She used to give me basic jobs, such as sorting clothing stock by myself, which is a two-person job, cleaning when no one else was and working in a cold storage room all day with no heating. She was rude and obnoxious, and would talk behind peoples backs and openly criticise other team members then act differently to their faces. She would also criticise the company and make life difficult for me alone, not other members of staff.

Once there was a miscommunication with shifts, and she decided to ring me up and shout at me down the phone, on the work WhatsApp group chat, and the next day in person. She used phrases such as, 'I am not your mum,' and described me as 'disposable, lazy, and inconsiderate.' She threatened my job, was openly ageist and constantly questioned my values. This was later disputed as a miscommunication, and I received no backlash from any other employee except her. I reported this situation to senior managers and got no help after this inappropriate and unprofessional display. I felt unsafe, threatened, and afraid to go back. The money I was being paid did not seem worth it for the amount of stress and strain this job had created on my mental health. I decided to leave the job rather than take any more of this abuse. I had lost a lot of confidence and had a big knock my self-esteem. This first experience was very unpleasant, and it put me off working for some while.

I have now found another job working with a far better and professional organisation, so don't give up. You may take some knocks, but dust yourself down and get back up to fight another day. This is what I did, and it later made me more determined to start my own online business, and to never treat others like that when I am a manager and owner. I also learned that giving something up is never a bad thing when it comes to your mental health and well-being.'

2.2: Complaints at Work

"Any fool can criticise, condemn and complain – and most fools do. But it takes character and self-control to be understanding and forgiving."

- Dale Carnegie

Antonia Fair's Story - Key Account Manager, Italy

'I had been working in the engineering business sales environment for over 15 years, which I thoroughly enjoyed, and life was good. I was keeping my head down and delivering the required outcomes for my role as a sales executive. For many years, I had taken great pleasure in building excellent customer relations and delivering first class customer service. Little did I know that this was about to become my potential downfall, and lead to an exceedingly difficult and stressful time in my career.

On a damp and dull Monday, I was sat in my usual place at my desk, when I saw my manager's name flash up on my mobile phone screen. I promptly answered the phone with my usual cheery hello and greeted my boss by name. I could tell this was not an ordinary call as I heard my manager take a slow, deep, and audible breath - then their words hit me like a sledgehammer. "There has been a customer complaint," he began. I did not really hear much after that; the horror of customer dissatisfaction was already spinning in my head. I was told at the end of the conversation that I was being suspended, and had to stop working immediately and cease all contact with colleagues and customers. I was formally suspended whilst an investigation took place, with no date set as to the outcome of the investigation and when or if I could go back to work.

The whole experience was surreal. It was analogous to being in the middle of a fast rollercoaster ride, with the wind blowing in my hair; laughing and happy, in full flow of maximum enjoyment, then the ride makes an abrupt emergency stop by hitting a brick wall. At the time of the conversation, I recollect the room seemed to spin around me as I gasped for breath: suddenly my world was in chaos and panic gripped my body.

I tried to calm myself by thinking about good customer engagements over the preceding weeks, and I reassured myself that nothing untoward had happened. Unbeknown to me, however, I had made a huge error of judgement.

In my efforts to try and help a customer to alleviate their work pressure, I had volunteered to approach a third-party provider with an open and generic question. The answer to this question would give insight as to whether a project plan would be viable or not, and therefore save a huge amount of time on both our parties. The customer had given me permission to do this, and I thought I was on safe ground because the question was so generic, requiring a simple yes or no answer. Unknown to me, the third-party company took it upon themselves to approach one of my customers directly. The customer was not happy in receiving the call and sent in a complaint to my employer.

The stress was unbearable over this suspension period. I felt alone and isolated, and did not feel that I could go anywhere for help. My mind was full of worries about what would happen to me and if I still had a job to go back to. The investigation took several weeks to complete, and the full details were kept confidential and withheld from me. I started to ask myself, how on earth would I ever be able to endure what was clearly going to be a prolonged period of intense stress?

I would like to share with you how I coped during this stressful time. I started small and I asked myself the following questions:

1. What does the core of this stress look like?
2. What does it feel like?

At that time, the stress felt like an anonymous, dark imposter that was slowly getting a grip over me. It was insipid, toxic, and all-consuming. I had to name it to give it an identity, to see it clearly for what it was. I dug deep and came to the realisation that the root source of this stress was based on several fears: the fear of losing my job, fear of not being able to pay my mortgage, and fear of losing my home. As a single parent with dependents, these were all very real threats. I decided I had to calm this monster within, and release myself completely from this creeping paralysis.

What did I do? I asked myself another important question: What had led me to this place, and what intentions were behind the decisions I had taken?

I promised that I would give myself a 100 percent honest answer, and then I journeyed inwards and did much soul searching. I concluded that my intentions had been genuinely pure. The situation had arisen from a gap in my knowledge, of which I was totally ignorant at the time. In other words, in this scenario, I was unconsciously incompetent. My desire to deliver superb service had been lost in translation. This revelation brought me immense comfort. The knowledge that I had genuinely tried to do my best, with pure intentions, was enough for me to make my peace. I reminded myself that an innate part of being human is to be capable of error. I then forgave myself.

Despite this, mentally I was still seeking some outside insights based on experience and knowledge. After all, the level of trust I had in myself at this point was incredibly low. A simple phone call and a few facts and figures thrown out to me by a seasoned ex-industry friend, who had been fortunate enough to work in a top echelon position, was the medicine I needed to begin my road to recovery. I realised that I was not alone in this scenario - many others had trodden this same path before me, and there

42

would be many others to follow me.

From this moment, I resolved that I would continue to draw on my years of professionalism by applying the same principles that I have always worked with to this situation. In other words, I tapped into an internal bank of resources that I had been unwittingly building up over the years, which were perfect to deal with the challenging situation I now faced. From this moment, I decided to focus only on the elements of this that I could control; everything else would be left out in the cold.

As the investigation rumbled on, I was still very much left in the dark. Snippets of details were being drip fed to me, and my mind was naturally straining and struggling to fill the gaps. Each exposure to this stressful situation came mainly from phone calls with my manager, which usually led to another exhausting onslaught of mindful overdrive and depleted energy. Then suddenly, out of nowhere, another stress reducer appeared.

A friend of mine popped up out of the blue and invited me to stay with them in Spain. I got permission to travel from my employers. By removing myself from the actual stressors completely, my stress levels began to fall further. Angst and anxiety were now replaced with the tranquility of a rural Spanish Villa, and my days began with long lies in bed and cheery greetings of "Hola!" from the locals. I enjoyed venturing outside into the sunshine. The focus of my day became the smell of warm, freshly baked pastries in the morning as I made my daily trip to the local bakeries. As a thank you to my friend for accommodating me, I cooked and cleaned the house each day. My friend warmly appreciated my efforts, and this became a new source of satisfaction. Completing these menial but essential household tasks provided the foundation for another emotional shift. Feelings of failure began to reshape into warm feelings of accomplishment again.

Slowly but surely, I was starting to feel re-energised and refocused. Earlier negative thoughts began to reshape into a positive mindset. This initial career catastrophe was beginning to morph into an opportunity. I pondered on the possibility that I was destined for other things.

Over those days, my mind began to calm itself, and with this calmness came a renewed ability to engage with my spirituality. I drew on my faith to feel protected and safe. This was certainly one place where I could talk freely and, because of this, I invested maximum time here.

Soon though, I had to return to England to complete the final phase of the hearing. Once back home, a visiting family member reminded me of the multiple times in my life I had faced and overcome adversity much worse than this. He reminded me of my strength in overcoming fears that had initially paralysed me, and that the thoughts which had once threatened the foundations of my self-esteem had now dissipated and gone away.

I now operate from a place of positive energy, telling myself there is always another job, always another way to make money to pay the bills, always another solution to uncover, providing I keep myself in check have more focus and self-control.

I am writing this now as a reflection of the past, as this stressful time was over 10 years ago. The reality is that the trauma of that initial phone call has never left me. Despite this, I have continued a forward-facing trajectory and gone on to achieve company awards and recognition.

My advice to others is that life can be a rollercoaster, and when one faces a stressful situation like this, seek a path to overcome the stress, and seek help and advice from those around you. The trauma can be long or short-lived depending on your attitude and self-belief to turn things around. This way you can start to enjoy the thrill of the ride of life once more.'

Trent Williams's Story – Teacher, Australia

'It was a text from a friend that started it all: 'Someone's made a complaint about you.' It was hard to wrap my head around it. The aggrieved party had accused me of breaking one of the cardinal rules of my profession, alleging that I had physically moved someone without their consent. The investigation that followed exonerated me entirely, and eyewitnesses spoke of my professionalism in the situation and how I had acted as a professional would. My employer acted professionally and made me aware of how things were progressing.

But sometimes, even though people are talking about how well you did, the seed of doubt is planted:

- – 'What if someone else makes a baseless accusation?'
- – 'What effect will it have on my future promotion chances?'
- – 'What are people saying about me?'

This all took a toll on me. I did not want to go to work, but I did not want to be stewing over it at home either. My employer put protocols in place so that my accuser and I were not in contact at all. They were not happy with my exoneration, though no further complaints were made, despite threats to take it to the media.

I needed help at this point. I was not coping by myself, and I needed to make a plan. My family were great support, but even then, it was not enough as my wife also had a stressful job and her own issues to deal with. Talking to people at work was not on the cards either; it would not have been professional to do so. Close friends were a possibility, but whilst I knew that their responses would have been supportive, I felt unable to dump all my emotions onto them over a sustained period.

There was only one solution - I would have to find someone outside and totally neutral to unload all of this onto. This was a hard step for the ego of a usually confident, gregarious male to take, but it was the only logical way to get myself out of this mental torture.

As a grown adult, it can be extremely hard to admit you need to seek professional help. There is a social stigma attached to it that is not helpful. It is not really a done thing to go up to people and ask, 'So, who do you see for your mental well-being?' As a society, we probably need to accept that we should be more open about it.

After I had sought help, I spoke about it with a few of my friends and colleagues. Most were supportive, but many were a bit taken aback when I said I had been for counselling. It is not something they thought I, as a usually confident person, would ever need, or that I would talk openly about.

Through my work, I was able to have funding to see a counsellor at a local clinic, and my work also let me have time to go and see them. Not only did this make me feel valued by my work, but also it helped me believe in myself, as they were willing to give me time and invest in me to get better. That was one huge boost.

The second was that my counsellor and I got on very well. They were superb at their job, and helped me go through the process of breaking down all my concerns, queries and worries, dismantling the shackles of doubt that had been dragging me down for the past few weeks.

As the doubt receded, my confidence grew, and I found my feet once again. Since that point, I have spoken about how counselling helped me to many people. It is important to recognise that it is not the only way to get through a difficult time, but it may be a help to some.'

2.3: Work Stress and Burnout

"In a culture fuelled by burnout, a culture that has run itself down, our national resilience becomes compromised. And when our collective immune system is weakened, we become more susceptible to viruses that are part of every culture because they're part of human nature - fearmongering, scapegoating, conspiracy theories, and demagoguery."

- Arianna Huffington

High levels of stress can lead to burnout if we're not careful, and the stories from contributors illustrate how stress can escalate if it's not handled in the right way. Burnout in business or home life can lead to an extreme state of physical or emotional exhaustion, as well as affect your mental health. According to the Mayo Clinic, burnout involves a sense of reduced accomplishment and possible loss of personal identity (2021). Burnout has become more prominent since COVID-19 for doctors, nurses, frontline workers, as well as business owners trying to survive. Recent research would suggest that many people who experience job burnout do not believe their jobs are the main cause.

The concept of burnout was developed back in 1975. Two psychoanalysts, Herbert Freundenberger and Christina Maslach, Professors of Psychology at the University of California, were working independently when their common research led to collaborative work with Professor Susan E. Jackson at Rutgers School of Management and Labour Relations.

They came to develop the Maslach Burnout Inventory (MBI), a tool used for identifying burnout. The World Health Organisation (WHO) also used the MBI as a framework to add 'burnout' to its international classification of disease and related health problems.

The MBI looks at 3 main areas of heath and mindset: exhaustion, cynicism, and negative self-worth. It also takes into account six workplace risk factors, shown below:

1. Workload
2. Sense of control
3. Reward
4. Workplace relationships
5. Fairness
6. Values alignment

Some common symptoms of job burnout include (Middleton, 2019):

- Irritability or impatience with co-workers, customers and clients
- Exhaustion, and lack of energy and ability to be consistently productive
- Lack of focus
- Low motivation and disillusionment
- Sleeping disorders
- Unhealthy eating, excessive use of alcohol and drugs
- Reduced satisfaction from achievements
- Regular headaches, stomach or bowel problems, and other physical complaints

If you are experiencing a number of these symptoms, then you may be suffering from job burnout. Consider making an appointment with a doctor or a mental health practitioner as these symptoms may also be related to health issues or even depression. If ignored or left unaddressed, job burnout can have significant consequences, including heart disease, high blood pressure or type 2 diabetes.

Causes of Burnout

Burnout can be caused by a variety of factors, for example (MindTools, 2021):

- Extreme changes in activity, such as when a job is by turns chaotic or monotonous
- An inability to influence decisions that affect your job, such as assignments or workload
- Lacking the resources you need to do your work
- Unclear job expectations
- Lack of social support, which can lead to a feeling of isolation
- Dysfunctional workplace (perhaps you work with an office bully, feel undermined by colleagues, or have a boss who micromanages your work)
- Poor work/life balance, which can lead to not having the energy to spend time with your family and friends

Job Burnout Risk Factors

You might be more likely to experience job burnout if (Cooks-Campbell, 2021):

- You try to be everything for everyone
- You feel you have little or no control over your work
- You identify so strongly with work that you lack balance between your work life and your personal life
- You have a high workload, including overtime work
- You work in a helping profession, such as health care
- Your job is monotonous

Claire Rogers's Story - Coaching & Consulting Director, California (www.itopiacoaching.com)

'I didn't recognise the signs that I was heading towards burnout until I found myself suffering from my first panic attack. Pre-panic attack, I projected an image of confidence and strength to colleagues, senior management, my staff, and clients; however, I was like a duck – smooth and calm on the surface, yet always frantically kicking my feet below the surface. At the time, I worked for an American Fortune 100 company, and like many individuals in today's society, I operated in a global environment accommodating multiple time zones, meaning I was contactable 24/7. Furthermore, constant re-structuring equated to increased working hours and unsustainable workloads, which saw me go from being an ambitious perfectionist and a high performer to becoming a highly stressed, burnt out, overworked leader.

My burnout happened in the blink of an eye. I didn't see it coming. It happened on a Saturday morning. It was grey outside, and I was exhausted. I couldn't seem to wake up. I felt like I was jet lagged - dazed and confused. Nonetheless, I had to get it together and head to my 5-year-old nephew's birthday party with my husband. I didn't want to go, but I didn't have a choice.

I walked into this dingy town hall an hour outside of London where I was greeted by 15 hyperactive kids running around playing with their nerf guns. I looked and played the part well: I put a big smile on my face and brought my extroverted personality out. But inside something was wrong. I could feel it. I didn't know what, but something was off. And that off feeling was making me really unnerved. Despite this, I managed to keep it together. I shined my light on the parents in the room and engaged and chatted with them.

A few hours later, we could finally escape. Thank God. My hubby and I started to drive home and that's when it happened.

We were talking about random stuff. Nothing too serious. When all of a sudden, I felt like someone had put a tight elastic band around my chest and was slowly squeezing the life out of me. My arms and legs started to go numb. My hands and feet started to tingle with pins and needles. I started to hyperventilate. I couldn't breathe. I frantically tried to pull air into my chest. I looked down at my chest where I could quite literally see my heart pounding away frantically. My body and mind were ravaged with an overwhelming, mind-blowing feeling of terror.

I've felt fear before, but this was next level.

'Oh my God. I'm going to die. I'm going to die right here in this car. I don't want to die. I've got so much more I want to do.'

I looked out the window in a state of utter stupefaction, like I was seeing clearly for the very first time. I wondered how I got there.

How did I get in this situation where I'm going to die?

Finally, something clicked in my mind.

Something inside me told me I was having a panic attack. I don't know how I knew. I just did.

Knowing didn't make it any easier. I was still ravaged with overwhelming feelings of terror, which lasted about 30 minutes.

By the time we got home I was a broken, fragile wreck, and I couldn't snap out of it. That tenacious, resilient, passionate girl that I used to be was gone. She left the building and wasn't coming back. I couldn't find her. I couldn't dig deep and force her to get back up again; she was gone. She was gone for 18 months.

Instead, a new girl moved in. And this new girl is terrified. Every day I wake up terrified. I shake uncontrollably. My heart is constantly pounding in overdrive. My body and mind are constantly flooded with overwhelming mind-blowing feelings of fear. I'm perpetually terrified of when the next panic attack is going to strike. And because of this, I developed a fear of fear itself. I went from being a girl that has trekked across the globe to a girl that's scared to walk into Starbucks for fear of not being able to open my mouth to speak; for fear of collapsing in a panic attack right there in the middle of the coffee shop.

Besides my husband and mum, I didn't tell anyone what was going on because I was ashamed. I was embarrassed. I thought I was weak. I thought I would be fired. I thought it was just me. And so, I hid the private world of hell I was living in. Emotionally in pain. Mentally depressed. Spiritually stressed. Yet physically, I smiled. I dressed the part. I acted the part. I deserve an academy award.

That first panic attack led to further panic attacks which eventually led me to sink into my own private world of chronic fear, anxiety, and depression, which lasted 18 months.

Ultimately, I was able to recover my mental health through meditation, running, changing my diet, quitting caffeine and sugar, and changing careers. All of this wasn't an instant fix – it took almost 2 years to recover my health.'

Natalie Lockyer's Story - Life Coach, Oxfordshire (www.natalielockyercoaching.co.uk)

'Stress and I have been friends for an exceptionally long time, and for the most part we get on brilliantly.

That might sound strange, but stress is not inherently bad. In fact, our stress response has evolved to ensure we survive. Stress does a lot of really fun things to your body. At the thought of perceived danger, our stress response gives us a heady cocktail of hormones - predominantly cortisol and, my favourite, adrenaline. It elevates our heart rate, decreases brain activity in the prefrontal cortex (the rational, problem-solving part of our brains) and short-circuits our bodies to perform without thought. For a short time, this is a great way to ensure we react to danger quickly. We fight, flight or occasionally freeze.

Short-term stress is able to bring us to our flow zone and shut out the rest of the world, enabling us to give a kickass speech, push through that final mile of a marathon, or jump out of a perfectly working plane (with a parachute attached) in the pursuit of growth and fun. In the short term, stress can be exciting, adrenaline-fuelled, heart-racing FUN!

Long-term stress on the other hand is really, really bad for us, and this is where stress and I have our falling outs. What the thrill seeker and public speaker in me loves, the caregiver and conscientious hard worker in me feels is a millstone wearing me down and burning me out.

In short, this has led to several periods in my life where I have experienced burnout due to stress. The most memorable was not even the year I nearly lost my nan, bought my first house, lost my mum's partner who was like a dad to me, lost my dad six months later and took a black belt grading in the martial art of Jiu Jitsu. That was a brutal, emotional, beautiful, and transformative year, but with a community around me and a lot of self-care practices and boundary-setting, I was OK - or so I thought. What I had actually done to survive that 12-month stretch was bury a lot of emotions and let my boundaries slip. In hindsight, that was a really bad idea.

Fast forward 2 years, and I have survived a relationship that brought me close to a post-traumatic stress disorder (PTSD) diagnosis, and was hiding under my desk in an open plan office because the final straw in work meant I couldn't make it to the bathroom to cry. My saving grace that day was a colleague who lay down under the desk with me like it was totally normal, looked me in the eye with empathy and compassion but not a hint of judgement and asked, "What do you need?"

What did I need? That one question gave me permission to be completely selfish. There was no demand to think of others, be a good employee, a strong daughter, a brave survivor, or a caring friend (all of which were parts of me).

Long story short, I needed to advocate for myself. I needed to tell people when their actions and behaviours where crossing what was OK for me, and I needed to know when to ask for and accept help. I needed to be more selfish, and take time out for me to do the things that let my body and my mind let go of tension and stress. And most importantly, I needed to feel - to lean into the pain, acknowledge it, learn from it, and then let it go.

Stress is our body's response to an emotional, physical or thought-based trigger. If you push down emotions or block out thoughts that are causing you stress, you will simply stay stressed. And much like that super fun, over-the-top friend who overstays their welcome, being stressed all the time is no good for anyone.

So now I walk a balanced road, calling on my friend stress when I need her. She helps me have confidence and courage when I am under pressure at work, about to give a talk or try a new crazy sport or activity. Stress helps me be brave and confident when I go into a room full of strangers or have a challenging conversation.

Afterwards, we part ways with thanks and well wishes, and I make sure I take time for me. I reflect on my thoughts, particularly the uncomfortable ones, and I acknowledge my emotions in all their beautiful rainbow of existence.

I'm not perfect: stress still outstays her welcome sometimes, but it's easier to recognise now and, with practice, I'm quicker to reset and reach out for help when I need it. I hope this helps you give yourself permission to do the same.'

Yuki Yamaguchi's Story - General Affairs Department, Japan

'I have been working overtime for about 70 hours every month from November every year. Even in Japan, these are considered long hours.

It is no exaggeration to say that I was living mainly for work every day, carrying out tasks such as year-end adjustments in November and December, company-wide management meetings in January, and in February, preparations for new employees (paperwork) to join the company in April. In addition to the accumulated fatigue and a lot of work (such as organising documents for about 30 new employees, preparing equipment, arranging housing, etc.), I also had to support a new staff member.

I was appointed as a trainer for the staff, which meant that new tasks were added to my workload, including how to delegate work, what could and could not be done, and giving regular and careful guidance. As a result, I trained the new staff member for only three weeks. The stress of all the additional work and having to train a new staff member caused me to suffer bass-impaired sensorineural hearing loss.

Sensorineural hearing loss (SNHL) happens when there is damage to tiny hair cells in the cochlear or the auditory nerve. The symptoms of SNHL include muffled hearing, difficulty understanding speech, sudden or steady loss of hearing, full or 'stuffy' sensation in the ear, dizziness, and ringing in the ear.

The new employee I was struggling to train was not bad, and he worked hard with what knowledge he had. However, there was a gap between the work he completed compared to other workers. Other members of staff also demanded my time, and they kept me informed about the guidance and support that this new staff member required. For example, I asked the new staff member to journal documents or letters by a person's name. He was not good at reading kanji (a system of Japanese writing using Chinese characters, used primarily for content words), so he could not organise the material as I had asked.

The learning process was difficult for him, so my boss and co-workers encouraged me to support him as I was his trainer. I arranged meetings with him to offer my support, but he still struggled to progress with the training. I became frustrated, as I was trying my best to help him, but he still could not manage to keep up with the standard and quality we wanted. I told my boss that I still had a lot of work to do in addition to training this new employee, and that I was struggling to juggle my own work whilst keeping an eye on him. This stress led eventually to a period of hearing loss.

My doctor advised that staying away from stress was the best cure. I knew my work was stressful, but I could not leave it. When I was wondering what to do, I decided to examine my weaknesses. My weakness is that I expect too much from the other people. Somewhere in my heart, I wondered why this man could not do such an easy task. So, I decided to change the way I think. I came to realise that this new staff member was working hard, though not to the standard that people around him wanted. Recognising the fact that he was a hard worker meant that I could ask him to step up and improve gradually.

It is easy to look at the negatives, but there are also positives wherever you look. If you pay attention to the positive things, your heart will also feel more positive about situations. I learned this through my experience of meeting him and suffering hearing loss. When you have a positive outlook, you do not care too much about the mistakes of others, and you can maintain your peace of mind. There are many things that can be stressful, but I have found that one way to deal with it is to look for something positive behind that stress. If you cannot find it, talk with others and ask for help and support.'

Lily Hart's Story - HR Manager, UK

'"Today is the tomorrow you worried about yesterday, and all is well." This message was strategically placed in our bathroom whilst I was growing up as an only child living in a small village with my parents. It was a happy time, but my mother was very shy and scared of everything, which rubbed off on me too. All I wanted was to fit in, and so I developed a way of coping so that no one would know what was going on in my head. I did not tell anyone how I felt. To the outside world I was absolutely fine, but inside I was scared and on high alert whenever there were new people or situations to conquer. It gave me pains in my stomach and I could feel the fizzing in my body whilst the adrenalin kicked in. Rational perspective would go out of the window and dark thoughts would invade my mind. This feeling of what I now know as stress never left me for long, whether it was exams, starting a new job, children being ill, or simply rushing to catch a train home from work.

Fast forward a few decades and I had a grown family and a career in HR in a great company working with wonderful people. I loved and embraced the challenges I faced, especially those where I could support others. The more difficult the challenge, the more I threw myself into dealing with it. Failure was not an option, and I cared far too much. As the company grew, my role grew, and despite requests from myself and others in the team, my manager was out of his depth during a period of constant change where so many of us worked long and hard. One of my colleagues and I supported each other by playing 'the Glad Game.' This was something I remembered from 'Pollyanna,' which I read as a child. In the book, Pollyanna finds things to be happy about even when she is sad. This helped my colleague and I to overcome difficulties and sorrows through positive thought.

I dealt with major personal family issues too, and invested the same energy in my family life as I did in my job. I was always trying to find solutions; I was always busy. I knew that constantly putting out fires was not an effective way to live or work, but I could not let anyone down. When I tried to work smarter rather than harder, I still became overwhelmed by the volume. I recognise now that my mental and physical health suffered as a result.

I always thought stress was a great motivator as it made me focus when a deadline was near, but no one can operate effectively whilst constantly stressed. Others went off sick with stress, but not me. I was invincible; I had to support others. I counselled employees and coached managers to recognise stress and manage it effectively. Why couldn't I do what I was telling others to do? My blood pressure was high; I was out of control, flying by the seat of my pants, and I was about to realise what stress can do. Sadly, one of our managers committed suicide. That was a stark message for me to change my life, and I felt this was my wake-up call to take back control of my life. I decided to retire at the end of that year. During my notice period I had major surgery, and whilst I was off sick, my manager went off too with stress. I knew that it could have been me, but thankfully I had stepped back and realised what was important in life.

Stress does not leave you: you will always face situations where the same plunge into overdrive 'flight or fight' mode happens when you are least expecting it. Everyone is different, and individuals have to find their own strategies to cope.

Whilst I miss the excitement and the challenges of business life, I have found more peace and joy writing poems, baking, and spending time with my family. Lockdown has been a joy for me, especially in the summer, sitting in the garden watching and listening to the birds and walking in the beautiful countryside where I live. My blood pressure has dropped, and I have learned to let go of the hurt and tried to embrace other joys in life. I still lurch into stress overdrive from time to time, especially in the run up to Christmas 2020, but I thank God for my blessings and realise I am one of the lucky ones.'

Chris Teague - Co-founder and Director of People Activation, Manchester
(www.peopleactivation.com)

'Imagine waking up each morning mentally exhausted, your jaw tense and sore from the vice-like grip in your sleep, your mind weary from spending yet another night working flat out on a problem. Imagine finding when the light of day came that the problem did not exist at all, and reflecting on your musings and trying to make sense of it all.

Finally, the moment of realisation came for me; I was stressed and had to do something about it.

Stress isn't a word many people would associate with me. In work, I am referred to as 'Iceman' and people describe me as calm, composed, organised and resilient. To this day, no one close to me would even know I had endured this period of stress, as I was determined not to be weak or let stress affect me. I was the founder and managing director of the business and must, therefore, be the rock for everyone and everything.

For the first three years of my business, I'd let stress consume my thoughts, my energy and all of my time. If I hadn't done something to help me change, there was no way I would see the business turn 14 this year.

I believed the success or failure of the business was down to me and me alone. The harder I worked, the greater chance my business would have of surviving and succeeding. Therefore, I shouldered the responsibility and the burden, rather than share it with my business partner and colleagues. I internalised it all, and spoke to no one. I wrongly believed I shouldn't burden others; these problems were for me to solve as I was the leader and head of the business.

Stress is mistaken as an ailment of the weak, but the only thing soft about it is that I didn't call it out sooner than I did. But late is better than never. The lightbulb moment for me was a sample meditation session organised by one of my colleagues. In this 45-minute session, we all sat, grounded our feet and were instructed to focus all our thoughts on our feet. The exercise made me very conscious of an unexpected part of my anatomy - my previously mentioned jaw.

Later that week, I had a routine dental check-up, and the dentist said 'Oh I see you grind your teeth!' This was a shock, as I didn't realise that I did. This confirmation helped me join the dots; subconsciously, I was stressed, and I needed to address the root cause.

I've always been a big believer in coaching, both in sport and business, and so I decided I needed someone to share my thoughts and feelings with. Crucially, this had to be someone who wouldn't judge me or see me as weak.

Early in a one-to-one coaching session, the coach asked me how I planned my days and my week. At the time, my answer was primitive; I have a to-do list. His follow-on question led to the most significant light bulb moment for me, 'How do you decide what to do from the long list of things?'

I realised that I'd adopted a 'whatever it takes' mentality to my to-do list, rather than assess what was important and why, and then correctly evaluate what it takes to accomplish it. I realised that I saw each day as being a day to complete my list. I didn't set myself the constraint of time, for example to complete a task between 09.00hrs and 17:00hrs. I worked until I accomplished my list every day, and each day this list would get longer and longer as I took on more and more responsibilities, most of which were not important, never mind urgent.

This coaching session taught me a technique that I use to this very day, almost 11 years on. At the end of each day, I think about what I need to do the following day and why I need to do it. I then assess how long it will take to complete the task and, based on the importance and the required time, I plot it into my diary. So, if it is important and requires a lot of time, I will do it in the morning, as that's when I'm most productive. The key is to stick to the time you have allocated for the task; the more you do this, the better you will get at estimating a realistic timeframe. It is so important to finish or move on at the end of the allocated time, as this helps you keep focused and build a 'ship it' mentality, whereby you either complete a piece of work or move on regardless, as this avoids procrastination and enables others to get on and do what they need to do. Remember, you are aiming to be better, not perfect.

The other techniques I've developed to help manage my day and subsequently my stress are:

- Declare a start and end of each day
- If disturbed when working through your tasks, ask, 'Can it wait?' 90% of the time, it can wait and therefore should
- Do not look at work messages and emails between the hours of 19:00hrs and 08:00hrs Monday to Thursday, or from Friday 16:00hrs to Sunday at 18:00hrs

- Aim to finish work each Friday at 16:00hrs to reflect on the week's successes and relax into the weekend

2020 has arguably been the most stressful year for my global live events business, which I have had to steer through a pandemic. Yet with the above techniques and a good fitness programme of running three times a week, I feel in control of my stress. I manage my energy and my focus rather than my time. You too can do this for the better of your health.'

Anna Gorst's Story - Children and Young People's Psychological Well-being Practitioner, England

'Imagine a line of shot glasses on a bar. You work from one end to the other, shot by shot, each hit flooding your system with alcohol. At some point, it becomes too much - your body shuts down and you stop drinking. When you come around you feel low; cold, flat, agitated, edgy. What might fix it? 'Just take another shot!' screams your body, 'I need to feel alive.' Addiction, right?

My journey with stress, as for everybody else, has been a long and winding one. Learned behaviour, hardwired responses, unhealthy habits and yes, as I have learned more recently, addiction. Having always prided myself on self-control with a (slightly smug) conviction that I, unlike others, most definitely did not have an 'addictive personality,' it came as quite a surprise to learn that I was in fact deeply involved in an addictive relationship with cortisol. The stress hormone, it transpires, is as addictive as a Class A drug. Never mind that I was the girl at the party who always knew when to say no to that final wine refill and stop before it was too much. Here I was at the age of forty–something being told by a highly respected scholar of neuroscience and psychotherapy that I was quite obviously addicted to stress. So, how had this happened?

I could list the obvious contributing factors; the sudden death of my father, a miscarriage, an unhappy marriage, a demanding job, divorce, house move and the cancer diagnosis of my best friend all in one year. The final straw was the suicide of a child with whom I worked closely.

If we look back further, I could note earlier stresses; my parents coping with the loss of my baby brother, the near-fatal road accident of my youngest brother, and maybe even an in-utero experience of stress hormones when my father's sister died in a car accident. Those hard knocks, each a hit of adrenaline – a shot at the bar – had been stored up, and had unknowingly contributed to feeding my addiction. In order to feel normal, I needed to be on edge, strung out, alert. And now I learned that this was not, at all, a healthy place to be.

I have always been a doubter when it comes to mindfulness. Self-care to me was self-indulgence. I am not the 'type' to do yoga, and meditation. Forget it – as if this over-thinking brain could ever stop for long enough! And yet...

With 6 months signed off work, a debilitating inability to think straight, manage my emotions, or achieve even the smallest task, it appeared that this whole stress addiction thing had started to get the better of me. I decided to take action:

Step One: If I wanted to feel better, I was going to have to accept that I was not well.

Step Two: I was going to have to accept that I should listen to the people who could help me get better.

Step Three: I was going to have to look at the things I did not believe in, and start to do things differently.

I was lucky enough to be able to follow a career change which gave me access to training and experience in this field. Now I manage my own stress with more insight, and I am able to work with children and young people to help them support their own mental health and well-being. I will always be grateful to the wonderful woman who identified my addiction and offered me a doorway out of it.

So, learn about trauma and trauma-informed practice. It is not always the big things – it's everything and anything which has triggered your adrenaline surges over your lifetime, whatever has taken you out of your 'window of tolerance' – those shot glasses which sent you to a place where you just could not think straight or function.

Once you have learned about it, it's time to let those Cortisol receptors die off. Stop feeding them. Allow your system to be calm and to function without the hit.

And the good news? Well, it's pretty simple stuff: sleep, eat well, drink water, learn to breathe, exercise, get fresh air, and yes, mindfulness.

For me, the greatest gift was breathing. Try 'box' breathing - breathe in for a count of 4, hold for 4, out for 4, hold for 4... Continue until you settle back into that window where you have perspective and clarity. Focus on letting your senses ground you. Count 5 things you can see, 4 things you can touch, 3 things you can hear, 2 things you can smell or taste, and finally one deep slow breath. It is not that difficult after all. And there's beauty in simple things.'

Tony Sargeant's Story - Business Owner, Cambridge, England

'Looking back now at age 70, I wonder why schools do not teach stress management skills, as we certainly all require it in today's fast-paced world.

After the Second World War, my parents (who did not have a lot) soon started seeing massive changes in Europe. The faster modern luxuries came to them, the more they wanted to give them to their children, as they had endured so much and wanted to give us what they could. By the time I was a teenager, life was starting to be a whole lot different, and jobs were in abundance. My first wage for one week of work was only ten bob (that's 50 pence nowadays, or 1 dollar).

In my case, I think stress is part of me, not something brought on by constant pressure from other forces. Let me explain: looking back it came down to 'the straw that broke the Camel's back,' as the expression goes.

I started work as an apprentice mechanic at the age of fifteen. I was a fast learner, and soon advanced to become a transport manager of a haulage firm. I was a very conscientious worker and wanted to show how good I was and that I was capable of doing any job put in front of me. The problem was that I took on this level of responsibility from the age of nineteen, and was far too young to be in the position of manager as well as a mechanic and breakdown servicer. I found myself working seven days a week and all hours, as this was financially very lucrative for me. The more I achieved, the more I said, 'OK, I will sort it,' and I found it hard to say no to jobs. Finally, I decided to change jobs and left to work where I thought it would be easier. In my new job, I would now just be one of more than twenty staff, without the pressure of managing everything.

How wrong I was. My interview was, I thought, in response to an advert asking for a motor mechanic, not a welder. The conversation went like this:

Me: Hi, I have come about the mechanic's job.

Interviewer: What's your name?

Me: Anthony

Interviewer: Tony

Me: No, it's Anthony.

Interviewer: If you want the job, it's Tony. Can you weld?

Me: Of course I can, why?

Interviewer: That's the job we want filling. You can start on Monday.

I was starting my first job in a massive company, despite the fact that I could not and never had done any welding in my life. I wanted to get a job, and said anything I had to to get it. This only caused me more stress, though in those days, no-one called it by this name.

Being born after the Second World War, there were no set rules on how one should grow into the new world. With technology driving the world forward, we all had to work hard to keep pace with the modern way of living. If someone else had it, you had to strive to have it too.

I was also married by age nineteen. I had a good job, and my ambition was to do well, as I needed to show that I was a man and thriving. My mother and father were going to be very proud of my achievements, I thought. I was a success. By twenty three, my first child came along. We had a new house, which also showed others that 'I had arrived,' and had become someone who showed that from a mere council house, one could become whatever they wished to be. Was this the foundation for finally cracking under the pressure in a stressful breakdown in my late forties?

From the day I started work to the day I walked away from my then multi-million business, I never stopped wanting more; more wealth, bigger homes, more fame, more recognition. Unfortunately, having reached the goal of being one of the top businesses in the whole of the UK, this ended up being the thing that finally that broke me.

I asked myself if I was ever ready to really have grown the business so fast, or at all. With all of the ups and downs, the money worries could not be handled by me alone, and I was let down by the banks and large conglomerates that promised large financial grants which never materialised. All of this stress came from wanting to be the largest business - one that rose from nothing to become one of the greatest.

All of this finally drove me to the doctors and eventually to pills and more pills until I was taking the maximum amount I could take. My doctor gave me the fright of my life and finally made me realise that I had to walk away from my business. At the time, I did not know how to. He told me, 'You are now on the strongest pills I can give you. You teach martial arts, do yoga and meditate, but still you cannot control your stress levels. If you do not stop work for good, your next step will be into a coffin.'

At fifty two, I finally sold the business, and my life started to become easier. I had paid a big price having had a mental breakdown in the last few years leading to me finally selling up. Until then, I had to keep the world thinking I was OK. I was trapped in a place where I did not wish to see anyone or hear from anyone; I would cocoon myself from the world and hide if the phone ever rang. The stress and fear would instantly return when I heard the phone ring, and it took many years to make myself answer it. Even today, I think twice before picking it up.

So, do we ever really recover from the (self-imposed, in my case) stress of life? If a valuable plate gets broken and proficiently repaired so that others can still enjoy looking at it, they may not see the crack, but the crack is still there.'

As you can see from Tony's story, he had a very stressful time in his life. He has now found peace through his teaching of Aikido, Tai Chi and yoga across the world. This has helped him to become more grounded. Tony is also a writer, and has published two books both available on Amazon: *'Takemusu Aikido: A Martial Artist's Journey of Discovery in Aikido'* and *'Keeping the Mind of a Child.'*

Useful Tips to Manage Burnout

Book time with your manager or supervisor to discuss specific concerns: this way you may be able to work together to change expectations or reach compromises or solutions. It is important to:

- Set achievable goals for what must get done and what can wait
- Seek help and support from friends, co-workers, friends or loved ones. If you have access to an employee assistance program, take advantage of these services
- Regular physical activity can help take your mind off work
- Try relaxing activities such as meditation, yoga, or Tai Chi
- Get more sleep, which restores well-being and helps protect your health
- Consider mindfulness. Mindfulness is the act of focusing on your breath flow and being intensely aware of what you are sensing and feeling at every moment, without interpretation or judgment. You can learn more about mindfulness in later in this book

CHAPTER 3: Occupational Stress

"People work for money but go the extra mile for recognition, praise and rewards."

- Dale Carnegie

According to CareerCast's annual 'Most Stressful Jobs' report, careers in the military and those that deal with public safety are considered amongst the most stressful jobs. In 2019, for the third year in a row, military personnel, firefighter, airline pilot and police officer were reported to be the four most stressful occupations. CareerCast uses a ranking system which looks at 11 types of demands in a job that evoke stress. These demands are listed below:

1. Amount of travel
2. Growth potential
3. Deadlines
4. Working in the public eye
5. Competitiveness
6. Physical demands
7. Environmental conditions
8. Hazards encountered
9. Risk to one's own life
10. Risk to the life of another person

11. Meeting the public

Top Industries Likely to Experience Stress	Likelihood of Stress
Local and National Government	92%
Telecoms	88%
Media and Marketing	85%
Healthcare	84%
Education	83%
Real Estate	83%
Travel and Legal Professional Services	79%
Retail, Catering and Leisure	78%

The chart above shows the most stressful industries in the UK (Perkbox, 2020). For individuals working in these industries, it would be wise to manage stress levels and have good coping strategies.

3.1: Armed Forces

"We must never forget why we have, and why we need our military. Our armed forces exist solely to ensure our nation is safe, so that each and every one of us can sleep soundly at night, knowing we have 'guardians at the gate.'"

- Allen West

Adam Jenkins's Story – RAF Flight Lieutenant, Basra

'In 2008, I was stationed in Basra, Iraq as the support officer responsible for infrastructure outside of the airbase. Some days would be spent in the office inside the protection of the airbase, and some days would involve visiting forward operating bases, Iraqi military and police installations in Basra city and the surrounding area. For 24 hours a day, you either wore your helmet and body armour or had it within arm's reach, as rocket attacks could happen at any time, day or night. All movement outside the airbase was via helicopter or armoured transport due to the very real threat of attack. The attacks on convoys ranged from sporadic rifle fire to shaped charge improvised explosive devices (IEDs) which would vaporise the occupants of a vehicle. The official working day was 12 hour shifts 6 days a week, which in reality became a standard 14 to 16 hour working day.

The days were long and the work was specialised, requiring meticulous attention to detail. I had to liaise with military personnel from different countries and cultures, as well as civilian contractors from the UK, Iraq and elsewhere. The work mounted up and there was constant threat to life. By most standards, this would appear to be an incredibly stressful environment, and I must admit that for the first week or so, it was. However, as I grew more accustomed to the environment and the routine, I began to relax into my work. There were other factors that also mitigated my concerns and greatly reduced my potential stress levels; I worked as part of a team, I had a boss, I had colleagues, I had a clearly defined role, I exercised daily, ate well, and socialised with colleagues who were experiencing the same stresses as I was.

One day about three weeks into my tour, our office cleaner who was a local civilian didn't turn up to work. I noticed because he was a very friendly character who would always say good morning as he emptied the wastepaper baskets in the office. I mentioned his absence to my boss who responded, "Keep your helmet on today." Now I felt stressed. What was going to happen? When? Sure enough, two hours later the sirens went off, followed immediately by the sound of the air defence guns and the sound of explosions as insurgents' rockets landed nearby. That was my first rocket attack. We all lived, nobody was hurt. It turned out that whenever our cleaner would fail to turn up to work in the morning, a rocket attack would follow. He must have been warned about the attacks beforehand.

Before going to Iraq, the RAF taught me about stress and various strategies for coping with a high workload. Eating well, getting lots of exercise and socialising with colleagues were key. I had managed to put all of these into effect when I got to Basra, but the one thing that I couldn't control was my own familiarity with being under threat. Before that first attack, I had just pretended that there wasn't really any threat at all. The moment my boss said, "Keep your helmet on today," the reality of mortal danger came flooding into my mind. I wasn't scared, just preoccupied. I couldn't concentrate on my work. I couldn't stop wondering what was going to happen. Would it be a rocket attack? Would it be an IED left on the base? Would it be nothing? Was I just being silly? After the attack, everything was back to normal. I wasn't preoccupied any more, I could concentrate on work again and get back into my routine. The next attack was fine, and the next, and the next. If our cleaner did not turn up to work, we kept our helmets on in the office. I guess what I learned from this is that we all try to control what we can in order to feel secure, and that while it's easy enough to believe that we accept the things that we can't control, familiarity with the uncontrollable is essential to maintaining balance. Understanding how you react to stress and becoming familiar with that sensation will allow you regain your composure.'

Steve Bander Wright's Story - Implementation Force (IFOR), Bosnia

'During my time in the forces, I have served in many situations which would be deemed stressful, some of which were not in times of conflict.

The war had raged for a long time in Bosnia and the United Nation peace force was failing in the eyes of troops on the ground, and for years troops could only observe and not take an active part. Orders were given so that IFOR would play a more active role. This meant troops would paint their vehicles from the United Nations (UN) white colour back to Green Disruptive Pattern Material (DPM) - camouflage. The task now was to stop the fighting by force. This now became a more heighted and stressful situation, but this was what I had trained for.

Troops were placed in zones of separation, and in a way it was like teachers telling kids to go to separate areas of the playground. The country had been heavily mined with no records of the location of where they were placed (as per the Geneva convention), and as more troops were deployed further into the country there were multiple mine strikes. Our job as the Explosive Ordinance Disposal unit (EOD) was to assist in mine strike operations to clear towns and villages of Explosive Remnants of War (ERW). Sadly, this also included assisting war crime investigators with investigating mass graves, as there were sometimes mines or booby traps left behind to deter excavation of these atrocities.

For three months, we were working in the Canadian Armour Officers (AO) clearing towns of munitions or removing bodies from the town, some of which had been frozen in the snow during the winter months. Having to go through this experience was part of my job, but a harrowing and stressful experience. I had to keep focused on the task no matter how grim it was. It was our task to remove these bodies and ERW, which took eight long months. At the end of each day, we would always do Physical Training (PT) to help de-stress, no matter how late we got back. Entering a minefield, there is no time to be overly stressed, as your mind must stay focused and there is no time to think about anything else. You never know when a mine may explode, and you can lose your life in an instant. We would try and diffuse the stress of this task with army humour and joking around. There was no point in overly stressing ourselves. In our minds, it was as simple as thinking in terms of either initial success or total failure. Part of our de-stress routine after returning to camp was doing the basics, such as the preparing your kit for the following days.

After deployment leave, we would be back on UK operations, and fortunately our boss at the time would send us off on adventure training. This could be kayaking, climbing, paragliding or some other sport. These adventure training programmes were vital for helping us to control and manage stressful situations.

Finding Live Explosives

This was foremost a training mission. We were training the American troops to conduct vehicle searches, using vehicles similar to what they would encounter in practice. During the lesson, I explained to them how they should approach other areas of the vehicles. As I was doing this, I showed them one area of the vehicle to examine and surprisingly a bag fell out. I looked up at one of the other Brits to see if they were playing a practical joke on me, and they began shaking their head and backing away. It turns out that these vehicles had been confiscated from known enemy combatants, and their specialist teams who were supposed to have already checked it had missed the bag. The bag was full of live explosives and parts to an IED that luckily had not been constructed. This was an extremely stressful moment as we thought we were in a safe environment within the confines of the camp.

Left Behind

There were multiple vehicles entering the city. Our role was to search for secondary devices, extract the injured and allow a safe recovery of the vehicles. At this stage, I was in charge of the team, sending men into an area of high risk (where they could quite possibly die), which was extremely stressful for me. On one extraction, a vehicle was hit. Fortunately, there were no casualties, but we had to search the surrounding area so that the vehicle could be recovered. During this operation the battle group left us behind, and we had to extract ourselves without the protection of the main force. The men were not impressed that we were left behind to fend for ourselves and make our own way back through the rubbish tp (an area in which IEDS were frequently placed). This was a frightening and stressful time for our team.

Once the tour had finished, we were sent to Cyprus. A comedian was sent to entertain the troops and we all had few beers. The following day we went to the beach to do some surfing, water skiing or just chill out. This had never happened on any other operational tours previously and at the time I thought it was a nice idea, but really, I just wanted to go home. I now realise that this time was there to help de-stress the troops. The things I learned in the forces helped me to deal with stress in the civilian world by staying calm and alert, and to have a routine and plan for the future. I also learned to have a backup plan in case Plan A doesn't work, and to find ways to de-stress like doing exercise I enjoy, such as running, cycling, and practicing martial arts.'

Josh Netherwood's Story - Her Majesty's Royal Navy, England

'Being in the Armed Forces and serving in Her Majesty's Royal Navy for almost 5 years now, I have seen, experienced, and coped with stress in several different capacities.

I would like to focus on a certain experience that can be the most stressful part of any sea-hardened sailor's career, which is called 'Defence Watches.'

Defence Watches are when the entirety of a ship's crew falls into a 'higher state of readiness,' whereby the ship is split into two halves in terms of responsibility. You have the Port watch, and the Starboard Watch. The two watches take it in turn to alternate 'on-watch' and 'off-watch.' Being a member of the Warfare Department, there will only ever be six hours on or off watches. Bearing in mind, in your own watch, in most cases, depending on the ship's positioning in the world and its tasking, you will find yourself having to do your job under constant pressure. There are many distractions and supervisors keeping an eye on you, which would put any calm human being under a lot of stress from the start.

In your off-watch, you have six hours to eat, sleep, go to the gym if you so wish, and then get woken up an hour before your next on-watch to wash and get fed. This does not allow much time to relax or de-stress.

As I look around at all my colleagues, and even myself, I can see that for the majority of people and myself for sure, the main cause of stress during these situations is having so many people around you, day-in and day-out. It's the addition of watchful and judging eyes in these scenarios that can make even the most experienced person crumble under strain and stress. This type of stress can be carried over and seen in everyday life, even for civilians. People may feel stressed that they are being watched or observed by their peers or superiors, and this can cause not only stress but anxiety in such situations.

Such stressful situations can have different and adverse effects on different people. Personally, some of the results I dealt with myself in this situation were over-thinking and being sleep deprived. It is sometimes very difficult to be able to switch off from work when you are feeling stressed, and the situation can constantly run through your mind during the limited

71

time you have to rest. Plenty of my colleagues were overtired and had short tempers as a result of this level of stress.

How do I personally get over my fears and stress in such situations and my life as a whole?

Firstly, make sure that whatever it is you are doing, you enjoy it. There is nothing worse than forcing yourself to get out of bed in the morning knowing you are about to take part in something you will not enjoy. People may go to their place of work for economic reasons, and the main part of working is earning. However, you cannot be internally happy and stress-free if deep down you do not enjoy or get anything positive out of your work.

Secondly, and most importantly for myself, the main way I manage my life and stress is to make sure I have a routine. During 2020, when we all endured numerous lockdowns, it became so important to stick to a routine. I found myself setting myself simple goals, tasks and targets for each day. This helped to set a routine and keep stress out of my life as much as possible. Simply by setting a regular time to get up every morning and to have completed my first task of the day (which is usually a quick tidy of the house) gives me a sense of accomplishment. Being able to plan my day helps me to vanquish stress just by knowing how much time I have and how to use it, which is not often possible for a member of the Armed Forces.

My message to others is that it is especially important to enjoy what you do throughout your professional and personal life. I believe that enjoying the little things is a main part of counteracting stress. Also, always remember that if you feel you are being watched or observed at work, it is not because anyone wants to catch you out - they are there to support you. Simply pretend they are not there and continue with your job as you normally do. Lastly and most importantly, find a routine that works for you. Managing my time and routine is one of the major de-stress components in my life, and can be the simplest one to achieve.'

Post-traumatic stress disorder (PTSD) in the military is often referred to as 'combat stress,' and is often linked to individuals fearing for their life or seeing others killed and hurt in explosions. PTSD is a common side effect of serving in the armed forces, and sufferers should seek medical advice (Gregory, 2021). However, it is important to understand that feeling 'unsafe' or deeply distressed and therefore suffering from PTSD can also arise from other situations and non-military jobs.

As one can imagine, military personnel deal with incredibly high levels of pressure that most civilians can't begin to imagine. This leaves these individuals vulnerable to the debilitating impact of PTSD. Soldiers returning from the Second World War were said to be 'shell-shocked,' and often stereotypically portrayed in war movies and television programmes. The characters would often be men suffering from breakdowns triggered by loud noises and threat of attack. The sad fact is that this is not a full picture of what PTSD is, and how it affects those currently serving in the armed forces and veterans.

Below are some experiences that soldiers with PTSD have described to professionals (Ministry of Defence, 2013):

- 'I woke up screaming'
- 'The sensations were running through my body, and I could recall smells and tastes from all my war tours'
- 'All the horrific and haunting memories came flooding back'
- 'I can't seem to remove harrowing images from my mind'
- 'I sometimes have flashbacks at the cinema or watching TV'

3.2: Police Forces

"Police officers put the badge on every morning, not knowing for sure if they'll come home at night to take it off."

- Tom Cotton

Research conducted by the University at Buffalo studied the impact of work pressure on police officers (2008). They found that work pressure can disrupt sleep patterns, raise blood pressure, increase stress and risk of heart disease, as well as prevalence of PTSD. Fluctuating shift patterns in police work can cause physiological disruption of circadian rhythms due to being awake all night. This can affect judgment and decision-making, leading to a double-barreled stress effect.

'Policing is a psychologically stressful work environment, filled with danger, high demands, ambiguity in work encounters, human misery and exposure to death,' said Violanti, a 23-year veteran of the New York State Police. 'When cortisol becomes dysregulated due to chronic stress, it opens a person up to disease,' reported Violanti. 'The body becomes physiologically unbalanced, organs are attacked, and the immune system is compromised as well. It's unfortunate, but that's what stress does to us' (University at Buffalo, 2008).

Research shows that intervention is necessary to help police officers deal with this stressful occupation. There are several support services in place to help educate those in this profession. This includes learning how to relax and how to think differently about things they experience. Post-traumatic growth (PTG) is the positive psychological change that some individuals experience after a life crisis or traumatic event. This phenomenon was identified by psychologists Richard Tedeschi and Lawrence Calhoun in the 1990s (1996). Based on their research, the pair described five categories of growth that occur over time:

1. Changes in how one relates to other people
2. Recognition of new opportunities, priorities or pathways in life
3. Greater appreciation for the value of one's own life, and life in general
4. Recognition of one's own strength
5. Spiritual or existential development

Adrian Trench's Story – Police Investigator, England

'I am an ordinary person; I work, pay bills and have aspirations. However, my work is challenging. I have been a police investigator for twenty years and been present on the worst day of people's lives. I have listened to the outpouring of emotions from victims and their families, and dealt with their needs within the confines of the investigation. I have then guided them through the long investigative process until its conclusion.

During an investigation, each moment has its stressors, right from the initial call. What information do I have? Is it correct or not as first reported? The first stage is getting to the scene and performing an initial assessment, identifying the victim, witnesses, suspects, and which forensic strategies and resources are required. All the time, information is coming at you from all directions; radio, telephone calls, emails, colleagues, and people all wanting to help. Everything requires assessment and analysis to form a working strategy, identify options and contingencies, take the appropriate actions, and record the rationale. This occurs with every new piece of information and continues throughout the investigation, because every decision matters.

Each investigation is different because every victim is different, whether you meet them or not. When investigating the death of a person you never meet the deceased, but you meet their loved ones, their spouse, their children, their parents, and their friends. An important role of an investigator is to be an attentive listener. This includes sitting down with victims, hearing the details of what happened, how they were lied to, trapped, betrayed, held down, violated, punched, kicked, stabbed, beaten, and threatened. Often, victims are left feeling powerless, broken and a sense of overwhelming grief.

A detective's aim is to obtain a satisfactory outcome for the victim, their loved ones, and the community. Hopefully, you can enable the victim to heal and move on, but every time you contact the victim you can risk triggering denial, anger, bargaining and depression.

You listen to the witnesses who also can be traumatised by what they have seen and experienced. You listen to the suspect. Whatever the investigation, you must remain calm and professional. You listen, you probe, and you examine, however bizarre or unbelievable. Each time you listen, you are analysing the information for evidence that proves or disproves the known facts, or provides new lines of enquiry. All the time, you must try to keep the rapport you have with the individuals involved, engender their trust, and keep the conversation going.

Every investigation has checks and balances regarding sufficient evidence and whether there is a realistic prospect of prosecution. Each step requires the investigator to engage with the victim and lead them through the process that can take years to bring to a conclusion. This is the life of an investigator. Now multiply this experience by twenty, or by thirty, and that is your workload of investigations. I am glad to confirm that, during lockdown, workloads were no longer as high as they have been in the past.

We all have coping mechanisms, and I had felt that I had excellent ones. I had my family, and they mean everything to me. I never spoke about my work at home and made sure I left work at work. I had hobbies and passions that enabled me to release the stress.

We all have dreams and we all have nightmares, but I started getting the same ones. It affected me badly, and I became withdrawn as my coping mechanisms no longer seemed to work. I became forgetful, and initially blamed my age. More than anything, I slowed down, unable to make decisions and act. I then started remembering the faces of every victim and distressing act I had been exposed to. I did not sleep, and I became short-tempered. Every relationship I had in my personal and work life suffered, but I just kept trying to carry on regardless. At the time, I did not see the spiral downwards or how self-destructive I had become. I felt that I had to shield the pain and despair I was feeling from the people I loved.

A change in life circumstances and role enabled me to simplify the stressors I faced, and after several years of rebuilding, I now have some understanding of what happened. It was not a single stressful case, but the continual stress of my job and empathising with victims of trauma over the years. My mind could not cope with the things I had seen, the things I had heard, and the weight of it all that I carried, and my mental health suffered as a result. You cannot fight yourself, because it is a fight you cannot win, and I wish I had sought help.

The good news is that I now have support in place. We all have good days and not so good days – that's normal - but now I look for signs of stress and for changes within myself. Instead of trying to tough it out and keep going, I reflect and use support services. I use a professional supporter to discuss matters of concern. The conversation enables me to think clearly, not overthink the issue, and reset my focus.

Following a traumatic event, I can attend a Trauma Risk Management (TRiM) session. TRiM is a risk assessment and support system designed specifically to help in the management of traumatic events. I would urge anyone struggling with stress to seek help, especially if you recognise anything from my experiences.'

Gordon Milward's Story –Retired Chief Superintendent, North England

'I joined a Northern police force at the age of twenty, a profession that challenged me from the first day and for the next thirty years. Whether from external demands or those emanating from within the organisation, stress was a constant for three decades; the degree of which varied at any one time. It's no wonder police officers don't claim their pensions for as long as they should!

It was the unpredictable nature of the job (amongst other things) that attracted me to it. However, with such variety comes a high degree of stress. These pressures are on top of the domestic anxieties all adults experience, such as family issues and dealing with home finances.

Self-imposed demands, such as seeking promotions or wanting to attain a specialist post in Motor Patrols or the Criminal Investigation Department (CID), added to the mix, and these stressors are not short-term; the period from advertisement, to application, to selection and finally interview is usually months.

Most of the time, if the demands become too acute, there is always the option of stepping back - a way out. The most intense pressure and extreme stress comes from situations where there is no 'emergency exit' - where an unexpected set of circumstances present themselves and you are the sole commander of that incident. These may include people in possession of firearms, high-risk missing persons (where there is a risk to life) and other incidents where the outcome may involve loss of life and adversely affect public confidence in the police.

These Critical Incidents (CI) are fast-moving, with outcomes that could be fatal and, in the case of the Commander (Silver level), jeopardise their career or even their liberty. There is much at stake, and all these aspects combine to heighten the necessity to successfully conclude the incident. That said, Commanders are not left unsupported; they receive regular training and opportunities to observe experts, such as firearms officers or negotiators in action (real or artificial). They are also supplied with advisors and experts in, for example, firearms or search tactics, as well as a note-taker to document decisions and the rationale for each. In addition, all strategic objectives must be agreed by a senior (Gold level) Commander.

Despite these support mechanisms, the unpredictability of each scenario and the pace of the ongoing circumstances makes each one unique, and thereby greatly stress inducing. There is a multitude of demands to be co-ordinated and addressed. It has at times felt akin to being a circus-class juggler!

I have dealt with dozens of CIs in my years as a senior ranking officer, including a report of men travelling by car to collect firearms with the intent of causing harm to others, people of pensionable age with dementia leaving their home in inclement weather and without appropriate clothing, and troubled adults standing on bridges over rivers and motorways threatening to kill themselves. A tour of duty as the Force Silver Commander could cover any number of such incidents, sometimes concurrently and on top of a range of other responsibilities across the entire area. Senior Commanders are expected to be all things to all people, all of the time.

One particularly stressful time is operating as the Silver Commander during media liaison, especially during live television interviews and press conferences. Back in 2008, a convicted murderer escaped from his prison guards whilst receiving hospital treatment. His offence and the circumstances of the temporary liberation combined to make the escape a national news item, and the resulting media interest was high. Dozens of journalists from television, radio stations and newspapers were all intent on prematurely apportioning blame for the escape and creating extreme public concern about a murderer 'on the loose.' This required extreme concentration in order to ensure the reputation of the police remained intact, and the communities where the offender lived and committed the murder felt reassured that the police response was effective and satisfactory. Whilst many of the issues raised during these press liaisons could be anticipated, you cannot predict every question, and given that my responses were being recorded for broadcast, the need for accurate and coherent replies persists for thirty or more minutes.

So, what tactics did I employ to manage my stress, given that too much stress affects performance and well-being adversely but a modicum adversely affects impetus, focus and drive?

The police service taught me useful adages that remain relevant now:

- 'Failing to plan is planning to fail'
- 'Healthy body, healthy mind'
- 'Planning and Preparation Prevent Poor Performance' (the 5 Ps)

My take-home message for you as a reader is that if you can attend training to keep your knowledge current, you should. When a stressor is likely to occur, get plenty of rest beforehand, eat sensibly and ease off the hard stuff. When faced with a challenge, identify contingencies and work through the 'what ifs.' Plan for them. Remember, if it can go wrong, it will. Know where to go for advice and do not be afraid to ask for help. Debrief once the dust has settled, but not too long after. Reflect on what worked well and what could have been better. Learn these lessons and remember them. Identify a mentor to use as a sounding board - someone who listens and understands.'

Managing Stress in the Police Force

The following tips for managing stress as a police officer have been adapted from 'Police Stress: 9 Tips for Avoiding Officer Burnout' (Flavin, 2018):

- Keep up to date with the law and legal procedures, as officers who are able to understand the law are far better equipped to make smarter decisions, which in turn helps to reduce stress
- Good physical exercise is one of the most important preventative

measures you can do to tackle stress and burnout. Frequent exercise can help with recovery as well as keep you more alert

- Seek professional support from doctors, psychologists or a local charity. Many organisations will have access to professionals to talk to
- Ensure that you are able get enough quality sleep. Lack of sleep can negatively impact mood and judgement. Form good and regular sleeping habits
- It's important to have trustworthy friends at work so you can build camaraderie and long-lasting relationships
- Sharing your thoughts with co-workers will help get things off your mind, which can also help to maintain emotional reserves
- It's important to have a strong support system, outside work as well inside of work. This support may be with friends or a community group

3.3: Child Protection Services

"Love needs no protection; it is its own protection. So long as love begets life no child is deserted, or hungry, or famished for the want of affection. I know this to be true."

- Emma Goldman

A research survey by University at Buffalo in the United States which looked at the levels of stress experienced by social workers found that 70-75% of them had emotional exhaustion (2008). The survey focused on a number of areas, including burn-out, emotional exhaustion and personal accomplishment. Surveys such as these show that social workers and those working in this sector can experience high levels of stress, as will be highlighted by the real-life stories in this chapter.

Karen Lambert's Story – Rapid Response Worker in Family and Children's Services, Canada

'I work in the field of Child Protection, where there are lots of demands for seeing children and families, interviewing and working with families with high conflict. There are Ministry demands, paperwork demands, organisational demands and the demands of the families I work with. In my job, I hear children talk about terrible things that have happened to them, and families talk about trauma they have suffered. After a day at work, I then come home to my own family, who have their own demands; such as mealtimes, cleaning up my home, driving my children to activities, seeing friends, helping with homework, and managing the stressors that my children face and want to talk about.

All of this can happen in one day in my life. An example of this is when I receive a work file and I conduct an investigation. Most recently, I attended a family home with police where the mother had been assaulted by her husband and was significantly injured. The husband was arrested, and I had to get the child and mother to a place of safety as the husband was going to be charged and then released that night (due to COVID-19, most people were charged and released with a promise to appear in court). I took the mother and child to the women's shelter and then assisted the mother in getting medical attention. I did not get home until 1:30am in the morning. At 8:30am that morning, I had to manage another file where a mother was having an access visit with her baby in the Neonatal Intensive Care Unit, as the baby was born early with an opiate addiction and was going through the withdrawal process. During the visit, the mother became angry and irate, accusing medical staff of stabbing her baby with needles, and she had to be removed by security. The mother was then placed in a psychiatric ward for a 72-hour hold and I visited her there.

After this, I got home and was exhausted, mentally and physically. However, my own children required my support too. It can be hard to walk through the door and have three teenagers coming at me with different needs such as homework help, a drive to work, dinner demands and a need to go to the store for something. All I want to do is sit down but I cannot, as I still have to be present and have enough emotional support for my own children, so keeping this in check is what I have to do. This is my work every day as I am on a crisis team and have to deal with high-risk situations, sometimes multiple times in one day.

To manage stress, I have a few things that I find very helpful. My own process is what I use for everyday stress (and I think my baseline is high stress), and I use the same process for stressful situations that are linked to a specific event.

I have spent time through my own education and work studying the brain and how trauma affects our brains. This knowledge is power, because having some understanding about the brain can provide a reason for why we feel the way we feel sometimes. Briefly, when our fight or flight senses are activated (which usually occurs during a stressful event or trauma), the stress hormone called cortisol floods the brain. When this happens, one can be on high alert and feel awake, jittery, emotional, or a lack of control or fear. Feelings of 'What the heck do I do now?' can be so overwhelming. When cortisol floods the brain, our amygdala (which manages how we feel our emotions) is awake and makes it difficult to sleep, think straight, make a plan, or basically do anything to solve the problem for at least one hour. While cortisol is diminishing, use that time to manage your stress. Struggling to solve a problem while cortisol is activated is only going to make a person feel worse and more stressed. This is the time for stress reducers and things that can help calm our minds down. What I find helpful is a hot bath - cliché I know, but I have one every evening. It is part of my routine and I look forward to it every day. Also, social time with friends and family is helpful, as well as trying to organise the home as well.

Ensuring a good routine is useful everyday so that you have a schedule. This means that you always know what is happening next when feeling of stress occur. Some of these simple things can be so helpful when things become stressful. My main stress reducer is teaching and training in Jiu Jitsu. It is a good way to relieve the stress of a long day. I go two times a week, and I enjoy seeing the people I teach. My mind can then focus on techniques for two hours and not the stressful situation that may be bothering me. Additionally, it is exercise, and regular exercise is healthy for the body, mind, and soul.

My take-away is this - listen to your body and your brain. Have an understanding of why you feel the way you do, and work through issues when you are calm and collected, because your brain will not function properly in the heat of the moment. Using your favourite stress relievers can help calm the body and brain in a short time, so that you are then capable of working through a situation.'

Peter Hinkley's Story – Social Worker, Australia

'I learned responsibility and resilience at an early age, helping to look after my brother who had learning difficulties, autism, and epilepsy. Unfortunately, he died in his early twenties due to complications with his epilepsy.

I was proud to be the first person in my family to go to university, and equally proud to get a First in Mathematics from a Russell Group university, which gave me a huge amount of self-confidence and opened doors to a career that could not have existed to my parents or grandparents.

By the time I was thirty, things were going exceptionally well for us. My wife and I had been married for two years and we had just bought our first house. We both had good jobs paying good money and with good job security. I really enjoyed my job; I was good at it, and I had had several promotions and pay rises. We were starting to think about starting a family. Over the next two and a half years, several events occurred which tested my resilience until I could no longer cope.

At work, I was offered the opportunity of a secondment. This was initially intended to be 3 to 6 months, and meant leaving the job I enjoyed and was good at to try something different. I knew I was not going to like the work as much, but as it was only for 6 months, I accepted it as a fantastic opportunity to learn new things that would have long-term benefits on my career. Unfortunately, things did not go to plan, and the 6-month secondment became 2 years. I did not enjoy the work, and felt trapped and bored; every day at work felt like Groundhog Day. Just over a year into the secondment, at Christmas time, my wife and I got the fantastic news that we were going to have a baby. The pregnancy went well and ultimately, we had a beautiful healthy baby girl. However, during the pregnancy we were unlucky and had several false alarms. Each false alarm was an incredibly stressful event. At 6 weeks, we had a miscarriage, and had to wait a week for a scan to confirm the bad news. On the day of the scan, it was revealed that we had not had a miscarriage at all! At the 20 week scan, our little girl had a hole in her heart. We had a horrible week waiting to see the cardiologist for a full assessment. Fortunately, this was another false alarm, and everything was OK.

In March of the same year, my father-in-law was diagnosed with asbestos-related lung cancer. His condition deteriorated rapidly and in parallel with the pregnancy. My wife needed a lot of emotional support dealing with the imminent loss of her father while simultaneously being pregnant with our child. Sadly, my father-in-law died just a few weeks after our daughter was born. The same week, after two years on the secondment that I had grown to hate, my employer put me at risk of redundancy. Then two weeks after my father-in-law died from cancer, my mum was diagnosed with cancer, and the prognosis was 50:50.

By this time, everything had built up and become too much for me. I still felt the need to support my wife, who was grieving for her father whilst being sleep-deprived from feeding a newborn baby. I was driving hundreds of miles twice a week to visit my mum in hospital. I found myself increasingly thinking about my brother who had died several years earlier. One morning I finally broke - I cried for an hour and went to my GP. I was diagnosed with stress and anxiety, and given a sick note for two weeks and some sedatives.

Time off work and sedatives did not help, so I went back to the GP and got another 2 weeks off work and more pills. I did not take the pills, but I did take the two weeks off and went to the seaside for fresh air, nice food and wine with my wife and baby.

I was given the 'good news' that I was not going to be made redundant. Twenty-four hours later I resigned! I am happy to say I made a full recovery (and so did my mum). I learned a lot about myself, which has helped me avoid suffering from stress and anxiety again since.

I learned not to bottle up my emotions, fears, stress, and frustration. I am now more open, and talk to friends and family about my feelings.

I got a new job with more work, more problems, more adversity and much more responsibility. Crucially for me, the responsibility gives control, challenge, and more enjoyment. Work stopped being frustrating and boring and became enjoyable again. I find it stressful, but a strangely enjoyable and motivating stress, which is not a problem.'

3.4: Lawyers and Solicitors

"The good lawyer is not the man who has an eye to every side and angle of contingency, and qualifies all his qualifications, but who throws himself on your part so heartily, that he can get you out of a scrape."

– Ralph Waldo Emerson

Hazel Shumaker's Story – Solicitor, Jersey

'As a solicitor of over 25 years, I have been used to stress and even thrived on it. I embraced the culture of maxing out my billing targets each month and pulling multiple all-nighters to complete acquisitions. Once I had moved in-house to work for a large corporation, I balanced being General Counsel and Company Secretary for a succession of increasingly large international companies, as well as bringing up a young family with a husband who often worked away from home. I even managed to find some time to pursue various hobbies over the years. The phrase 'continuous progression' describes me perfectly, whether at work, home, or play.

In recent years, I have moved roles reasonably frequently, once due to a corporate takeover which led to me looking for a new role, then again when the role I found was not exciting enough. After 20 years of being a General Counsel and Company Secretary, I ended up in a place where I didn't like the people, and they didn't like me – a first for me. This coincided with several other non-work-related issues, resulting in me experiencing first-hand a type of stress I have been lucky to avoid for most of my life.

Helpful stress enables us to learn quickly, hone our skills, sharpen our wits, think on our feet, and run marathons - literally or metaphorically. In essence, it helps us to get the job done. Unhelpful stress does the opposite. It can manifest itself in various ways. I became less tolerant, and my concentration lapsed as I found it more difficult to remember where I had left things or what I needed to buy. I couldn't summon up the energy to do as much exercise as before, I ate more junk/comfort food, drank more alcohol, failed to sleep as well and suffered from more headaches. At home, I talked continuously about work and stopped being much fun to be around. At work, I started to second guess myself, lost confidence and became more introverted. Of course, these changes did not happen all at once, and for a while I did not recognise how much stress I was under. Once I did, I set about identifying the causes of the stress, and put in place a plan to eradicate what I could and manage the stressors I was not in control of.

Just as we carry out an MOT on our car or an annual service of our heating boiler, it is incumbent on us all to keep checking in with ourselves - to assess not just our physical health, but our mental health as well. I have found it helpful to create two lists – what is going well in life and makes me happy, and what does not. The first list helps me to count my blessings which, when suffering from unhelpful stress, is not easy. The second list helps to identify each unhelpful stressor. Once I understood what was making me anxious, I started to look at what I could do to change the situation.

Taking this forensic approach suits my personality, but I would urge others to try it. Finding time and space for this introspection is not easy, but I have found it to be worthwhile. You need to be honest about your own role in creating or exacerbating a situation. You can involve others in your deliberations, as long as you chose the right person, though this does require bravery that you may not feel up to.

The process of taking control in this way, whilst potentially stressful in itself, put me on the path to relieving some of the unhelpful stress practically immediately. Even recognising what was beyond my power to change opened up options for me. Having a plan to address the cause of the underlying stress has also enabled me to address the symptoms too. I am back to doing more physical exercise, eating more healthily, drinking less or not at all, and sleeping better, which in turn has led to me having the brain space to tackle the bigger issues of changing jobs, house, etc.

Unhelpful stress is a part of life, rising from time to time in varying shapes or forms. Recognising it early and dealing with it means it remains manageable, enabling you to optimise your potential.'

Matthew Price's Story - Criminal Prosecutor, Sweden

'When people ask what I do, I sometimes offer up my job title as a complete explanation: 'I'm a criminal prosecutor.' Sometimes, I offer a more vague and blunt description: 'I argue with people for a living.' In either case, my answer is usually met with the same response: 'Oh, that's really interesting! It must be stressful!'

The truth of the matter is, my work is incredibly stressful, but not in the way that most people might think. Working as a prosecutor is inherently high-conflict and adversarial. In my day-to-day work, I encounter judges, police officers, defence lawyers, court staff, civil servants, and members of the public. I've had a front-row seat to nearly every aspect of the human condition that you could imagine. Sometimes I meet people on the worst day of their lives, and others on their best day. I have witnessed people in states of intense anger or sadness, and I have seen some people show one another levels of compassion and grace that I hadn't thought possible. I have laughed with some, and cried with others. My role in the criminal justice system is to present a case firmly and fairly to the Court, and to do my best to see that justice is done. Invariably, this means that people are going to disagree with me, sometimes passionately. The job requires thick skin, sharp elbows, and a big heart.

The moments of high, dramatic stress rarely come, if ever. The real-life courtroom is not like what you see on television; it is, for the most part, a reserved, polite, and orderly place. Some might even call it boring, and most of the time they would not be wrong. The true stress of the job is realised in the countless hours of painstaking preparation, agonising over strategic decisions, and trying to manage a punishing workload. Stress resides in the knowledge that every case demands the very best of your skill and expertise. Any respite that comes with the conclusion of a case is short-lived: as soon as one case closes, a different one joins the queue. Lawyers in general, and criminal lawyers specifically, are renowned for having a poor work/life balance. Mental health disorders and substance abuse are rife in our profession, and it is a grim stereotype that criminal lawyers tend to die early rather than retire.

My most stressful time as a lawyer was not the time a judge screamed at me to leave their courtroom (it's a long story, but it was actually a case of mistaken identity), or the time an accused person threatened to 'smash my face in' (in fairness, he was having a very bad day, and I don't think he meant anything by it). No, my most stressful time as a lawyer was not a single event, but a process.

One summer a few years ago, I agreed to take over a case from a colleague who was going through a difficult time with his family. With a mere month to prepare the case in addition to my normal case load, I agreed to take on a two-week jury trial. This put a significant strain on my schedule, and at the conclusion of the jury trial I expected to have two weeks of preparation time before starting another three-week murder trial. It was tight, but manageable.

Things did not work out as planned, and my two-week jury trial soon stretched to four weeks, obliterating my preparation time before starting the next case. By the end, I had spent nearly three months working almost every waking hour on complex litigation, inside and outside the courtroom. I could barely function due to exhaustion. I should mention that my particular ordeal isn't unusual in this profession – many trial lawyers will go for months (or years) at a time without a break. I quickly realised that the pace I had set for myself was unsustainable. I wasn't sleeping or eating properly and, as I had no time for recreational activities, I was truly miserable.

Stress can motivate us to achieve, but it can also take a toll on our health and well-being, and the relationships we share with those around us. With age and maturity, my priorities have shifted. Although my job is important and demands my best efforts, I try not to lose sight of what is truly important - my family, my friends, and my health. After all, just because I argue with people for a living, doesn't mean I should make it my whole life.'

Tips for Lawyers and Solicitors

Legal professions are regularly among the highest reported most stressful job areas. In 2014, 96% of 1,517 solicitors surveyed by the Law Society said they felt negative stress in their occupation. If you work for a big firm, find out about available resources such as mindfulness, yoga and stress awareness courses. Keep a close eye on the number of long hours you spend working, and try to get the balance right through honest, open conversations with your manager or HR team. If you are working in a small firm or by yourself, this is harder to implement but still needs to be reviewed.

The key to keeping on top of your stress whilst managing a busy workload includes:

- Identifying what will help you thrive and not just survive
- Having a flexible approach to work and developing your resilience
- Set a limit on your case load by refusing some clients and passing them on to other colleagues
- Challenging the veracity of negative thoughts as vigorously as you would challenge an opponent's case
- Seek excellence not perfection, as you are human and will make mistakes
- Accept that you will lose some cases
- Have a support network of friends, family and encouraging work colleagues
- Take breaks during the day
- Plan for contingencies
- Keep your mind flexible
- Team building to help with motivation and camaraderie

3.5: Farming

"Farming is the riskiest profession in the world since the fate of the crop is closely linked to the behaviour of the monsoon."

- M.S. Swaminathan

Farming is one of the ten most stressful occupations in the world.

Researchers have found that farmers experience a demanding work environment coupled with long hours all year round. Farmers who have poor social support can develop stress, anxiety, mental health problems and depression, which can lead to suicide. Farmers and their families face many stressors which are related to the physical environment; this includes economic difficulties, such as lockdown and Brexit rules in Great Britain. Other stressors include the changing structure of farming families and the uncertainties associated with farming, which can be detrimental to famers' mental health.

Two of the most identified stress factors among farmers are worrying about finances and workload.

Financial Worries

Money worries can arise due to irregular and uncertain income as well as the accumulation of debt, as farming requires a large capital investment for equipment, food for animals, vet bills, machinery and much more. There are many government regulations and a mountain of paperwork required to operate within the farming industry. Many farmers have no choice but to take a second job to supplement their income, rather than lose their farm when it is running at a loss. Farmers have struggled with a 40 – 50% decrease in net farm income since 2013. The number of farmers filing for liquidation and closures has risen to a level not seen since the 2008 recession. Meanwhile, production expenses and interest rates are increasing, putting family farmers in a vice that is forcing many to call it quits, or consider worse.

Workload

High workloads, especially during peak times such as harvesting or calving, can cause huge pressure on farmers. There is also time pressure to get products to market and retail groups as quickly as possible. The most reported symptoms of farmer stress reported were fatigue, sleep problems, irritability, low mood, and high rates of stress. When farmers are highly stressed, their health is impacted by chronic back and respiratory problems, as well as farm-related injuries. The Health & Safety Authority report that the fatality rate in agriculture is far higher than any other economic sector, and unfortunately a large proportion of all fatal workplace accidents occur in agriculture. When farmers visit their doctor, it's not easy for them to accept advice to take a vacation or change to a less stressful job. Their role as a farmer is at the root of their identity; it's their culture, not just a job. Farmers are very loyal and feel burdened at the possible loss of their land, which may have been in their family for generations.

Ties to Livestock

In the past, things like foot and mouth disease have added to emotional stressors for farmers. This is especially the case when farmers lose animals through disease, floods, drought, hard winters or other adverse weather conditions. Farmers have a close connection to their animals, and feel their loss when they die or have to be put down. The mental health of farmers is one of the biggest challenges currently facing the sector. Recently, the Royal Agricultural Benevolent Institution (RABI, 2021) reported that almost half of the farming community (47%) were experiencing some form of anxiety, and 36% were probably or possibly depressed.

Ted Brandon's Story – Farmer, UK

'Dairy and sheep farming has been in my family for many generations. I have a dairy farm with a herd of 150 cows and my brother has a sheep farm. It has been a labour of love, and can be extremely rewarding. I look back with fond memories of our 2 children growing up with farm animals and nature. Our children have now left the farm to pursue careers, one in engineering and the other in the army. This left my wife and I with half a dozen full-time farm workers and occasional part-time helpers to tend the farm.

Over the last few years, I have been constantly stressed and unable to sleep properly due to the worries and pressures of farming life. I had high levels of anxiety and a bout of depression, but I couldn't take holidays or take time off because I was too worried about who would run the farm. I would sit in a paddock after a hard day's work feeling lonely, isolated, tearful, and drowning in the day-to-day pressures. It was all grinding me down; it seemed that we were losing more money than making it. Over the years, supermarket chains were wanting to reduce prices for milk, which reduced my profits for the farm as I had to deal with downward milk prices during the 2015 dairy crisis. More recently, supply chains were disrupted following the lockdown imposed to suppress the COVID-19 outbreak in March 2020. COVID-19 reduced demand from the hospitality industry which meant some farmers like myself were unable to sell our milk, and had no option but to dispose of it. My veterinary bills were sky high because of problems with my dairy cows.

Looking back, I never really recovered from the impact of foot and mouth disease and BSE (bovine spongiform encephalopathy – also called 'mad cow disease'), a progressive neurological disorder of cattle that results from infection by an unusual transmissible agent called a prion. I still feel the pain from the loss of our cattle who had contracted BSE and died horrible deaths, and had to be removed from the farm to have their carcasses incinerated. Government subsidies have been a lifeline for me and many farmers, especially when prices or environmental conditions have been volatile. The uncertainty of changes to subsidies added even more stress. It was a harrowing time in my life, and I even contemplated taking my own life when things got very dark.

At this point, my wife intervened and invited a good friend and fellow farmer around. She put us together in a room until I started talking. Looking back, this was the best thing that could have happened, as I don't know how much more I could have taken. This started the ball rolling as I really needed help. Talking about mental health hasn't come easy for me as I am a private man, and I was reluctant to seek formal help. After having support and advice from like-minded farmers who understood what I was going through, I realised that help was long overdue. It was a tough uphill battle, but I had an amazing supportive wife who made it easier than going through it by myself. I don't know what I would have done without her. My brother and sister-in-law became a lot closer to us, as they seemed to be doing well, but were also struggling. We made a pact to help each other and make cuts and investments wherever we could. We decided to sell part of our land to private property developers. We also have plans to open up a shop to sell local produce from other farmers, including organically grown vegetables, chicken eggs and meat. This will help us to diversify our brand, and bring in much needed cash flow.

I hope this story helps fellow farmers out there and encourages you to start talking about your stress and problems before they become too much to handle.'

Help and Support for Farmers

It's important for farmers to seek local support, which is more likely to be used and trusted. However, there is variability in farming communities' preferences for support. Partnership approaches that enable access to a range of services through a single point of contact are likely to be most successful. Find a support service that is multi-dimensional and can cater for the wide range of stressors that impacts the farming community.

3.6: Aviation

"There's only one job in this world that gives you an office in the sky; and that is pilot."

- Mohith Agadi

Kathryn Atkinson's Story - Flight Instructor, England

'As a flying instructor, dealing with high stress scenarios is a frequent part of my job. I have plenty of stories about sudden weather changes, aircraft malfunctions, and the inevitable excitement that ensues when teaching student pilots how to land! However, I find that this type of stress is over and done with very quickly: it's the cumulative stress that poses the real danger.

Back when I was a student pilot, I remember distinctly a day when the stressors in my personal life came to a head and completely caught me off guard. I was doing an intensive one-month course to earn my private pilot licence; my grandfather had passed away earlier that year, and my dad had recently fallen ill and been admitted to hospital. I was of course aware that I was stressed, but remained resolutely single minded, pressing on with training, determined to finish within the time frame as planned

I was due to fly solo that day - alone in the aircraft while my instructor supervised from the ground. All seemed fine until I was lined up on the runway about to take off. Out of the corner of my eye I noticed that one of the switches was in the wrong position. I quickly looked around the rest of the cockpit and saw that it wasn't the only thing wrong. Then it hit me - I'd missed out a whole section of crucial pre-flight checks! If I had messed up something as simple as following a checklist, then what else might I mess up in flight? I decided taking off wasn't a good idea and taxied back to the parking spot instead. I just hadn't appreciated how much of an effect my personal problems could have on my ability to fly.

With the safety-critical nature of my job, I now take it very seriously when it comes to recognising in myself when the stress is building up, making me physically or emotionally fatigued. If I notice I'm getting clumsy, forgetful or snappy with people, it's time for some early nights or to book some days off. Safety aside, being grumpy with students is unfair and puts undue pressure on them. At best, the lesson is thoroughly unenjoyable: at worst, it's setting them up to fail. Stress can also come off as nerves, and no-one wants to fly with a nervous pilot! I do my best to always put on my 'pilot persona' when I get in an aircraft - calm, confident and with a smile on my face. Admittedly, some days that's a lot easier than others.

When it comes to work stress leaking into my personal life however, I'm not nearly as adept at noticing it before it escalates. On one embarrassing occasion, I was doing an evening kickboxing class which finished with some light sparring. My partner caught me with a knee to the stomach and I went down in tears. The coach ran over to check how badly I was injured (assuming it was an accidental low blow) and I had to explain that I was not hurt at all - I was crying because the previous week I'd had a partial engine failure after take-off and barely made it back to the airfield.

In the heat of the moment, I had made an emergency radio call, tried to troubleshoot the problem, navigated back to the airfield, reassured my student, continually assessed which field I would glide into if it completely stopped and ultimately made the right airmanship decisions to get us safely back on the ground. There had been no time for panic. After a week of bottling it up and trying to ignore it, taking a light body shot had been enough to make the stress spill over. I guess it had to come out somewhere.

I am lucky enough to have people close to me who recognise when I am struggling, and will call me out on any uncharacteristic reclusive behaviour or tetchy attitude without taking it too personally. I am someone who tries to bottle things up, but it just does not work. Acknowledging stress and taking action to let it go seems to be the answer, otherwise I end up taking it out on others then becoming even more stressed from the guilt! When I am doing well on the stress awareness front, I talk things out with friends and family, and if no one is available I write it down. Usually just the act of discussing it is enough to calm things down, but if I am still stressed after that then at least it is out in the open where it can't sneak up on me!'

Stress in Pilots

Career Cast ranked this job as the third most stressful job in 2012 (Career Cast, 2012). Becoming a professional flight instructor or airline pilot can be quite stressful, as it can involve many responsibilities for people's lives and many risks (Hansen, 2015). There may be numerous sources of stress which can increase the dangers of flying. These include three main groups of stressors; physical, physiological, and psychological (Pratt, 2012):

Physical Stressors - These may include factors within the cockpit environment such as lack of oxygen, noise and vibrations.

Psychological Stressors - These may include the pilot having to deal with personal relationships, financial problems or the loss of loved a one.

Physiological Stressors - This may include things like illness and fatigue, lack of sleep and insufficient nutrition.

Financial Stress - Many pilots may have to pay up to £100,000 to gain enough flying hours and then pass all the tests and exams to become a licenced pilot, both practical and theory. It may take many years before these loans are fully paid off.

Other Stressful Factors - Additional stressors can include luggage not being ready, someone being late on a flight, very tight turnaround times in airports, and on occasions losing a take-off or landing slot. Food poisoning and other illnesses can also prevent flights from happening as scheduled. During COVID-19, a number of pilots were furloughed, and some were only getting 40% of their pay until the UK government stepped in paid 80% of the salaries.

Coping Methods

'Caging the Monkey'

Some pilots are trained to deal with stress using the 'caging the monkey' training process. It is said that under stress and pressure, we resort to 'monkey brain thinking' and can over-react due to brain chatter going into overdrive. This can lead to poor decision-making and panic if the 'monkey' is not calmed. Part of the process is taking a moment to breathe and properly appreciate and think about the stressful situation you are being faced with. This could be things like an engine fire, smoke in the cabin, or some other emergency. Each pilot would ask the other for their thoughts and evaluation of the situation by swiftly reviewing all the facts at hand. This calm evaluation, combined with cross-referencing and years of experience and training, will ensure better decisions and outcome. This way you can see the threat at hand with a rational mind.

Taming and caging your monkey mind will provide all of the following for you:
- Clarity of mind
- Greater focus on the present and on the task at hand
- Improved quality of sleep
- Increased sense of calm and well-being

It's a good idea to have a conversation with yourself and try to better understand your monkey mind if it gets over excited and out of control (Eulenstein, 2021). This will help to calm it down so more rational decisions can be made. When your monkey mind is in full swing, calm it down by having a conversation with it. Stop for a moment and listen to try and understand what your monkey mind is saying. Once you have the answers, you can better calm the monkey mind and help make better decisions.

As we can see, pilots use a variety of methods to assess the situation at hand and stay calm. Even though most of us reading this chapter are not pilots, we can still take away some useful tips for dealing with stressful situations in life.

3.7: Health Care

"It is health that is real wealth, not pieces of gold and silver."

— Mahatma Gandhi

Terrence Whitcombe Price's Story - Nurse Endoscopist, England

'I have had a varied career history, working both within and outside of the NHS. I have had high intensity jobs, working as part of a team and on my own. I always thought I had good coping mechanisms and the resilience to shoulder more responsibility, so I always sought out doing or helping more.

I knew I could be grumpy occasionally, but I put it down to being tired, juggling too many things and looking after other people's needs (constantly). I never thought that stress would affect me significantly. That was before my late 40's, when I was progressing in my career as a Nurse Endoscopist.

I became the manager of the team, and so had lots of extra responsibility. With this came the opportunity to do more advanced endoscopy. I already do most things in endoscopy, and this was a step up in terms of clinical responsibility - higher decision-making, higher risk.

I completed the training and obtained certification (this is a rigorous ordeal in itself) for this advanced level of work. I now found myself in a position where I could not say no to any extra clinical work. I did all (general) procedures, and I now also did this extra level of work which only a small team of five Consultants and myself could do. So, I was asked – daily – to pick up extra work. This meant not only having to change my schedule around, but also that I was doing more and more.

In endoscopy, we have different managers for different services. Different managers would approach me, not knowing that the other managers had approached me with the same request – can I do more? Can I pick up this extra list? Can I do this task for them or look at this bit of work to help them out? Please, pretty please…?

Initially, the individual managers did not realise that this was happening to me. However, when I informed them that I could not keep up with all their requests, the trend for coming to me first was already established and it was a hard habit to break. It continued in this vein for many months.

After some time, I realised that I generally didn't feel well most of the time. Nothing major, but I just felt unwell and worried more. The most significant thing I felt was anxious all the time and I could not sleep. I'd never had that problem before, so it really bothered me. I was tired and found it difficult to concentrate. I worried a lot about it. Most of all, I really resented how I was being used at work. I did try to discuss this with one of the managers, but she was not sympathetic and continued to have the same expectations of me. This bothered me greatly, and so I eventually spoke to my line manager about it and had a small break down. I was tearful, which I hadn't expected. Neither did she, and it really made me feel concerned that I was 'cracking up.' Fortunately, my manager was very supportive and helped me out straight away. We formulated a plan to re-organise my work, and she spoke with the managers and explained that I was under too much pressure and they needed to reduce their expectation of what I could realistically do.

The NHS Trust recently started to take stress and anxiety seriously, and they have instigated open forums for all staff (including very senior and experienced people) to talk about how they feel about pressure and difficult situations at work. This makes all staff feel like the Trust cares about how they are coping with working for the NHS, particularly now when it is at its most pressured and under-funded in its history.

As for me, I'm OK. I realise that working too much is not productive. I am more aware of stress and the impact it has on me. If I look after myself, I should be around for a lot longer to keep providing for patients. I think it has made me a better manager too. I am conscious of protecting my team to get the best out of them, not the most.

On reflection, I should have realised earlier that it was affecting me, and spoken out sooner. I tried to 'soldier on' but this, with hindsight, was not the right thing to do. Talking to somebody is always the difficult first step, but talking is what is going to help you see clearly that you need to make changes to help you sort it out.'

Vladamir Ambramov's Story – Doctor, Wales

'A normal day in my job and for all doctors is stressful. In one day, I can be running non-stop for 8 to 12 hours, and then be on-call. I have patients, doctors and nurses demanding my time. I have hospital management on my back. I must sometimes console families when they lose a loved one, or empathise with a patient who is critically ill or told that they have an inoperable tumour. I am up to my neck in paperwork and my brain is full of information. I need to make rapid decisions, sometimes without adequate information. It's like a pressure cooker - each day I am faced with delicate medical decisions, and if I make an error or miss some important piece of information, the fall out is disastrous, to the people I care for as well as to my professional standing and reputation. I could be sued based on these decisions which have financial consequences, so I spend a good percent of my income on legal insurance.

A recent poll from the American College of Emergency Physicians found that 87% of emergency room doctors experienced more stress during the pandemic, and 57% of ER doctors say they would be concerned for their jobs if they sought mental health treatment.

On a bad day, the emotional strain of dealing with difficult or very ill patients is draining. I would go home and have extraordinarily little time with my family, or be stressed and irritable, resulting in arguments for no reasons. I would sometimes deal with the death of a child, a mistaken diagnosis, or someone dying unexpectedly and having to wonder if it was my fault. Perhaps me or one of my team made an error, and as head of department I am accountable for it. Days like this can drive doctors like me over the edge. I have been there, and it is a dark place. Without going to much detail, a patient died right in front of me from a ruptured aortic aneurysm. The scan had looked normal; the aneurysm was in the chest and ruptured into the thorax, which is very unusual. I found it hard to sleep that night, and for many nights afterwards. I sought help from my psychologist and spoke to colleagues who I respected and understood what I was going through.

I had to review my own health as I wasn't getting enough exercise, I already had high blood pressure, and was on several pills for diabetes. Adding high levels of stress to this mix was not good. My wife supported me through this difficult time which I truly appreciate, and I managed to book some time away from work to recuperate. I started to spend more time with my children who were growing up fast without me realising. I went back to work on a phased return and made plans to share responsibility with other senior doctors. In time, I became more aware of my stress triggers and made adjustments to cope.'

Rachael Gue's Story - Paramedic and Photographer, England (www.rachelguephotography.co.uk)

'My career in the NHS began as a student paramedic in 2012, and I graduated and registered as a Paramedic in 2015. Stress is something I have battled with daily; mostly good stress, but also some awfully bad stress. Anxiety is something I have battled with throughout most of my life, most likely from childhood. I had a very good childhood, but anxiety has always been a part of me. With the stresses of being a paramedic coupled with anxiety, there were days I did not think I could continue with my paramedic career. Being a paramedic comes with stresses and demands of all kinds:

- Working with colleagues for up to 12 hours that berate you over the littlest things

- Disagreeing with others regarding treatment or the correct care pathways for your patients
- Being belittled by accident and emergency staff in front of your patients
- Driving to fatal accidents at 3am in the morning with heavy eyes
- Being audited and the smallest mistakes being pointed out to you
- Low mood and anxiety after 12-hour night shifts.
- Imposter syndrome (thinking you are not worthy of your position, feeling like a fraud)

Most days, I dealt with these like any normal person would. However, when coupled with personal life stresses or challenges, I was then faced with very unwelcome periods of acute anxiety.

For reasons mentioned above, I can think of numerous times during acute periods that I cried before work, after work, at work. It wreaked havoc, and acute periods of anxiety almost destroyed my career - but I am still here doing what I love. How is that, I hear you ask?

There are many things I have done to combat anxiety and low mood. Number one was recognising why I chose the career of paramedic in the first place. I am not here for anyone else other than my patients and me. I love that my hard work and determination can help save the lives, and not just by restarting hearts - a paramedic's main and vital skill is communication.

Talking to patients has made a difference. Being there for patients when they are alone has made a difference. Listening to their life stories has made a difference. My patients and most of my crew mates were a reason to turn up to do the job I love because I have made a difference in someone's life. You also don't need to be a paramedic to do this.

When times became very tough, I stepped away from ambulance shifts and considered other avenues, in addition to changing personal life circumstances. This was one way of eliminating most causes of stress and I am now loving life as a paramedic/emergency care practitioner in a minor injury unit. This may change in a few years but that's also OK, because I will then reassess and see what I can do to improve. This works for all professions or lifestyles. Find ways of changing your life for the better, physically and mentally. Do it for you!

Recognising when something is not right for you is a positive step, even if at that point you don't know what to do. That is OK - take your time and find your way.

I have reached out to family, very close friends and my partner for help. Whilst they have all also struggled at times, they have continued to support me in every way they can, for which I will be eternally grateful. I have been through hours of counselling in addition to my own therapies, such as martial arts, sport, and photography.

Throwing yourself into things you love doing is the best recipe to overcome most types of stress. I know it's not easy, and I admit there have been days where I have struggled to go to Jiu Jitsu or get out with my camera, but once you get yourself into a routine, you will find that stress will quickly diminish and you will regain control.

My take-home points to all reading would be:

- If you are not happy, make a change. Whether in your career or lifestyle choices, go back to the drawing board and change to make yourself happy. It is never too late.
- Sit down and do things for you. Take some time to just sit and breathe.
- In times of low mood or anxiety, think of a colour. Mine is yellow. Sunshine = happiness.
- Try new hobbies. I am always trying new things. I have recently started painting and oil pastel drawings. I'm no Van Gogh, but its therapeutic and a good source of stress relief. And of course, I whole heartedly encourage getting out there with a camera (phone, DSLR, film) and taking photos on any adventures.
- Always have something planned to look forward to. This doesn't have to cost money or even be a big thing.
- TALK, TALK, TALK - I cannot emphasise this enough. Don't bury your head in the sand. Opening up always makes you feel better, and your friends and family do really want to help and guide you. If you feel you are unable to speak to friends or family, then

contacting your GP for an appropriate referral would be mostly beneficial (I would also encourage those who can rely on family to also do this).'

Tim Sorsky's Story - Chiropractor, Brazil

'I am a chiropractor, which means that I have regular close contact with hundreds of people each month. I see people suffering with various types of pains in different parts of their bodies. Over the years, I have come to recognise the role stress plays in everyone's lives, especially in relation to pain, mental health, and well-being.

The body is a fantastic and intricate machine, made up of physical, emotional, and chemical components - the so-called 'triad of health.' Stress can be physical (a fall, a car crash etc.), emotional (death of beloved, work issues, family etc.) or chemical (foods, drugs, alcohol, cleaning products etc.) in nature. When stress arises in any of these systems, the others will try to compensate by working harder. Sometimes they override the faulty component by successfully restoring health, whereas other times the faulty system brings everything else into chaos.

The more we ignore stress, the more it grows and chronically damages our body by increasing levels of inflammation, creating hormonal imbalances (especially by overworking our adrenal glands, where cortisol is mainly produced), and impairing tissue repair, cellular growth and much more. This will lead to more pain, which over time will turn from acute to chronic, wreaking havoc in every cell of our body, creating the right environment for disease to proliferate.

When I was young, I struggled to manage stress in my life. I have been aware of being stressed since I was in my early teens for one reason or another. Over the years it got worse, to the point that during my university years I developed panic attacks and social anxiety. I never really tried to focus on the root of the problem; instead, I managed to ignore how I was feeling by being highly active and sporty.

I started to finally understand the importance of stress during my postgraduate studies and when I began working. Years went by, and I slowly shifted my awareness, trying to cultivate my spiritual dimension through daily meditation, walks, psychotherapy, and cleaner eating. It was helping, but then I suddenly stopped all my healthy routines at the beginning of the COVID-19 pandemic. I stopped meditating, practising sport, and all my other hobbies, replacing good habits with bad ones, one at a time. Loneliness and the inability to express my feelings brought my stress levels to a new high, causing me to get accustomed to a constant state of 'burn out.' After re-living my past through another panic attack, I understood it would only get worse. I knew I had to take a break, and realised that the single most important thing for me was finding someone to talk to.

Talking more, especially with people I trust and feel comfortable being honest and vulnerable with, as well as moving my body daily with long walks, helped me greatly to cope better with my stress.

It makes me feel uncomfortable to talk about things like this, but I know I'm not the only one that has struggled with life lately, for one reason or another. Being open and vulnerable with that bunch of people in your life that you can really trust and rely on can help you find that lost balance once again.

Finding the motivation to talk about it helped me overcome my divided mind, and all other aspects of my life slowly improved too. We are social animals, and we need real connections to remind ourselves of the magic that life is.'

Tips and Advice to Reduce Stress for Medical Professionals

Some workplaces run wellness programs offering yoga, meditation, photography, and other classes designed to reduce stress and encourage a healthy work/life balance. Several hospitals have benefits, such discounted gym memberships, an on-site massage service and physio, as well as help for employees to figure out how to handle stress at work in healthcare jobs.

Compassion Fatigue

Compassion fatigue is a term which describes the stress that comes from caring 'too much.' It can strike any healthcare worker, as being compassionate and empathic is the one of the main reasons for joining the healthcare profession. Strategies for dealing with compassion fatigue include increasing social support, rejecting feelings of self-blame and guilt, and participating in community or charitable events.

Many medical professionals have shared their tips for dealing with their stressful occupations, a few of which are discussed below (Shadowfax, 2013). Some healthcare professionals will practice 'professional detachment.' This is when the health care professional tries to maintain a sense of distance from their day-to-day tasks and crises. This can mean suppressing their natural urge to feel sympathy for suffering patients. Whilst this may help in the short term, it can be detrimental if taken to extremes. Sympathy and compassion should be delivered in a measured dose, used on a case-by-case basis, and balanced with one's own mental state and capacity.

A number of health care professionals will take some time to deal with bad experiences. Some professionals will blame themselves and feel guilt and shame if some form of error took place, and it may cause extreme stress and anxiety. Some choose to erase their mistakes from their memory, however avoiding the issue may exacerbate the problem. It's a good idea to informally debrief with a trusted partner, superior or mentor.

- Talk through the case, reviewing your actions, outcomes, and emotional response to the situation
- Your mistakes may have been due to a system error or cognitive bias, so it's important to seek out the root causes to improve the quality of your own care and that of your team
- Keep a sense of perspective and try to stay positive
- Take a break, go outside, and take a few deep breaths. Try to remember the big picture

"There is only one boss - the customer, and he can fire everybody in the company from the chairman on down, simply by spending his money somewhere else."

- Sam Walton

It's well known that owning a business can be very rewarding, and at the same time extremely stressful. Many thousands of hours and money could have been invested. Alongside this there could be large overheads, loans to pay off, and responsibility for employing and managing staff. The stories featured in this chapter highlight some of the highs and lows of running a business, and the strain it can put on work life balance and relationships.

James Owen's Story - Managing Director, UK

'In my role as the Managing Director (MD) of a small to medium sized enterprise (SME), I have had a fair few stressful situations to contend with. The daily running of your own business can be quite stressful. Knowing that you are responsible for providing everything to keep the company running, and that the company provides the money for the roof over your family's heads and the food on the table, is rather a lot to think about!

The biggest source of stress I have found as an MD is money. Management, the prediction of income, and the allocation of funds to properly balance the business are all constant sources of stress. If you take your eye off that particular ball for a moment, things can quickly become quite unmanageable.

When I was asked to write about stress and how I manage it, a few experiences popped straight into my head. However, one in particular was definitely a high point of stress so far in my life. This involved my first business partner pulling the rug out from under me and closing the business without my consent, and in the process taking the entire cash balance of the company.

To cut a long story short, I decided early in the partnership to trust my shares in the company to his named party so that we could open a business bank account. This didn't quite work out in the way I had hoped. We had several discussions about how we were, or rather weren't, working together, and I offered to buy his half of the business in order to keep our friendship safe from the rigors of business life. At the time he agreed, and said he would formulate a price.

A few days later, I was locked out of the company banking without warning and started to receive emails from his chosen liquidator. I was informed that as an employee (not owner director as was the reality) my employment and all links with the company were being terminated.

The bottom fell out of my world. The company I had worked on building for years was suddenly being taken away from me, and there was nothing I could do. My business partner and his entire family ignored all requests to open communication channels and I was left totally alone, without a job or business.

At this point, I had twin 6-year-old boys to think about, a partner who was finishing her degree, and rent and bills to pay with no money. I had no savings, in fact I had a large debt from my previous bad life decisions, and I was staring into a rather large abyss.

My stress levels were through the roof when this happened. For a day or so I was basically non-functional. I thought my life was over: I was a complete failure and a fool. I sat in my bed and did nothing but play out all the failures in my head.

It was at this point that the group of people I call my 'inner counsel' rushed to my aid. I am truly blessed to have them, and not a day goes by that I am not grateful for each of them. One by one, they put their metaphorical (and literal) arms around me and picked me up. They told me to get going again, get back on the horse, and pick myself back up.

By sharing what happened with my inner counsel, they talked me through it, and got me ready to go back into the business world again. I cannot emphasise enough the importance of reaching out to those closest to you in times of stress!

I am typically a pragmatic, driven, and stoical person in my approach to life. I do not like to be a burden on people, or give them my 'baggage' to carry. However, a vital piece of stoic philosophy is to give yourself the advice and consideration that you would give your best friend in that situation. I can testify through many personal experiences that your closest friends and family are there for you, just waiting for that call for help. If your best friend reached out in their time of need, would you help them? Well then, there you go!

Whether it's a phone call on my drive home, a vent over a cup of tea in the kitchen when I get home, a Jiu Jitsu session with some of the best people I know, or just a beer and a half-drunk conversation, my inner counsel **always** helps me deal with stress. Sometimes they tell me to stop moaning about nothing and get on with it, sometimes they let me cry on their shoulder (more than once for most of them).

If you experience stress that begins to overwhelm you, share it with someone! Exercise, diet, and good people are my keys to navigating this stressful world. I can only repeat myself again and say share your feelings and thoughts so that people can help you!

I did start again by the way. I took out a crazily high percentage business loan and started it all again from scratch. This year, the company I run with one of my inner counsel has turned over just shy of £1 million! Not bad for a ruined, stressed fool with nowhere to go.'

Derek Clayton Jones's Story – Business Owner, England

'I've never been great at managing stress, but a few years ago the mechanisms I used were pushed beyond their limits when the 3 most important things in my life all came crashing down.

Firstly, I found out my wife was having an affair and my marriage was over. While I was processing that news, a week later my mother - my only surviving relative - was told she only had a few months to live. I took some time out of running my development company and moved in with my terminally ill mother so that I could look after her. Shortly after the sad loss of my mother, the business that I had been building for 20 years collapsed.

I could have probably dealt with each of these problems on their own, but they hit me in quick succession and I found it hard to cope. It felt like things were spiraling out of control. I was stressed and irritable, not getting much sleep, tired and restless. I realised I was depressed and went to see my GP, where I was referred to some psychiatrists. Unfortunately, my experience was not great. I had hoped to get counselling, but they would only see me if I went on a course of medication which I was not prepared to do. Instead, I tried to cope on my own; I found solace being with friends and drinking too much, but was ultimately avoiding dealing with my mounting problems.

My need for escapism continued and I left the country on an extended break travelling around New Zealand. It was there, on the other side of the world, that I realised running away from my problems wasn't working and that I had to go home and try to get my life back on track. I cut my holiday short and got on a plane back to the UK.

When I was growing up, there was a part of me that tended to push back when I was the underdog; a need to prove to others that I could do better and bounce back. It was this determination, along with an acceptance of where I had found myself, that I turned to for strength.

I decided that I would make a list of all the challenges I was facing. I was very methodical about this, and as each day and week passed, I tried to work through each problem I faced in order of importance. I had to sort out the mounting paperwork which I had neglected, and I worked diligently to get through it. This way I could compartmentalise and isolate each issue. It wasn't easy, and it took discipline and persistent effort over 12 months to make things better. I sought advice and support from friends and spent my free time training in several different combat martial arts to help with stress relief and lingering depression.

I did get divorced, but found a new relationship and got married a few years later. I am very happy, proud and privileged to have a wonderful wife and family. I managed to get some money back from my old company after its liquidation, and was able to start again and build it up to become something better than it had been. The loss of my mother will always be with me, but I have many great memories that I treasure.

Those of you reading this story could be hit by many stresses and terrible worries in your life. It's important to keep believing in yourself and put a plan together to tackle all the things that need your attention. Get help and support from friends, try to take positive steps each day, week or month, and seek counselling if you can get it. Someone once said to me, 'It's not what happens to you, but how you deal with it that counts.' This phrase has stuck with me and urged me on.

You will have knock backs, so expect them. It's not about how many times you get knocked down, but the number of times you are willing to get back up and fight for yourself and your family.

I am still very methodical and things still worry me, but I am in a far better place now than I was 15 years ago. I have good health and a happy family. Like everyone, I still have difficulties that I face, however I work hard to look at each one of these as a challenge and not a headache. I hope you find something in my story that may help you.'

Richard Robinson's Story - Language School Business Owner, Argentina
(www.robinsonsinstitute.com)

'I have always enjoyed international travel, and during my time in Argentina I fell in love with the country and people, so I moved there from the UK. I began teaching English in 2010 for several different institutes in the city of Buenos Aires, but by 2012 I was running my own business, giving classes freelance and managing a couple of teachers who were giving classes to other students who I did not have the time to teach. It is hard enough to manage one's own time, but managing the time and actions of others is much trickier.

Starting a business is no easy feat, especially in another country and in another language! I had to deal with messages and calls from students who said that their teacher had not turned up for the class and that they had been waiting for them. It was then up to me to ascertain why the teacher hadn't turned up for the class. Some of the reasons were that they were ill, they had overslept, they forgot, and one teacher (who was soon to leave the country) was hungover! It was then up to me to relay this information to the usually angry student, and attempt to repair the damage by rearranging the class. Sometimes the class had to be refunded, which was not good for business and tainted the institute's reputation.

As soon as I received such a message from a student or teacher about a situation, I felt that it was another burden to deal with, and began to feel stressed. The stress lasted until I had decided upon the best course of action and resolved the situation. Having to deal with this regularly made me very anxious. My mood would tend to deteriorate and I would rush to resolve the problem, which in hindsight was not the best thing to do as I would often be stressed and upset. This also affected the relationship with my girlfriend. It seemed to her that I was taking out my stress on her, when she had nothing to do with the situation that was making me stressed.

In order to combat this, I began to take my time to digest the information first, so I would not fly off the hook and potentially make things worse. I now try to see things from the students' and the teacher's perspective, which facilitates resolving the issue in a way that both would feel content with.

One recent example of this was when a teacher notified me on a Thursday that she couldn't teach any more classes with immediate effect as she had to return to her home country urgently due to family issues. She had classes scheduled on Friday and Saturday that had already been paid for, and that meant I had to find replacement teachers as soon as possible and explain the situation to the students. Naturally I felt myself becoming stressed, but I tried to calm down and think rationally. I messaged other teachers to see if any of them were available to cover the classes. I also sent messages to the students explaining the situation. When I started receiving replies to say that one or two teachers were available, and from students saying that they understood the situation and that they awaited news about their courses, I started to feel better and the stress began to diminish. It helped that I had worded the messages well, explaining the situation in a way that meant the teachers were more inclined to help out, and the students understood that sometimes these things happen in life. It ended up being a very busy day that Thursday, but with some rational thinking and calmness I managed to resolve the issue without getting too stressed and allowing it to affect myself or others around me.

My take-home message is to try and stay calm and digest the information, then explore solutions and options before acting.'

4.1: Managers

"In times of stress, the best thing we can do for each other is to listen with our ears and our hearts, and to be assured that our questions are just as important as our answers."

– Fred Rogers

Jim Bass's Story - Director of Operations, UK

'On August 10th 2018, there was a major incident at my place of work, which tragically resulted in one colleague losing his life and another suffering a life-changing injury, who did return to work after a long rehabilitation. With over 350 colleagues to manage (all of which were part of a close-knit group being located at a relatively isolated facility with significant family ties and long company service) and having both served on the emergency response team and been in a senior leadership position, I felt a tremendous responsibility for this event, and put myself under enormous pressure to support those affected and ensure an optimal return to work situation.

My stress in this situation was derived from many factors: grief for the affected colleagues and their families, concern for the mental well-being of people worried about their friend's recovery and their own job security, people's feelings of guilt and blame, dealing with the immediate physical remediation of the site, the investigation and working with authorities, planning for the restart process (which resulted in a challenging reduction in the workforce), and working too many hours to try help everyone and fix everything as soon as possible.

Stress management theory states that, while some stress is a positive driver of performance, too much can inhibit it, and the build-up of many smaller stresses can be equally as stressful as one or two larger factors. Everyone is unique in what factors and levels constitutes enough or too much stress, so being able to recognise our limits, and to subsequently manage a situation, our behaviour and response is crucial, yet far harder than it sounds.

I recognise that I had an extraordinarily strong support network in and out of work, as well as a routine to fall back on, which meant I could concentrate my energy on the extraordinary events. First and foremost, I talked a lot with my wife in that period. We only briefly discussed the work situation, but she provided a calm and supportive environment. I called my parents regularly, and spoke to some old friends with whom catching up was a source of solace. My children were a great way to forget my concerns for a while and, as ever, exercise provided mental and physical benefits. Teaching and training at the Jiu-Jitsu club in Southampton and running by myself in isolated areas provided the benefits of social and contact activity, as well as individual time to think and consider events.

At work, I interacted closely with many people, and the support and open discussion was incredibly beneficial for everyone. Conversations with two of the directors, mutually supporting each other and talking openly about the effect this was having on our colleagues, were particularly helpful. I also forged a new relationship with an individual who had commanded warships in the Royal Navy, who provided a new perspective and support. The company provided professional counselling and, despite working closely with two amazing gentlemen on the incredible program they delivered, I rebuffed their gentle suggestions and avoided any one-to-one conversations for myself, not wanting to recognise or acknowledge that they would benefit me. However, after sitting in on a particularly difficult group session, I was coaxed into a brief individual conversation and was able to air what was bothering me, understand my thought processes and deal with my feelings.

The impact of different stressors on individuals and their ability to cope with overall stress levels varies significantly. I believe that you can improve your ability to manage stress, both through study and understanding, and practically through implementing coping mechanisms. The challenge is for an individual to recognise what factors are most stressful for them, what an acceptable or unacceptable level of stress is, and develop their own coping mechanisms early enough to be effective. You will sub-consciously be doing some of this already, but may need to develop your awareness and consciously focus on beneficial activity, reducing negative behaviours (over-intake of alcohol, lack of sleep etc.) or eliminate sources of stress – again, far harder than it sounds.

Coping mechanisms can be physical and psychological: music, exercise, rest, hobbies, games, TV, and everyday routines are some practical tools that can reduce physical and psychological stress. The counselling team also shared some simple physiological tips to ensure self-care, as it is natural to withdraw from or simply neglect basics such as exercise, rest, food, and water when under duress. However, I stress one crucial mechanism for everyone, which is human contact. I would much rather the events described had not transpired, but ultimately it was the old and new relationships and shared support with so many people that was most powerful in enabling me and everyone to emerge from that most difficult and stressful of times.'

Frank Birkenstein's Story - Banking Industry Sales Manager, Sicily

'I was fortunate to be promoted at work, which meant I had to travel 200 miles each Sunday and stay in hotel rooms for a few days over an eighteen-month period. It was an exciting new role, which involved working at head office with new people. The downside for me was being away from family and friends, and having to work long hours in a role with extraordinarily little appreciation from senior managers. After a period of 18 months, I was able to secure a regional sales managers role working from home, which I thought would be better for me. The management role created a different level of stress, and meant having to be accountable for a team of talented and strong-willed salespeople. I had big sales targets to meet and inherited a team of individuals who were not used to me or my management style. Some members of the new team found the change in management style a challenge, and there followed a period of adjustment.

This period developed in stages I referred to as storming, norming and performing. We had to overcome some difference in opinions (storming), set new rules for normal working practice with each other (norming), and once we all settled down, we would start meeting our goals better (performing). I had to learn to adapt to their way of working and vice versa, which sometimes led to some heated conversations before things finally settled down. Some individuals would complain and spread rumours behind my back just because they were upset by me asking them to closely follow company processes and avoid breaching local banking compliance rules. These false rumours would get through to senior management, which then led to me being closely monitored. I felt that Big Brother was constantly looking over my shoulder, and felt betrayed by some members of my team. While many team members liked my management and coaching style, others did not. I felt that I had to refrain from micromanaging and using more of a carrot than stick approach. I decide to give people more leeway to make their own decisions. I was disappointed that some team members felt that they couldn't approach me directly with their concerns so we could talk through them, and instead went behind my back.

This led to a many sleepless nights, anxiety and self-doubt, as well as shock and surprise to find out that my team members would act this way. Things did eventually settle down, and I was also asked to use more carrot and less stick - which is what I thought I was doing, but sometimes others can perceive things differently, especially when there is a change in management. It took some time to start to trust some of my team, as it was not clear who had made these confidential accusations. These things should be kept confidential to protect individuals, but at the same time it's important to know what the feedback is so that action to improve can be made. The good news is that the team is performing well, and things have settled down.

This was not an easy time in my life. To keep myself motivated I had to believe in myself, that I was doing a good job, and most people were happy with me. I had some excellent team members who were incredibly supportive. I also have a wonderfully supportive wife who was there as a shoulder to lean on. I had to adjust my ways of working so I could get the best out of people.'

Edwin Gupta's Story – Civil Service, India

'About five years ago, I took a promotion at work that had me stepping into the role of manager of my former team. This was a group of people with whom I had worked for many years and forged some pretty close friendships. As you'd expect, I had the usual doubts: Am I management material? Will it be awkward supervising friends and former peers? Will the added responsibility impact on my work-life balance? It took about a year before I started to feel at ease in my new role. It definitely added a layer of stress to my life, but this was counterbalanced by a feeling that I was challenging myself, expanding my capabilities and broadening my experiences. Sometimes I think stress is easier to manage when there is a counterbalance, such as a reward or positive outcome at the end or along the way.

About mid-way through my second year, the experience changed abruptly with a sequence of events that would push my coping abilities to their limits. In the span of the next eleven months, I learned that five members of my team (or members of their close families) were facing life-threatening or debilitating illnesses. In that same span of time, I learned that a former colleague (the previous manager of our team, in fact, and a role model of mine) had passed away suddenly in her sleep. I had experienced illness and loss in my life before this, but not on such a grand scale and in such swift succession.

The close relationship I had with each of these people, coupled with my role as their manager, compelled me to do everything I possibly could to support them. Unfortunately, the personal strain of internalising their struggles and overloading myself with efforts to help were just too

116

much to handle. My normal coping mechanisms for stress broke down, and the result was a complete drain on my mood, my focus, my happiness and my health.

Luckily, I had support. In fact, there were two things specifically that I did which helped me get through this exceedingly difficult stretch:

1. I listened to the people closest to me. My wife knows me very well; she was able to read my cues, and she knew when things were becoming too much for me. She was the alarm that I could not hear ringing inside myself. Sometimes we think we have things under control and miss those signs that our loved ones can help us to see more clearly.

2. I asked for help. My job was stressful enough, along with other existing pressures outside the workplace and in my personal life. The added strain of trying to process the many challenges my colleagues were facing was overwhelming. I knew that I needed some advice to get through this. There is an unfortunate stigma around seeking help through therapy or counselling - that it somehow signals a weakness or instability in a person. Please let me reassure you that this stigma is false. It takes courage to ask for help, and no one person has all the faculties to deal with every situation. I found it greatly beneficial to speak with someone who could look at me objectively, and who was trained to listen to me and help me build on those coping strengths that I already possessed. It would have been a much harder road had I tried to walk it alone.

I wanted to share this particular story because no matter how adept we are at dealing with stress, situations sometimes come up that push us beyond our threshold. Counselling did teach me a few things, but most of all it provided me with some reassurance and a little more insight into my limits!'

Denis Aubert's Story – Sales Manager, France

'By the spring of 2012, I had been working as a Sales Manager in France for a global European Biotech company for several years. During that time, I had been recognised by my previous boss and my peers as being a leader who delivered consistently well by meeting objectives, offering valuable contributions to the broader team, and developing my own team into a high-performing group of sales representatives.

The company's major product had received authorisation for two new license indications at the end of 2005. The expectations for a significant spike in sales on the back of these positive changes were incredibly high. At the same time, the local health service was going through a massive change in its statutory structure. The sales in France were low, and were deemed as being an underperformance by the parent company. As such, my own stress levels increased day by day, as the sales just seemed to be flat-lining. Despite using all my previous experience of people management, business planning and business analysis, nothing seemed to change the sales trend for my region. I coped with my own stress levels by regularly reminding myself that, as a team, we were doing all the right things. We were a confident, young, and energetic team, and it was more a matter of time before we saw the anticipated uplift in sales.

However, the French senior leadership team started to panic because of the lower-than-expected sales returns. The consequence of this was that the services of a small team of external leadership pharmaceutical professionals were brought in to guide us and help us on this perilous journey, and set us on the path to high performance. However, their style and culture were at odds with that of our own. Some would call their culture one of high performance; others would call it a bullying and harassment culture. This was stressful, since change in the workplace inevitably brings about stress and anxiety. I coped with this by embracing this new team and, wherever possible, supporting them and trying to build positive relationships.

During this period, twice-monthly 'in-depth' business reviews became the norm, where one would expect to be questioned, challenged, and grilled on every aspect of the business and the performance. The inquisitors were made up of senior sales and marketing leaders, and the inquisitor in chief was the newly appointed leader of the group. This was a particularly determined and focused individual, who consistently challenged us. I felt that he was unfair, and was regularly bordering on bullying in the way he conducted himself.

My stress levels during this time were off the scale. Having a business review one week, which lasted more than 3 hours, then subsequently repeating the exercise the following week for a similar length of time, seemed unnecessary and counterproductive. Following that second business review, I was invited back down to the office to have a further chat. The verbal invitation sounded positive, and I was looking forward to exploring some of my ideas. This was not the case, and during the meeting the 'chief inquisitor' and his supporting manager took a further opportunity to challenge, harangue and bully me.

This was the last straw - I had had enough of this type of behaviour and my stress levels peaked. I felt that this was unfair, unwarranted and was certainly not going to continue any longer. I sought solace in reading the Human Resources policies from top to bottom to seek redress for what I had been experiencing. I followed the Company Grievance procedure to the letter. After several further meetings, including a significant one with the most senior leader, I ultimately received a written apology and subsequent verbal apology for the way in which I had been treated by both the 'chief inquisitor' and his supporting manager.

During this unpleasant period, I was not sleeping, not eating properly, and my family relationships were put under significant strain. I know that what I have described, and probably much worse, happens every day for so many people in the workplace. However, my way of coping with the stress was to focus on the problem itself. The bully was essentially causing the stress and adding significantly to the existing stress caused by low sales and low performance. When I achieved some level of control over the situation and addressed those negative behaviors by my seniors, this gave me a sense of relief and helped me to function more effectively, both at home and work. I know it is hard to challenge our superiors, but it is important for everyone to have a voice and to have a fair hearing.

My key coping mechanisms for stress are as follows:

- Share with friends what is on your mind to gain their insight and maybe a different perspective
- Regularly reflect on and remind yourself of your own skills,

abilities and qualities, and the reason you are in that position
- Address the issue with the individual, and seek to understand why and what is going on
- Understand your rights - what is right and what unacceptable behaviours are
- Listen to your family, and do not be too proud to listen to their perspective
- Lots of exercise, dog walking, and running'

4.2: Business Through Lockdown

"Retreating to indefinite lockdown culture would mean surrendering what makes life worth living, a far more tragic cost than anything inflicted by a virus."

- Claire Fox

The global COVID-19 pandemic has been causing havoc across all parts of our society and our lives. Sufferers and family members have dealt with a myriad of problems, ranging from experiencing flu-like symptoms to having to deal with tragic loss of life. For many businesses, the impact is magnified as employees have been taken ill, and raw materials, goods and services are in short supply and high demand, depending on the industry. Trying to run a business when there is no pandemic is difficult in itself, and can cause a great deal of stress and anxiety. The stories in this chapter give you some insight as to how some businesses have coped through the various lockdowns.

Phil Redhouse's Story - Finance Director, Indonesia

'2020 has been a very tough and challenging year for everyone. The impact of the COVID-19 pandemic has had a pervasive impact on the lives of millions of people, affecting their work and personal lives.

I have a personal life and the same stresses and strains as everyone else. I have young children whose education has been disrupted by COVID-

19. I have a parent with a pre-existing condition that makes them potentially vulnerable to COVID-19, and an elderly grandparent at great risk from the virus.

As a company director, I am legally responsible for the health and safety of around 1,500 employees, which is a huge pressure, especially when faced with the unprecedented and unknown events of COVID-19. More specifically, as the Finance Director, I feel the weight of responsibility to protect the long-term financial strength of the company, as this has a direct impact on the long-term viability of all the jobs of the people who work for me. I am acutely aware that, if I fail, all those people could lose their jobs, which would affect their mortgages and their families. The lockdown caused a collapse in our turnover and huge losses during the spring of 2020 before the business could adapt to the changed trading conditions.

Many people do not appreciate the scale of the problems businesses face. A vocal minority refuse to believe things are as bad the media, government and company portray, and some staff have been uncooperative in adapting to new working practices. It is immensely frustrating, and has put jobs and businesses at risk.

In summary, 2020 has been an incredibly stressful year! I have made it through the year with a few strategies for coping with stress. The following lessons I have learned during COVID-19 and previous experience that I use to deal with stressful situations:

Self-Awareness and Honesty with Yourself

I do not think it is possible to deal with stress unless you can recognise what is causing the problem. Personally, I have the mindset and experience to deal with a lot of problems, but there are certain things that I know I will struggle with. It can take a lot of personal courage and self-awareness to understand your own vulnerabilities, but that is the first stage towards addressing stress and making positive changes.

Personally, I struggle with the cumulative effect of lots of small issues in my personal and work life more than individual big events or issues. I also feel stressed by problems that affect me but are outside my control to resolve. Obviously, I cannot fix COVID-19, therefore this has been a particular challenge this year.

Accept It, Deal with It, Get on with It

The choices that I have made in my life are what have put me in the position I am in. Therefore, I am responsible for myself and I am going to sort it out. I do not have to do everything myself, I can get help, I can share my problems, but ultimately it is incumbent on me to initiate whatever needs to be done. Obviously, in 2020, I was not responsible for the havoc caused by COVID-19, but it was my choice to accept the job of Finance Director and so I had to sort out the problems that arose in its wake.

Once I have identified the problems, I make a list and prioritise them before I start fixing them, one by one. Issues that are causing me stress will not get any better if I ignore them; they will build up and accumulate with other problems, making them less and less manageable. For me, attacking the problem head-on and fixing the issue is the only way to make it go away and stop the stress. I accept that I can only do one thing at a time, so I fix the problems one by one and keep going.

Share, Take a Break and Switch Off

Prolonged and excessive stress is a bad thing, but I recognise that a certain amount of stress is normal and useful. I accept that I am never going to escape stress completely, nor do I think I would want to totally escape stress, but I absolutely need to have some time without any stress.

I find sharing my worries, frustrations and anxieties helps enormously. Once or twice a week, I have a 20-minute rant to either my best friend or my wife about problems at work. I know that this does not help fix the problems themselves, but it is amazing how much feel better I feel after 'venting' for a few minutes. A problem shared is a problem halved!

I ensure that I have one day off each week for family time and hobbies. Normally, I practice martial arts, which is a great way to switch off from everyday life and focus on something else. Unfortunately,

COVID-19 has interfered with this during 2020, so instead I have discovered that I love playing with Lego, even on my own for several hours after the kids have gone to bed.

I also find cutting the grass very relaxing and therapeutic. During the spring and summer, I made sure that I found the time to mow the lawn twice a week and forget about all of life's stress for an hour or so.'

Tony Gill's Story - Physiotherapy Business Owner, Bristol (www.bristolphysio.com)

'I personally believe I cope with stress extremely well, and am extremely resilient to stress. My internal answer has usually been, 'Roll up your sleeves and get stuck in, and it will all work out OK. The enemy is always indecision, so make a decision, live with the consequences, and it will work out fine.'

My wife, however, would tell you a different story; a story of a man who becomes intolerant and snappy, whose sleep pattern changes, and who becomes more insular, grumpy and less communicative when stressed. Maybe the real me is somewhere in between these two characters.

Let's get few things clear here. COVID-19 has had a significant negative impact on my business and income this year. My company will almost certainly end up in the red by the end of the year, and my personal income will have dropped by 20-30%. Nonetheless, this is not a true reflection of how my family will cope. I have a good life with financial security. My wife and I both work for the NHS part time, and we have both had non-symptomatic COVID. The reality is we are well equipped to survive this disease on all fronts.

How do I know this? Why am I not worried? Well, that is more complicated.

My hard-working parents passed on their own ethic of work to me, and have been huge influences in my life. My parents sent me to boarding school, which was a baptism of fire. While I managed to float in this 'sink or swim' environment, life became a lot more black and white in respect to 'getting on with it.' I don't necessarily think this was a good thing, and I would never send my own children to this type of environment, but I do owe a debt of gratitude to my school as it tempered me and hardened my ability to ride life's emotional rollercoaster. I still experience the highs, I just do not really have time to dwell long on the lows. The older I get, however, the more I wake up at 3am with my brain whirring, coming up with solutions to problems.

Work has always been a saviour for me. I have learned that working harder, rolling your sleeves up, and getting on with it seems to work well to survive. Deep down, I tell myself to stop moping and 'get on with it.' Is this really helpful? In the short term, yes, but in the long term, the jury is still out!

What do I do when I am not working? I climb as well as teaching and practicing Jiu Jitsu. Halfway up a climb, you cannot decide to give up - stopping and hanging on would be rather fatal!

Jiu Jitsu has allowed me to practice and get better at a chosen art. The better I got, the exterior reward was another level or belt. Internally, this has been a huge source of self-belief, which has helped me to understand that hard work brings reward and that I can achieve anything.

Both climbing and Jiu Jitsu reward me physically and mentally for my effort and achievements. I have adopted my learning from these areas in my life, and use them to manage pretty much all aspects under my control. I now cycle a lot more and love downhill mountain biking. There is no time to think; you react instinctively and roll over the bumps and drops. At the end, with your heart pumping and a big grin on your face, you normally whoop, 'What a ride!'

So, back to business. I am a physiotherapist, and run my own physiotherapy company in Bristol. The healthcare sector in the UK will weather the financial effects of COVID-19. Yes, we will be poorer, but we will survive. Even in lockdown, we kept 30% of the business alive via Zoom rehabilitation, so I am confident things will turn out OK. This calmer time also allowed me to spend more time with my family. For a person who had very little free time, COVID-19 gave me time. Yes, at a monetary cost, but I could afford it, and this experience will shape how I live my life going forward. For me personally, it might have been a blessing in disguise.

Unfortunately, this will not be the case for millions of people, and

I feel for the people I know around me whose lives will be significantly worse.

I am sanguine about the reality of COVID-19 and the effects it will have on the survivors. I am sure my sleep will be interrupted from time to time over the next year or so. I will snap a little at times, and I will withdraw for a few days, but then I will roll my sleeves up, smile at my boys as they giggle and laugh, and remember that they are really my life. The joy and happiness they bring me outshines any negative experience life has ever brought me. If you want my advice, find something in life that makes you happy to the core of your soul and allow this to bring a smile to your face. When life gets tough, remember that happiness and its importance in your life. Nothing else really matters in the grand scheme of things.'

Simon Toy's Story - Managing Director, England (www.performanceassociates.co.uk)

'Having been involved in running a business since 2001 that focuses on the psychological aspects of performance, I have never viewed stress as either good or bad, but rather as a stimulus, provided by life's experiences, that causes either a physical, emotional, or cognitive response. When we cope well with a particular stressor, we experience eustress (good stress). When we deal badly with a particular stressor, we experience distress. Good coping strategies results in more eustress in our lives, whereas poor coping strategies creates more distress in our lives.

This may seem like a simplistic approach to dealing with a subject that affects all aspects of our everyday lives, whether at work or outside of work, but I genuinely believe it is that simple. Unfortunately, this does not mean it is easy.

Another element that feeds into our perceived levels of stress relates to our own, self-generated expectations for our lives. The concept of 'my perfect life' and our continual urge to measure ourselves against this perfect version of ourselves can create distress for those of us who feel we are continually falling short of our own expectations. Temporarily reappraising our expectations, at least for the short-term, can be a greatly beneficial exercise.

Due to the global COVID-19 pandemic, the past 10 months have been an extraordinary period for many of us, and one in which the topic of stress has hit the headlines, often under the banner of 'well-being.' As I have worked with clients to help them deal with the stress associated with the pandemic and all its ramifications, it has provided me with an opportunity to reflect on my own ability to cope with the uncertainty it has brought me.

For 20 years, my paid work has typically involved face-to-face meetings with clients, with barely any virtual work. Probably 99% of our income was generated in this manner, so when the UK government announced the first lockdown in March 2020, our business was severely compromised in terms of income generation. Even when lockdown ended, the severe restrictions about how people could meet and interact meant that our old model of working was impossible, because every single one of our clients reverted to working remotely. As the main bread winner, 2 children at university, and a partner having to deal with being an 'essential worker,' the prospect of not earning money was a distressing one to say the least, and a long way from my 'perfect life.' So, what happened?

After an initial panic, induced by the fear of not being able to provide for our families, my business partner and I had to seriously redefine our offering to clients. Working in a partnership, I knew I had a colleague and friend I could rely on and who was going through the same range of emotions as me. We quickly redefined our roles and responsibilities to reflect how we could change our business model. We also reached out to others in a similar situation to discover how they were coping, and then tried to apply what we learned to our own situation. This social network of colleagues and associates that we had strong long-term relationships with proved essential in these trying times.

I have always exercised, but during lockdown I found the routine of daily activity a lifesaver. Whether it was cycling, using the gym when able, or just daily walking with my family, physical activity helped me maintain a more positive approach to life's daily challenges. Coupled with this, I focused more on what I ate and how much water I drank to ensure that I did not slip into the lethargy often associated with distress. Apart from work colleagues and my family at home, social interaction via the numerous virtual platforms became the norm, and enabled some degree of social interaction with the friends we could no longer visit.

Sleep is another factor that suffers during distress, so I created a 'sleep routine' including mindfulness exercises which I believe has been very beneficial.

The result? Our business has never been in as strong a position as it is right now, and I believe that the changes forced on us by the government's response to the pandemic will positively change the way we do business forever. My wife and I have had more time with our children at a time when we probably would not have expected it, and that is something to cherish. With no time spent travelling to and from business meetings, I have managed to exercise more and eat in a more structured way, resulting in me losing weight and gaining fitness. I also use a watch that measures my stress score, which is lower now than it was back in March 2020, so something is working.

In summary, not everything is great. Not being able to socialise and go out with friends and family is not nice, but things could have been a lot worse. By applying a few simple strategies to maintain as much social contact with those who matter to us as possible, working collaboratively with close colleagues, actively seeking other people's perspectives, and looking after your health in terms of exercise, diet and sleep, it is possible to create eustress from a situation that could easily escalate into distress.'

Princeton Walker's Story - Pharmaceutical Supply Chain Senior Manager, UK

'The world as we know it changed in March 2020 when we experienced a once-in-a-lifetime global event that has so far taken over 2 million lives. COVID-19 hit the UK 4 months after it originated, and we were unprepared. We had to think on our feet and make decisions and policies on the hoof. These decisions affected lives and enterprise, with dire consequences in some cases.

At my place of work, we had engineers on site at several locations across the globe, and the priority was to return these people to the UK. This posed difficulties as borders were closing daily and rules on travel were changing almost by the hour. This situation had a stressful and emotional impact on my engineers who struggled with the enormity of it all.

As a leadership team, we had the core responsibility of preparing our position, our responses, and to ultimately protect our employees and business. It was at this very point that the cracks began to appear in our organisation. The key people in positions of accountability and responsibility started to panic, and struggled to cope with what was occurring in the UK and indeed the world. The keystone characters of our organisation quickly crumbled into the grooves in the floor and left others to take lead. I was truly fortunate, as in my past I served for Her Majesty's Armed Forces as a Special Forces Soldier, where decision-making in critical situations was drilled into us. Life or death responses were second nature and heavily relied upon by the wider team. I took a natural leadership role and began to make proposals and policies where others found it difficult and stressful. This gave the leaders comfort that direction was being set, and their input was a contribution as opposed to creation.

Losses to revenue, fear-stricken staff, health risks due to shielding, impact on employees from their own network outside of work, and many more stress-inducing events tested the very mettle of our team and, on occasion, they did not fare well. Being the figurehead of reason and stability as self-elected task master gave other members of the team confidence that they could focus on and deal with the situations they were living with, the risks they personally had, and allowed them to take a back seat in the whole circumstance. One member of staff was suffering from long-term COVID-19, and fatigue was really impacting on their lives to the point that they had become a recluse and their confidence had dropped. They required some extra help and support to get them through this difficult period.

I look at stress very differently to most other people, to the point where I do not recognise it as a big feature in my life. I strive on conditions that others find difficult, and revel in the opportunity to be a guiding hand in the most trying occasions. It was quickly identified that this situation was not going to go away any time soon, so the reinforcing of the policy we had set was instrumental in ensuring that we had a consistent message across our businesses, both in the UK and in the USA, where our sister site was suffering a much worse fate.

Back home, the situation was not much different. Our neighbourhood is quite elderly and relies on support from family and friends for day-to-day interactions. With the whole country on lockdown, no one visiting, and restrictions on who could travel, it was easy to see that our community was going to suffer as a result. One good thing that came from all of this was that people went out more, exercised more and took walks when they perhaps did not before. With our neighbours being out and about, we got the chance to engage with them (respecting social distancing protocols), and got to know more about how life was in their world.

Through these interactions, and the fact that we had good weather for a change, we were able to promote a more village-feel to our street and everyone took on a natural position to help each other and make life just that bit more bearable and take the stress away. The anniversary of Victory in Europe (VE) day was upon us and this allowed for celebration, bringing everyone into their front garden to have 'Afternoon Tea' with music from the 40s blaring out of speakers in windows and singing along to Dame Vera Lynn after a rousing Sir Winston Churchill Speech.

Looking back upon that time now and reflecting on the months that followed, stress took on many shapes and sizes. We used the existence of it to remain steadfast in our resolve, and I think it was this that gave us the energy to host more garden parties and to immerse ourselves in the community culture, reducing the impact of COVID even if only a little bit.'

Tom Ive's Story - Raven Forge Business Owner, West Yorkshire, England
(www.ravenforge.com)

'My brother Sam and I started Raven Forge, a medieval weapons and clothes accessories business, from my living room on the 1st of October 2019. We had a small cupboard full of axes and a dream to quit our respective jobs as a plumber and physiotherapy assistant. The business was going great and grew exponentially, which was an utter joy and the absolute best we could have hoped for in a new venture. This rapid growth in our business did not come stress free. We had several different types of stress. The stress of starting a new business, stress from home life, wife stress and family stress, brotherly stress, financial stress, about every imaginable stress available to two brothers selling axes from a two-bedroom terrace house.

Like the rest of the world, we could not have foreseen COVID-19 landing in March 2020, and the new lockdown rules in the UK. By this time, our company had a steady turnover and more than enough income to employ some staff, so we had decided to get ourselves a central office in the village that we lived in. Just 5 days after moving into our new offices, Raven Forge HQ, the nation went into full and unforgiving lockdown. This was compound stress for us: we were already dealing with a huge boom in business and massive changes in our working and home lives, not to mention the business going from zero to absolutely nuts in just 5 months (I am not bragging - rapid expansion and success is stressful enough on its own without all the other things that were going on!). So, overall, I've dealt with my fair share of stress in the last year.

A lot of people say that when you have a lot on, it is no surprise that you're stressed; I think this is counterproductive and not the full story. I like to think of stress as the by-product of bad management and miscommunication, not just with everyone else, but most of all with oneself. This is not to say that I do not get stressed; I can sometimes be the most poorly managed bumbling idiot around. The point I am trying to make is that knowing what types of things cause me stress helps me to take direct steps to tackle it.

People say that deep breathing, a nice walk, and yoga are the key to stress relief, but these are all fundamentally acts that bring your heartrate down and give you space to think temporarily. When you get back to the thing that is causing you stress, be it work, school or your home life, then the problem at the root of the stress is still there, permeating stress, meaning that it is only a matter of time before you will become stressed again, despite your yoga, breathing and the lovely walk that you went on. The only way I have found to deal with stress in a permanent and progressive way is to deal with the root cause of stress, making numbered lists in order of priority. It is so easy to cherry pick the easy stuff on your list and pat yourself on the back for having completing a few check boxes before losing steam. If you are working down the list in a methodical way, your short-term stress might go up very temporarily, but your long-term stress will drop in a permanent way. If your stress is coming from relationships, be it with your boss, your partner, or most importantly yourself, make sure to have the long conversations needed to clear the air and make yourself heard. This includes conversations with yourself. Despite popular opinion, this does not make you crazy - it's just thinking out loud, and thinking is great. I'm not always great at practicing these things myself, as I spend large amounts of time being stressed, but I've always felt that knowing the root cause is the key to overcoming it.

I believe that we all have the tools required to not put off stress but destroy it, and make way for clean and clear thinking and progress. You've got this!'

Hannah Stacey's Story -Theatre Director & Facilitator, Leeds (www.hannah-stacey.co.uk)

'Every industry has unique stresses in the workplace, and the theatre industry is no exception. As an artform that relies on the presence of mind and body, there is little room for human error. I could speak about the stress of arriving in a space and realising your workshop is not suitable, the feeling when an actor drops out of a rehearsal or worse still a performance, or even the thrill and pressure of a show night where your creativity will be judged. However, there has been one main and constant stress that has affected every theatre industry worker this year - COVID-19. Overnight, theatres were 'recommended' to close, meaning that freelancers lost contracts, all with no guidance for when our industry would recover or any initial government funding.

On the 16th March 2020, I had just finished rehearsals for a performance in London and was in tech. That evening, the beginnings of a lockdown were announced. Over the next two weeks, any plans and shows

I had booked all disappeared. For the first 4 weeks I experienced a range of emotions, from joy at spending more time with family, playing online quizzes and catching up with old friends, to sheer confusion, upset and rage that the creative industries were being left out to dry with no support for the beautiful venues or their workers. I completed daily online workouts for feel-good dopamine boosts and attended Zoom meetings to feel engaged with loved ones, but there was a constant dread and confusion about what the future held. There were so many questions that couldn't be answered by a newcomer in the industry or by a respected Artistic Director.

There came a point where I think everyone realised this wouldn't be going away soon, so we all did the natural thing and began to adapt. Upon this realisation hitting me and multiple days of questioning whether to stay in an industry I loved and had worked hard to be in, I decided it was time to be productive and start making opportunities for myself. My main guidance here that I would give to anyone and everyone is making lists. I know this doesn't work for everyone, but having a list of goals to achieve keeps me active and focused. These of course weren't all work-related, and there had to be fun ones in there, such as painting, relearning an instrument, and sorting out clothes that hadn't been worn in forever. I forced myself to consider that if COVID continues to paralyse our theatre industry in 3 months, 6 months, 9 months... what would I have wanted to achieve? In the short term; what can I do to stay active and keep my brain ticking creatively and artistically? In the long term; in one year's time, where do I want to be professionally, and what would be useful for me to do? This is where I began my list:

- Make a website
- Contact creatives to start making Zoom theatre projects
- Join Zoom webinars to learn about theatre companies, roles, relationships etc.

I made lists of anything and everything to stay motivated. When creating these targets, you need to remember to reward yourself. Allow yourself to feel proud and have that chocolate treat, or a break to get a cup of tea. Also include short-term tasks that are simple; nothing looks better than a day with 10 ticked off to-do items!

I could lie and say this relieved my stress, brought me comfort and has left me feeling proactive and motivated. 2020 still brought stress from not being eligible for the Self-Employed Income Support Scheme (SEISS), every job having too many applicants or being withdrawn, and the 'theatre saving' £1.57 billion still not being distributed months after its announcement, causing more theatre closures. But writing to-do lists with targeted completion dates kept me motivated to prepare for when theatres reopened and to support fellow creatives in their collective dread.

This lockdown has been hard on us all. My final piece of advice is to stay honest and kind. My recent Zoom event, 'In This Together,' showed individuals coming together to support each other and express their current problems and fears. It connected to audiences due to its honest and hard-hitting nature, as we see the characters struggling. In this show, and in real life, everyone is struggling in some way or another, and in stressful times we need compassion and honesty. I always aim to create a safe, open and honest workspace, online or in person. I don't want to set unrealistic expectations, or for people to go away feeling stressed that they don't know the whole picture. Level with people, tell them when you're stressed or simply do not know the answer. Some of my most reassuring talks with creatives have been the ones where they've honestly told me what they're waiting on and what their current plan is. Try and keep a positive mindset, keep planning realistically, and be honest and kind.'

Antoinette Evans's Story - New Business Owner, England (www.jwel.com)

'When the government announced an international lockdown, I believe a spectrum formed in society; one end being depressed and not moving from the couch, the other end hyperactively improving overall health. I danced along the spectrum, my stress and commitment levels fluctuating from day to day. They now predominantly fall somewhere in the middle. I remain active, by running or walking 4 miles on average a day, with a deteriorating grasp on 'how to socialise' due to living alone. I only had a delightful little dog and FaceTime chats to keep me company. I knew I would grow bored quickly, so I had to think of ways to keep myself active. I have had several hobbies in the past, but only a few of these I could do alone at home to keep my mind occupied. I made a vow to perfect the skills that I could do alone and indoors. I also had no Wi-Fi due to a broadband issue with my provider for 4 months, so I was restricted in how many hours I spent on Netflix and YouTube. I made music as I was a Disc Jockey (DJ). I painted and did a body detox, as well perfecting my cooking for several months as downtime. Predominantly, I was busy typing at least 9 hours a day, writing a business plan for a new business idea.

I occupied my mind, tackling isolation as if I were stranded on a desert island, slowly but surely becoming more and more bored of any activity which didn't involve propelling my business. Work became my obsession. At this time, my finances suffered because I had no time to spend on selling. I didn't eat, I was severely stressed, and I went down to about 7 and a half stone.

My motivation has always been to live a better life as a self-employed individual working from home, and sometimes it's easy to forget that I'm actually living. Prior to lockdown, I worked in the jewellery industry and was test trading on eBay. I had a brand idea that I took to the Prince's Trust, a charity that helps start-up businesses. I knew that lockdown was the perfect time to build the foundations for a business because for the first time, the rest of the world was on pause. By October, I had finished my 30-page business plan, and was fortunate enough to win the 'Young Innovators' award from Innovate UK.

I had all my products photographed, edited, and was ready to populate the website. I planned a giveaway promotion that I wanted to run alongside the business, and by November 5th 2020, I had printing, packaging, and a finished website ready for Christmas. Due to delays, I couldn't populate the website with one of the collections, which meant that Christmas sales were affected. This caused me additional stress due to the uncertainty of when I could be ready. I didn't allow this to stop me; I simply changed my goal to prepare for sales by Valentine's Day. My plan was to have my products on Etsy, a useful platform for selling and promoting my goods. This was the first time I outsourced any of the work to do with my business, and low and behold this only caused further delays, meaning I had to do the work myself in the end, which was frustrating.

I smile now when I look back on this time, as my attitude towards setbacks has changed. Business setbacks used to be disheartening, but now I enjoy them because it means I can figure out a new way to try something, which is exciting. Now I have my business across 4 platforms, working towards a 5th, and fully ready to come out of lockdown and launch into face-to-face retail. With the support I've received by having business mentors provided to me by the Princes Trust and Innovate UK, combined with my degree in Fashion, PR and Communication, I have been able to produce a lot of work myself that I would have otherwise had to outsource. I divide my time effectively, making sure I work from 11 am to 8 pm, 5 days a week.

I make a to-do list and cross off as much as I can in a week. If I can do 3 things a day then that's perfect; if it's only 1, that is still good because I'm doing something towards my end goal. My drivers are fear and excitement, which go hand-in-hand with stress and anxiety. I try to use them to my advantage, but they used to hold me back. I was even prescribed medication, but after taking it for 3 days I realised that my anxiety was more manageable without having an addiction to prescription medication. I tried cognitive behavioural therapy, but that also didn't work for me. Lastly, I tried professional counselling for the third time in my life, and this time it really worked. I never gave up on trying to improve my mental health because I realised that internalising happiness is so important.

By being able to compartmentalise my emotions and feelings, I was no longer working just to distract myself. Before I had my business, I used to socialise to forget about how I felt, but when the government lockdown took socialising out of my options, I was forced to look at myself. I now enjoy being alone and how I spend my time. I work to watch my business grow, and I'm much better at being organised because I'm no longer thinking about pointless things such as regrets or my place in society - my business is my only focus. I'm not saying it's a healthy way of living, but it's a much more enjoyable experience than the way I was living before.'

Practical Steps Managers and Business Owners Can Take to Reduce Stress

As a manager, you are in a leadership position and accountable for your team's work, helping them to achieve company or organisational goals and key performance indicators. You also must balance the needs of the team and the company, as well as your own personal and family needs. When under stress, your mood and behaviour can change from calm and reasonable to agitated and unreasonable. This is unfortunately very common. As a manger, you are constantly multi-tasking and having to deal with urgent or important issues. There are many reasons for this, including pressure on managers to deliver, as well as extraordinarily little support, training, or appreciation from senior management, leading to demotivated managers, teams and reduced productivity overall.

Many managers plan by blocking time in their week to allow time to catch up on administrative tasks, which requires them to be free from all meetings, calls and miscellaneous interruptions during this time. This blocked off time will help you to manage your workload better and reduce stress. The amount of time you can block off will depend on your workload. Some managers can also use this time to exercise at home or go for walks. Your place of work may even have an excellent fitness centre. After exercise and a shower, you will feel invigorated, clear-headed, and ready for a productive morning, afternoon or evening. Build a support network of trusted colleagues - people whose judgment you respect and to whom you could readily go to for an objective point of view during troublesome situations. You can't fully lead a team and give your all if you are not both mentally and psychically robust. Similar to using an oxygen mask on a plane, you must put your mask on first so you can help others.

Guide to Managing Stress

Triggers – Watch out for what triggers your stress response.

Mentor – Seek a mentor you can talk to and vent your frustration.

Flexibility – Having a flexible style of management will help you adapt to the different styles of working of people in your team.

Listen – Active listening will help you get to know your team better and understand their needs and concerns.

Document – Write down and make a note of conversations and emails so you can refer to them as reminders.

Empathise – Team members may be going through many personal situations, such as family illness, divorce, break-ups, death of a family member, friend or even pet, finance troubles etc. It is important to empathise with your employees, and see how you or others can help to support them, or allow them time off to sort out their worries and concerns. Also consider how many work demands you lay on them.

Confidentiality – Keep discussions confidential as you need to maintain the trust of the team.

Inspire – Be inspired by your team and think of ways to inspire them. Find out what motivates each team member, and work out ways to help them keep motivated.

Recognition – Recognise the good things your team are doing instead of focusing on failures. Find ways to celebrate individuals and their achievements, e.g. something they have done to help customers, clients, the business or other teammates. If you can, offer some form of reward, such as vouchers that are separate from any bonus scheme.

Expectations – Set a clear set of objectives and visions for the team.

Charity and Community – Consider doing a team-building exercise, such as raising money for charity, feeding the homeless, doing sponsored events, or cleaning up local parks etc. This helps with camaraderie by working towards a common goal.

Avoid Favourites – Try to avoid over-complementing one or two people over others as it doesn't always go down well with other team members, even though you are trying to share best practice.

Team Charter – Write a team charter that everyone abides to in terms of ways of working and engaging with each other that are respectful and trusting.

HR Support – Have a close link with your HR department so you are aware of what support is on offer. Many organisations offer help and support through occupational and private health providers if advice and counselling is required.

Relax – Plan times for yourself and your team to have fun, relax and socialise.

Review – Have regular catch-ups with your team members (these do not have to be about business or work.)

Vision – Create a vision for your team which involves their input so that they feel they are part of the process and can contribute to it. This will make people more motivated.

Feedback – Ask for feedback on how you can improve in your management style such as:

> STOP - What can you or your team stop doing?

> START - What new behaviour or idea can you and others initiate?

> CONTINUE - What can you continue to do that is already going well?

Approachability – To help gain the trust of your team, try to be more approachable

Useful Tips to Help Reduce Business Stress

"Seek first to understand, then to be understood."

- Stephen Covey

Below are 6 highly effective ways to keep your stress under control, no matter what is happening in your business and personal life.

1. The Why

Remind yourself why you started your business. Was it to provide quality and value for your clients and customers? Was it to get away from working for someone else? Was it because you wanted to change the world?

Sit in a quiet room and those passions and enthusiasms will flood back and help fuel you. Take time to think through your stresses and adjust your life so you can relax more often. Tell yourself that this too shall pass, as tough times come and go.

Regularly remind yourself of what's going well and right for your business, rather than focusing on what's not going your way. Imagine you are a soaring eagle and see the big picture from this viewpoint. You will be surprised: most of you will see that many things in your life are going well.

2. Action

Find a pen and some paper, and write a list of all the things that are going well in your life. This can include business, family, health, and anything else you can think of.

Take your time writing this list, as you will be surprised at how long the list becomes. What do you do with this list? Well, place it somewhere that you can see it on a regular basis, such as your fridge, mirror, or computer.

Now the magic begins, as this will quickly lift your mood, perspective and attitude.

3. Prioritised To-Do Lists

You may find that you have a big 'To Do' list which can clutter your mind, reminding you of all the things you haven't done. Prioritise your list into Important, Urgent and Later. Some things that we need to do are urgent, and we tend to do those first instead of doing the important items. This will help us to refocus our minds and set a clear path. You may find yourself moving certain things on your list from one column to the other. Keep reviewing these on a weekly basis so you know that what you are planning to do is going to help you move forward and also reduce your stress. Discuss this list with key people in your business and your partner if you have one.

Important	Urgent	Later

When you have a to-do list, also have a list of all the things you have done in the last month. This will help you review things more clearly compared to what you have already achieved. Circle the most important items on the to-do list, and prioritise from there.

4. Massive Action

Taking the right massive actions will help the business and reduce your levels of stress.

Some of you may feel that you are at a point in your business life that things have become so poor and bad that you feel hopeless. These types of feelings can be paralysing. If we look at some research about this, we come across a concept in psychology known as 'learned helplessness.' This can lead to us failing to respond or act to improve our circumstances. It may sound extreme, but it happens more than you think. An example is a smoker who repeatedly tries and fails to quit. They may believe that nothing they do will help, and therefore stop trying altogether.

The term 'learned helplessness' was coined by American psychologists Martin Seligman and Steven Maier (1967). They were conducting research on animal behaviour that involved delivering electric shocks to dogs (which of course would never be allowed today). Dogs soon learned that they could not escape the shocks, and would not try in subsequent experiments, even when it became possible to avoid the shock by jumping over a barrier. This phenomenon has also been observed in a number of animal species, as well as in humans, and is known as learned helplessness.

By taking action you will avoid the pain and stress of a situation. You can regain a feeling of control and possibility by taking the first step proactively and taking action. As your situation improves, it will boost your confidence and encourage you to act further.

5. Ask for Help

You may find that, as a business owner or enterprising employee, it was your drive and energy that got you to where you are. This is understandable. However, at the same time, these decisions have also got you to your current stressed state. I realise that external factors like lockdown due to COVID-19, the crash of the stock market, and natural disasters may have also impacted your business. Therefore, it is important to have a mentor or person not involved in your business to offer you advice without any emotional or financial attachment.

There are other places that you can turn to for advice, such as the Citizens Advice Bureau, LinkedIn, Facebook business groups, other business owners in the same line of business, or even other business owners in different fields. They may be able to offer advice, or simply listen to your stresses, which may well help you solve your own challenges. As they say, 'A problem shared is a problem halved.'

6. Create Order by Having a Clean and Tidy Environment

If you're feeling stressed and overwhelmed, one way to cope is to create more order in your immediate environment, such as your office, home or car. Wayne Dwyer, a renowned personal development author and speaker, once said, 'You can tell the state of a person's mind by the state of their car.'

The tell-tale signs of an untidy car, office or home may well suggest a lack of self-care and increased levels of stress. By taking charge of your surroundings, your feelings of control will also increase. This allows for a better and calmer working environment.

Take the Pressure Off

There are several studies linking happiness with service and dedication to others. When we are focusing on our own problems, we are blinkered and cannot think of anything else. By focusing on others, it changes our psychological and physical state, and can be a welcome distraction. This helps with balance in life, as many people who are stressed in business and the corporate world are busy thinking about their own problems and issues rather than others (Reynolds, 2013).

Better Breathing

Take a deep breath. As you exhale, imagine all your problems and stress leaving you. Do this just 10 times, and I bet your feeling of stress has dissipated significantly.

CHAPTER 5: University and School Stress

"Education is the most powerful weapon, which you can use to change the world."

– Nelson Mandela

Student life brings with it exciting new opportunities and experiences, as well as unfamiliar environments. Many students will have to deal with many different stresses such as studying and exams, having to live away from home, finances, and regular bills such as rent, travel, books, meals, mobile and broadband. Some will make new relationships and suffer heart ache without loved ones close by for help and support. Mental health problems and stress are high during these student years. This chapter shares some student stories and offers some helpful tips and advice.

5.1: Student Life

A recent report by The Insight Network and student organisation Dig-In, University Student Mental Health Survey (2017), found that one in five students has a current mental health diagnosis. The survey also found that almost half of the 19,000 students surveyed had experienced a serious psychological issue for which they needed professional help.

Marwah El-Murad, project manager for higher education at the Mental Health Foundation, said, 'More than half of adults who have experienced a mental health problem say that it started before turning 24.' His research also showed that University students are at a high risk of developing mental health problems. They are also less likely to seek help, and if they do, they face challenges due to the lack of available support.

Student stress can be caused by several factors, including emotional and financial problems (Active Minds, 2020):

- Loneliness and homesickness
- Relationship difficulties
- Worrying about exams and re-sits
- Struggling to deal with money or dealing with large debts
- Struggling with study and life balance
- Writing essays or dissertations to deadlines

Trevor Badridge's Story – Student, England

'Taking three A-Levels is no easy business. Your whole future depends on some exams you can only take once. At one of the most important times in my academic career, I didn't make the grade. The exams that did not go to plan were my Year 12 mocks; these exams decided my predicted grades, for which I needed above 3 As. In the exams I got A, B and C. I revised for months in advance for these mocks, and when I finally took the exams the inevitable happened - I burned out. The stress and exhaustion from revising, and the pressure of getting straight A's in the many exams before, finally got to me. Whilst doing the exams, I was also preparing to speak at a national conference the day before, which added to my stress. When I received the results, I was devastated; the grades, and hence the future I wanted, had disappeared. I asked my teachers what I could do to get those A's, and they gave the simple response of, 'Prove how much you want it.' My confidence was demolished, and I was too stressed to know where to begin to turn my grades around. I was at an all-time low. All that was going through my head was that I wouldn't get my dream career and would have to think of a plan B.

I had a great support network: my teachers were supportive and reassured me there were other ways of getting the grades and career I

144

wanted. My parents were not disappointed in me, as they understood the stress I was under and were keen to help me get back on track. The only person that was struggling was me: I felt disappointed in myself as I had never received a grade this low. I took a backseat from my usual activities of sports and music as my first instinct was to stop everything. However, after a few weeks I managed to find some solutions, as I realised that wallowing in self-pity was not the way to go. I had to be proactive and tackle the problem.

The first thing I did was let myself recover from the amount of stress I was under. I needed to click the reset button. For the two weeks after I got my results, I did the bare minimum of just doing my homework, and went to every sporting practice and every music and drama rehearsal. The next step was evaluating what went wrong and how I could stop this from happening again. This was simple: I had to look after myself whilst maintaining getting straight A's. I created a 'stress score,' and at the end of every day I would rate how much capacity I had on a scale of 1-10 to help manage my stress. As well as that, I made sure I did the things I loved outside of academia, whether that was music, drama or sport, as these things made me relax and brought down my stress score. The third thing I did was talk to people and ask for advice. I went to my teachers and asked what I could change for the next exam. I also went to the school counsellor for someone to talk to. It was an accumulation of all these things that meant that, during the next exams, my grades began to climb. When I applied to university, I had above the requirements I needed, and felt I was better able to control my stress.'

Sarensen Peters's Story – Interior Designer, France

'My daughter's final year of school was extremely difficult for her and for me. Halfway through her mock exams while she was 17 years-old, she started to feel the pressure. She would study for hours, stay up late and study at weekends - a very conscientious student. On a few occasions, she would come home from school and have a big meltdown. I tried to console her and give her hugs, but most times she was too distraught and would start saying things like:

- I am hopeless
- I will never pass these exams
- It's a waste of time
- Why did I ever choose these subjects?

I offered help and understanding, but many times it would end in arguments, emotions over-spilling, and swearing. The next time our daughter came home from school in a bad mood, I gave her space and 15-30 minutes in her room to calm down. I would then offer her some tea and cake or something I knew she liked to try and cheer her up. I asked if she wanted to talk about it and responded accordingly. When I started to offer more help and advice, like getting a tutor or mentor, she would get angry and upset again so I backed off. In the end, she opened up more to me and we set up a study plan which was above her desk in her room. This had a plan with blocked off time for each subject. She found that helpful because she felt more in control. Later, she also asked for a private tutor and buddied up with friends to support each other.

We later discovered that she was self-harming, which came as a shock and was an exceedingly difficult time for all the family. This self-harm started happening when she found out her boyfriend was also seeing another girl at the same time, which pushed her over the edge. When we tried to reach out to her to talk about this, she got angry and closed herself off. We also reached out to her friends to see what they knew and if they could help. They said that they knew, and they were trying to help her and do what they could. Our daughter wasn't happy that we went to her friends, so she went back into her shell. We asked a cousin that she was close to reach out to her and thankfully this got her talking and accepting help. Over time she opened up to us, and we managed to talk the issue through and get her the help and support she needed at this time in her life. We were surprised to read about how common self-harm was in teenagers, especially young women.

Once things settled down, we planned some down time so she could either see friends, or we could go to the park or cinema together. Most nights we would have dinner together with no TV, no phones on the table, and just enjoy each other's company. Dinner became a good chance to talk, as before this she would spend all her time in her room and eat food there.

The good news is that our daughter passed her exams and got a place at university in the course she wanted. Of course, the stress of university is a whole new story in itself!

My advice to parents is to be patient, calm, and try to listen to and give your child space. If they don't get the results they need then it's not the end of the world. Be prepared to be there if this happens, and help them reset their goals. We also told our daughter that some of the most successful people in the world never graduated from school or college, and that didn't hold them back. We also let her know that her father failed many exams, but he stuck at it and now he has good salary, a nice car, a good job and a comfortable home. Exam results do not define who we are, and it is our job as parents to love our children anyway, no matter the outcome.'

My Story: Raj Soren - Asian Society President, Manchester

'I first started experiencing stress at university when I was president of the Asian society in Manchester. I took on this role to try and get experience in a leadership role, and so that I could support my Indian, Pakistani, and Bengali community. I remember organising an evening party at a local night club in Manchester, England. We had booked the venue, but the owners said that they 'expected a certain clientele.' I remember thinking at the time that this was a strange thing to say. On the evening of the party, some 150 of us arrived at the event, mostly Asian with some Black and White friends. They allowed 30 or so people to enter then they stopped any more from entering. They did not tell us why they stopped any more entering even though I asked them, and I reminded them that I had booked the event. In the end, there were 150 upset and disappointed party goers who had to go elsewhere for the evening. I later found out that the night club owners were being racist and did not want their club to be associated with Asians. This was back in the mid-1980s, which was totally unacceptable then as it is now. I ended up filing a lawsuit against the night club with the support of the National Race Equality Charity, but unfortunately the owners changed their business and dissolved the company to avoid being sued. This same night club started under a new company name, and thus avoided being prosecuted. Hopefully this experience taught them not to act in this way again, but it is also possible that they continued to show their prejudice under a different name. Other night clubs in Manchester had heard about me taking a club to court for racist behaviour, so the word was out. In their eyes I was trouble, which meant that they would not let me in other similar clubs, and I would have to go to other venues instead. I did not mind, as I had at least made a stand against this despicable behaviour.

Another stressful incident occurred when I had organised a joint Asian society and Jiu Jitsu club long weekend trip to Amsterdam. We had a party of twenty in our group and had arranged to meet the coach at a local hotel near Manchester airport. We were informed that there was going to be another group already on the coach before our party was picked up. When the coach arrived, we were surprised to be told that the other group were an all-male football team. They were already drunk by the time we joined them. Shortly after we joined the coach, the other group started making inappropriate comments and gestures to the women in our group. One of them was so drunk that he was urinating on the floor of the coach. This was very intimidating and frightening for many of our group. I had to tell the coach driver that this was not acceptable, and we could no longer continue travelling with this group as we were concerned for our safety. The coach driver agreed that we should turn back, but he was also worried about the repercussions of this decision as the football team would be upset and angry, and as they were already drunk it could be very volatile situation. We wanted to avoid an already volatile situation becoming worse and then our members being assaulted.

The driver finally stopped the coach about 15 miles along our journey at the local motorway service station. I had to explain to the group leader of the football team that our group was scared, felt intimidated and were being harassed by his drunk teammates. I had to explain in a calm manner that we could not continue our trip to Amsterdam with this level of behaviour. He was upset by this decision, and after calming down he

148

seemed to come to his senses and understood. When he and I informed his teammates, they became incredibly angry and upset, and started swearing and threatening me and members of my group. This made it even more imperative that we had to end our coach trip and return to our pick-up point. After 45 minutes of heated discussion, we all finally agreed that the driver should turn around and go back. This was a harrowing experience for me and for those in my group. We got back safely and got our money back (and the football club apologised for their behaviour), but this certainly added to my stress levels that year as president.

This was a difficult time at university, as my emotions were constantly up and down from dealing with these situations. I felt that I had disappointed my friends and society members that year, even though most things were out of my control. I had to learn how to stay calm in these situations, and to seek help from my student's union solicitors and race equality organisations. I had many sleepless nights, and was starting to get twitches and palpitations. My girlfriend at the time (who is now my wife) was my rock, and her incredible support helped me get through this difficult time. I had to re-learn to breathe better and avoid hyper-ventilating, as I was only taking shallow breaths which made me more anxious.

My take-home message to others is that, if you are ever faced with situations like this, remain calm in the face of adversity. I had to appeal to the football team captain's empathy so that he realised how scared and intimated our group felt. In the night club situation, again I had to stay calm and, in the end, seek legal advice. I quickly learned that year how to handle aggressive, drunken football teams as well as racist night club owners. I had people I could trust to lean on, like my girlfriend and other close friends around to support me, as well as the student union.'

Advice for Students

Time Management

Students often get stressed when meeting deadlines, and can feel like they are running out of time to complete something. Students who cope well with deadlines divide their work into urgent and non-urgent tasks, and important and non-important tasks. These same students have found that the following habits have helped them:

- Creating a written work schedule
- Breaking tasks down into manageable chunks
- Planning accordingly

Sleep

Sleep and rest are usually the last thing on a student's mind, as they may be too busy studying, having fun, seeing friends and going to parties. Regular good sleep helps the body and mind heal from the day's activity, and acts as a refresh so the body can handle the next day and beyond. Stress can interrupt your sleeping pattern, so it is important to plan a bit of time to relax before you go to sleep, as this can help the quality of your sleep. Try different ways of relaxing such as taking a bath to wind down, watching your favourite TV show, or sitting quietly and reading. Avoid too much screen time before bed by switching off laptops, phones and tablets at least an hour before going to sleep. Other distractions from sleep can be include the lure of bars, clubs and Netflix. Social media such as Instagram, Facebook, Snapchat and TikTok are additional distractions from getting a good night's sleep.

A good sleep routine is vital for better mental health and stress management. Ideally, plan to sleep at the same time and wake up at the same time each day so you can aim for seven to eight hours sleep. If you do study in the same room as you sleep, try to separate your study space by placing your study materials in a cupboard, out of sight and reach. If you have tried all of the above strategies and still struggle to get enough sleep, then consider visiting your medical practitioner to double check that there are no underlying issues.

Mindfulness

Mindfulness is a relaxation technique, originating in Buddhism, which is becoming an increasingly popular coping mechanism for those tackling stress or anxiety. There are several ways to practice this, including through smartphone apps such as Mindfulness, Calm and Headspace. Several books are also available on the subject as well as many YouTube videos. Other useful apps include Calm Harm, Student Health App, Stress and Anxiety Companion, and WorryTree.

Spending and Saving Tips for Students

It's important to keep track of your spending. Some students tend to manage money using apps, while others write down how much they spend in a diary or even create a spreadsheet on income and outgoings. This way you can see how much you spend each month. Things to include in your spreadsheet include income from student loans, parental contributions, part-time jobs, scholarships and bursaries. Also include regular outgoings, such as your rent, mobile phone, food shops, heating and Wi-Fi bills. Other expenses may include travel, books, socialising, and gifts for birthdays.

The table below should help you with keeping an eye on your finances.

Monthly / Annual Income	Amount
Student loan	£
Bursary	£
Parental contribution	£
Part-time Job	£
Scholarships	£
Other	£
Total	£
Monthly Expenses	**Amount**
Accommodation	£

Course fees	£
Travel	£
Food	£
Car	£
Socialising	£
Utility bills (Gas, electric, water)	£
Other bills (mobile, WiFi etc)	£
Insurance	£
Other	£
Total	£
Income Minus Expenses	£

Below are some tips Daniel Higginbotham has shared to help students save money (2021):

Food Shopping

It's better to do a bigger, cost-effective shop at a supermarket and buy unbranded items as opposed to well-known brands from more expensive local shops. Planning meals in advance will also help reduce the temptation for takeout food. Look for bargains at the end of the day when many items are more like to be discounted. Consider preparing packed lunches rather than buying a sandwich or going to a coffee shop. Share the cooking with your housemates and plan your daily meals in advance.

Travel

Most universities are either city-based with excellent public transport links, or campus-based with everything on your doorstep. Student rail, bus and subway cards can offer big discounts on your travel. Share taxis if there is no other safe form of transport. Avoid buying a car unless you can really afford to run it, as this can be a heavy drain on your expenses. Local buses remain one of the cheapest ways to get around.

Student Discounts

Look for the many student discounts available, ranging from essentials to fashion, music, and technology. Check whether you're entitled to any student discounts or weekly/monthly passes on the services you use. Sign up to apps that offer immediate discounts when you shop or eat out. Sign up for discount codes or voucher schemes.

Bills

If you are sharing a student house, you will have bills to pay for, such as gas, electricity, water, and broadband. This is when it's worthwhile using comparison websites to get the best deals and keep costs down by saving energy. Also set up regular direct debits, so these utility bills are paid automatically each month. This will help you to avoid any late payment charges. To avoid tension with house mates, make sure people are paid back as quickly as possible.

Books and Materials

Buy your course books secondhand wherever possible. Do not fall into the trap of buying all the books on your reading list, as you may be able to borrow some from the library. You can find cheap secondhand copies online via Amazon, eBay or through your university, and can sell the books when you no longer need them.

Banking

Move to a student banking account instead of a current account, as this will better serve your needs. With a student account, you don't pay for an overdraft, and the money borrowed won't accumulate interest like with some regular accounts. Shop around for the best deal - take your time and choose wisely. Certain banks will offer interest-free overdrafts, discounts on rail cards, travel and insurance, freebies, discounts, and gift vouchers, and make you pay less for borrowing in an emergency or if you overspend. Keep comparing offers, and switch banks if you need to in order to take advantage of the best deals.

It's important to keep to the terms of your overdraft, stick to the limit, and always repay what you borrow on time. This way you build a good relationship with the bank and you can go to them when in need.

It's worth having more than one bank account for separating different pots of money. You can deposit savings in one account if it offers better interest rates or cash bonuses. You could put your student loan and wages in one account, then transfer money to a separate account for paying bills and direct debits. Providing you meet the account conditions, there's no reason you can't mix-and-match accounts.

Avoid Credit Cards

Most students cannot usually obtain a credit card, as they have no regular monthly salary. If you do have a credit card, be strict about paying off what you owe each month, otherwise there are high interest payments.

Use Apps to Save Money

Certain apps, such as Monzo, Plum, Squirrel and Moneybox, can be set to automatically save 10-15% or more into your savings. This limit can be set by you and is an easy way to save for holidays, emergencies, or anything else you might need cash for in the future.

Debt Management

Many students can unfortunately accumulate large debts very quickly. They may have large outgoings and extraordinarily little income, or find it difficult to manage their money. The strain of owing money not only has a negative impact on your mental well-being, but it can also affect your studies, emotions, and relationships.

Handling Debt

With the cost of living and all the fees associated with student life, it's understandable that several students can build up bills and quickly get into debt. Students may receive emails and letters demanding payment for overdue bills. Make sure you avoid using quick-fix, pay-day loans at all costs.

It is important to try to keep calm and seek help as early as possible. This way, your mounting debt can be quickly resolved. Ensure that you open and deal with all correspondences so you are up to date. Store all letters and bills in a box or folder as you may need to refer to them later. Students should not hide the full extent of their debts, as it is important to be honest to family, friends, university services and outside agencies; this way those helping you are fully aware of the extent of your problems.

Prioritise Debts

Make a list and separate your priority from your non-priority debts, as shown below, and detail all income and outgoings:

Priority	Non-priority
Rent	Overdrafts or loans
Course fees	Credit or store cards
Utility bills gas and electric, TV licence	Unsecured personal loans
Mobile	Money borrowed from friends or family.
Speeding fines	

Whilst it's still important to clear non-priority debts and take them seriously, the penalties for not paying them are generally less severe. Highlight all unpaid debts and repayments due. Plan what you can afford to repay from any available income, and apportion this among priority creditors. If you write to your creditors and propose a new repayment offer, they can usually be quite understanding. To help with your creditors, prepare a financial statement to let them know of any exceptional circumstances. Ask for help if you are not sure how to prepare a financial statement. The other option is to ask the creditors to freeze the interest on any debts while you renegotiate terms.

Talk to Others

Do not suffer in silence or feel embarrassed about your debts. Share your money worries with family and friends as they can offer moral, if not financial, support. You can also approach university student services, as they are also there to offer help and advice. Some establishments can signpost you to money advisers who can often provide one-to-one support. If your institution cannot offer help, contact debt charities, self-help groups or money advice services, such as Step Change or the National Debtline, where you will receive free and impartial advice.

Like all things in life, looking after your finances takes discipline and effort, so set yourself a realistic budget. Be prepared for real change by cutting back on social and leisure spending. Students can still have fun at university without going into major debt. Consider asking other student friends who can manage their money better what tips they have. Consider taking on a part-time job, but be aware of balancing work and study.

Packing for University

Below is a useful list to help you pack:
- Clothes for all seasons, plus smart wear
- Coat hangers
- Wallet or purse
- Bed linen, including sheets, duvet, blankets, pillows and pillowcases
- Towels and personal items, such as toiletries
- Mobile phone and charger
- Extension lead
- First aid kit

- Torch
- Rail card
- Washing detergent and cleaning items
- Kitchen items and some food to keep you going for the first week
- Medicine
- Electric socket adaptor (for international students)
- Stationary, including pens, pencils, notepads and highlighters
- A list of important numbers in case you lose your mobile phone
- Laptop and any cables and chargers
- USB stick
- Notepads
- Games and sports equipment
- Umbrella
- Family photographs
- Desk lamp and fan
- Drawing pins for putting up photos or posters
- Kitchen equipment and utensils, including cups, saucers, plates and cutlery
- Toaster and kettle
- Tea towels
- Washing up liquid
- Corkscrew, bottle opener and tin opener
- Vegetable peeler
- Measuring jug
- Grater
- Cling film
- Tin foil
- Recipe book
- Pots and pans
- Knives and chopping board
- Baking tray
- Plates and bowls (microwavable ones are a good idea)
- Glasses and mugs

If there are items that you have forgotten to pack, it's not the end of the world. Most things can be bought from nearby shops or collected from home later. When packing belongings, it helps to separate them into manageable chunks and bring a couple of helpers if you will have to make lots of trips.

Remember to bring documentation and important files you may need to identify yourself. New students should remember to bring two forms of photo ID (you'll need this to collect your campus card and when going out during fresher's week), any official documentation sent by the university, and any details of student finance arrangements. You'll also need a letter or document with your address on, as this might be needed to register with a local GP. If you have a car, you may need to apply for a parking permit.

Some universities may also give you the opportunity to pre-order bedding and kitchen packs. These bundles can be in your room on arrival. Some universities require that electrical items have been Portable Appliance Tested (PAT) tested, or that you can prove they are less than two years old.

Study essentials include:
- Pens, pencils and highlighters
- A4 file paper
- Ruler
- Lever arch files
- Eraser
- Stapler
- Hole punch
- Diary/personal organiser
- Notebooks
- Post-it notes
- Laptop
- A portable hard drive

Tips for Writing a Thesis

Writing a research project or dissertation can be an incredibly stressful experience. First, let's understand what assignment stress really is and how it manifests. Stress can increase when you realise that the project or assignment you had initially planned for is no longer working out as it should (EduGeeksClub, 2020). Your efforts and research may no longer support your thesis, or experiments are not on schedule or working out. The first step to tackling this stress is recognising it.

Some tell-tale signs of stress include:
- A lack of desire to continue working on your dissertation
- Fatigue
- Inability to work at your full potential
- Feeling down and unmotivated
- Negative thoughts about your ability to finish the paper on time
- Impatience and irritability
- Bad temper
- Poor sleep and constantly feeling tired

The causes of dissertation stress are numerous, and include:
- Approaching deadlines
- Struggling to make meaningful progress due to an over-complex subject
- Work piling up and too many things to do
- Lack of sleep
- Struggling to write
- Lack of help and support
- Negative feedback from supervisors

Below are some tips for dealing with stress when writing an important assignment or dissertation:
- First, put yourself in a positive mindset
- Plan and organise your time and your project
- Achieve every milestone that you set
- Take a day off to spend with your family and friends
- Get quality sleep and wake up early
- Ask for assistance from a professional academic writer
- Ask for help from professors and others who have already completed their thesis
- Relax

You will finish the paper on time if you follow your plan and stay productive. Trust that your results and productivity will increase when you are able to manage and reduce your levels of stress.

Ingrid Curl shared her tips for planning and writing a dissertation with Times Higher Education (2016):

- Be prepared to review and rewrite each chapter a number of times
- Write a rough draft as you go so that you can amend and update it
- Write a coherent piece and restructure where necessary
- Have someone help you who has a critical eye and can read objectively
- Check with your college or university as to the preferred reference style
- All references in your thesis need to be cross-checked with the bibliography before submission
- Use helpful software such as EndNote or Paperpile to manage your bibliography from day one
- Stick to British spelling if in the UK and be consistent, or use American spelling in the US
- Use one dictionary and stick to it as they vary in their use of hyphenation
- Be careful not to plagiarise

5.2: Teaching and Lecturing

"If you are planning for a year, sow rice; if you are planning for a decade, plant trees; if you are planning for a lifetime, educate people."

– Chinese Proverb

Jaime Morrish's Story – Associate Professor, Japan

'The word stress has a lot of associations, both good and bad. Some people tend to thrive under the additional pressure that certain stress gives us, while for other people it can have the opposite effect. It is fascinating to think about stress and stressful situations, and how each individual copes differently with them. As with many things in life, there is no right or wrong way; it is up to each person to find what works best for them. The following is just one of many situations that I could have chosen in which I have faced stress. My particular field of work, teaching, is nothing like the life and

160

death situations that people in the armed forces, frontline medical or other emergency services face on a day-to-day basis, but it still has its challenges.

I am an Associate Professor at a fairly large, private university in central Japan. I am the co-ordinator for two of the courses taught in our Foreign Languages Department, and as such am solely responsible for the students on that course and the full-time and part-time teachers. I have a position on the entrance exam committee, as well as being a speaking examiner for the Cambridge University Language Proficiency Test (IELTS). In addition, I am about two-thirds through my PhD, so suffice to say I am usually busy every day! Many people think that people who work in education have it easy as we have long holidays, but that is far from the truth. Ask pretty much any teacher, and they will tell you that the majority of work starts when the school year ends, as that is when we have to do all our marking, endless reports and then plan and prepare for the next academic year. I am not complaining - far from it, I enjoy my job - I am just trying to dispel a few myths!

The year 2020 will certainly be remembered for many reasons. For myself, it was a massive learning curve. Almost overnight the teaching staff at my university, myself included, were expected to become technology gurus, counsellors to both students and staff, and medical experts, all while still being expected to deliver the same content and classes that we would normally do in a pre-COVID world.

The situation was not helped any by the lack of top-down, decisive action. At first, we were going ahead with face-to-face classes, then we were delaying the start of the school year (which usually begins in April not September), then we were cancelling the first half of the academic year, until eventually it was decided that each university would decide its own course of action. My workplace decided to start the year online after a 4-week delay, and re-evaluate the situation after the summer break. During this time, I had teachers contacting me asking me what the situation was on a daily basis, as rumours started to spread of people being laid off or told to take an 'extended vacation.' This did in fact happen to a few people that I knew, but generally speaking, most people teaching at universities in Japan were able to hold onto their jobs.

I completely understand the uncertainty that occurred when things started getting bad around April, as this was a new and unprecedented situation for everyone. Unfortunately, not everyone was as understanding as I was, and this added to my stress levels, as teachers, students, family members and administration staff all wanted to know what the plan was, when nobody had one. Many people regard me as a very laid-back individual who never gets stressed out or worked up, and although this may be the appearance I give, inside it is usually the exact opposite. There are a few techniques that help me give off an outward appearance of calm, including breathing exercises, trying to think through a situation fully before acting or speaking, and not overreacting in a good or bad situation. However, pretty much all the of the various methods I use to stay calm can be attributed to physical activity, or more specifically, martial arts, in one way or another.

Breathing techniques – When you are at the end of a four or five-hour grading and you are completely out on your feet, just breathe. In through the nose, out through the mouth.

Not overreacting – When you are faced with multiple attackers carrying various weapons, you have to make an internal decision of what you are going to do first, but also have a plan B, C or D lined up if your first plan does not work out.

Keeping an outwardly calm appearance - Zanshin is the Japanese term for this, which could equally be called keeping a 'poker face.' You will never see a more textbook example of this than when sumo wrestlers win a bout. They will never rejoice, even if they have just won the grand tournament. This concept of 'Zanshin' is taught in every Japanese dojo I have ever visited, Kendo, Judo, Aikido, Jiu Jitsu and many more. It teaches respect for your opponent and to never show excitement or joy when you win, but to also not show despair when you lose - keep everything in balance.

This is one of the things that I think is most important; balance. Things may be bad now, but they will get better: things may be great now and by all means enjoy it, but just be aware that things may not be quite so rosy for everyone else or around the corner. I was taught by my sensei from very early on that when we enter the dojo to train in Jiu Jitsu, we 'rei' (bow), and that entrance signifies that I am now focused on my training for however long I am there. If I have been having a terrible day, then I leave it in the changing rooms, and for the two hours or so in the dojo, I do not think about outside stressors. I apply the same mindset to work; if I have had a bad day, then the moment that I step back into the house I leave the work stuff at the door (although I do not 'rei' when I enter my house!). By all means I can talk about work stuff, but my wife does not deserve to have me in a bad mood or stressed out because of something that happened at work. This has become a bit trickier when working from home, as the boundary between home and work gets blurred, but I find it can be something as simple as walking into a different room or taking a shower and then getting dressed in non-work clothes and leaving the struggles of that day until tomorrow.'

Adam MacQueen's Story – Head of Science, Cornwall

'It is ironic that I was asked to write a piece about how I deal with stress, considering that for the last two weeks, this is all that I have had to contend with. I am the Head of Department in a large secondary school in Cornwall. I manage 22 members of staff, run a very busy department and when I am not working, I (with my wife) care for three brilliant but exhausting children. This year has been challenging for all of us.

I feel that school children have also had to contend with a massive amount. Cancelled exams, isolation, remote learning, kept in year group bubbles, dealing with financial worries due to parents losing jobs, and then there is also the small matter of learning schoolwork. It has been my job this year to continue to engage, motivate, support, cajole and, at times, hold to account, these students as they continue their school experience. In addition, we as a staff team have had to adjust to a whole new way of teaching. We are not allowed near the students. We must move classrooms lesson to lesson to try to maintain year group bubbles, which means that Science teachers are not in Science rooms. This makes doing practical work, which is an essential part of Science teaching, impossible. Just to make life harder, students who are isolating have to join lessons from home, and I.T. in schools does not work fabulously well.

My staff are tired, emotionally drained, frustrated, and feel that they are not doing a great job. They are angry at the situation and they are angry for the ramifications of COVID-19 on the students that they teach. It is me that they come to and vent their anger and frustration on, and that is fine. That is my job. I have a mindset that I work for my staff, not the other way around, and so it is my job to make their life as easy as possible. This may consist of me dealing with troublesome parents, or challenging senior leaders on policies that are not welcomed by staff. It must be said however that this is a rare occurrence, as I am very fortunate to have a senior leadership team who go out of their way to support and care for our health and well-being.

All these challenges have caused my stress levels to elevate substantially over the course of the last few months. The kicker has been the last week, when my COVID-19 app pinged and told me I had to self-isolate for 8 days. If you had told me a year ago that I would spend a week stuck in a caravan teaching all my classes via the internet from ten miles away, I would have laughed in your face. However, this is what I have just finished doing. Lesson after lesson, I have had to try and manage a class, deal with connection issues, get the students to complete tasks and actually teach them over the computer. The students have been in the classroom, with a supervisor, and I have taught via an old laptop and visualiser to the best of my abilities.

Whilst this appears so far to be a cathartic outpouring of 'woe is me,' I am not looking for sympathy. I am merely trying to put some context to the stresses that many people like me are having on a regular basis. So how have I managed this stress? I do not profess to have all the answers, and all I can do is share what I do to try and alleviate the daily struggle as best as I can. I don't always win, and there have been days where I go home, give in, and just go to bed. However, overall, I am very positive and feel that I am coping as best as I can. The first major stress relief is my family. I have a very patient (if anything, too patient) and loving wife and children.

My wife has picked up the slack and has acted as a very good sounding board when I need to vent. I would offer this as one of the best bits of advice I can give - talk and share problems. I have made it a policy for all my staff that we all talk openly and freely. We make a point of checking in on each other, and none of us are afraid to say we are having a bad day. This is so important. I see so much machismo in workplaces, including my own. This is especially prevalent in men. We should not feel the need to hide our emotions if we are not coping, and yet many of us do. It is not a failure in life to be stressed: it is a failure to not recognise when we are struggling and ask for help.

The biggest mechanism I use for alleviating stress is exercising. I enjoy all aspects of physical exercise, especially martial arts. I have been a practitioner of Jiu Jitsu for nearly twenty years, and I find this practice very therapeutic. Jiu Jitsu is a full contact martial art, and sadly COVID-19 has put a stop to face-to-face training. However, lockdown has presented opportunities for problem solving and finding solutions around this. I have been running online training sessions with members all over the country and the world. There is nothing I enjoy more than the post-workout endorphin rush after a hard training session. It may be that you have not done any exercise for a while, but I would implore you to give it a go if you are stressed. A long walk in fresh air or multiple burpees both serve as an excellent tonic to tackle those feelings of stress and anger.

Stress is constantly around us, and I have no doubt that it will continue to surround us for the foreseeable future. However you deal with stress, it is important to do so, and never ever allow yourself to get to the point where it completely envelopes your being. If you do not think you can cope, talk to someone. There is always a solution.'

Tom Dugmore's Story – Associate Lecturer, England

'Causes of stress can take many forms, so it can be hard to identify specific factors, but generally people seem to consider being overworked, excess worries, and fatigue as being big drivers, which seems to match my own experiences.

Certainly, having a lot on my mind has played into a stressful situation for me previously, which can then get amplified into having trouble falling asleep, which in turn leads to an inability to focus on jobs well, which leads to them building up, hence having more on my mind. It's something that can quickly turn into a very vicious downward spiral, and knowing how to break that cycle is hard. As a child, I ended up seeing a child therapist to help me with mental strategies to deal with this.

Fast forward several years, and I think I now deal with stress much better. I will use an example of something that is commonly associated with stress, which hopefully people can relate to or learn from - writing up my PhD thesis. Anyone who has been through this will tell you what a mammoth undertaking it is to collate everything you have done over 3 years and write it all up, particularly if you are working as well. Stories of long, sleepless, coffee-fuelled nights, exhaustion and mental fatigue are pretty much par for the course, especially as the strict deadline for submission looms.

Early on, I was having a typical week, working all day in the lab to finish off a couple of key experiments and then sitting down as everyone was heading home to start processing my data from the day and writing everything up. I had had a couple of days where I stayed until nearly midnight just staring at the screen, desperately trying to work my mind into getting some more down. I was worried that my progress was painfully slow, and I would never be able to finish if I stayed at that rate. However, on this day, I had stayed for a couple of hours already, and had spent the best part of the last hour looking at my latest results and trying to work out what they meant in the context of my work. It was the night my sports club met for training, so I decided to go along and enjoy a drink in the bar with my friends afterwards. 4 hours later, I returned to the office, looked at the screen I had left, and instantly saw the answer to the problem I'd been trying to solve. Immediately I sat down and began to write, staying for another couple of hours writing solidly before calling it a night, reflecting to myself that I had written far more in those two hours than I had in the past 2 days.

At that point, I resolved to prioritise quality of time spent writing up over quantity, and immediately found myself being more productive. If

I found myself stuck for something to say, I would stop and work on something else, maybe processing some data or updating tables of content (this was before the Word plug-in tools that would do it automatically for you) or having some dinner, doing a household task, or even just going for a walk to clear my head. By not forcing myself to devote needless hours to a task when it just was not happening, I could make sure other jobs were not building up around me to add to the mental workload, and was able to maintain and enjoy a decent work-life balance.

It's not always easy, but I have tried to maintain this approach to my work-life balance going forward by trying not to get phased by the amount of work I may have to do, but to simply pick one off the list and mentally block all others out whilst I work on it. Once mental fatigue sets in, I do not try and force it; I stop for a break, or go to work on the next task, and try to make sure it is different so I can shut the other one out entirely. For instance, if my current task is a desk-based one for work or household admin, I will switch to something like mowing the lawn or washing the dishes. As many jobs sometimes come along at once with strict deadlines, it gets hard at times, and the late nights have not gone away, but at least they are the exceptions rather than the rule. It's still important to keep a list of your jobs somewhere, otherwise blocking them out to focus on one can inevitably lead to you forgetting all about one from time to time!'

Rhianna Gately's Story – Teacher, England

'In the couple of days before I turned twenty-two, my whole world turned upside down. The country went into lockdown, and my dad died unexpectedly. Only days before, I had been stressing about how I was going to plan for my next set of lessons as a trainee teacher. I thought this was stressful, but it was nothing compared to the emotional turmoil of what I faced next. I came to a crossroad: my two biggest stresses determined how my life would move forward now. I had lost my dad, and wondered how I could continue what I had set out to do for myself. I did not know what this would mean for my family, and I was worried about how my life would change. My family were at the forefront of my mind, of course, and I was so worried about helping everyone else and being perfect for everybody that I did not even look at myself. I created stress by not prioritising my own emotional needs. And the worst part was that me being this way was less helpful to other people than focusing on bringing back my own happiness.

There were two main ways that I got back on my feet – by separating my thoughts, and talking. I decided to focus on one thing at a time. The first, and most basic, was completing my degree. I considered my work in a different way. Instead of thinking that focusing on my work meant I was neglecting my family's needs, I thought of how my determination would help me to feel accomplished and make my family proud. It also meant there would be one more thing that I could tick off the list to make way for others. Instead of stressing about everything at once, I managed one thing at a time.

Secondly, I spoke to people about it. This was the more difficult of the two. I struggled to understand my own emotions, which led to me dismissing them and making them worse until they overflowed into a much bigger, and more damaging, wave. I thought that if I could not articulate how I felt, then others would think I was stupid. I was wrong. If anything, speaking to others about how I felt allowed me to understand myself better too. Especially given my situation, speaking to others allowed me to share my story and listen to others. No matter your situation, you are never the only one. I even went to counselling - which is something that made me previously feel uncomfortable. I thought that my experiences of stress were not 'bad enough,' and that if I went to counselling, I would be wasting their time. Every feeling is justified, no matter how big or small it might seem compared to others. I learned not to compare myself to others but to only look at myself and what I needed to do to improve. I would now recommend counselling to anybody who is going through a tough spot.

Using these two methods, I feel as though I now have more control over my own emotions. There will always be times where too much has happened too quickly for me to ease the flow before it erupts. But now, more often than not, I can sense when I begin to feel stressed and I can rationalise it more. I can divide it into individual tasks and, where possible, discuss this with somebody else too. Now when anyone I know is stressed, I tell them to try and unravel all of the things that are stressing them, write them down if it is easier than talking, and start with one solution at a time.

Since that time in my life there are things that are still difficult, but that have become easier - such as the death of my dad. I have also achieved great things, like starting a new education course in something that I truly love. I have high hopes for what I can achieve in the future, and whilst I put pressure on myself, I try not to create stress. So, when I am working (now on something that I love), I switch off from the rest of the world, put my phone away, and focus on the task at hand. One thing at a time.'

Tips to Reduce Stress for Teachers

Below are some helpful tips to reduce stress for teachers and lecturers:

Time Management

Delegate items to other people in your teaching team, colleagues, or even ask parent volunteers if they are available. The type of things you can delegate to volunteers are photocopying, pencil sharpening, tidying work spaces and tracing.

Aim to get at a good night's sleep of 8 hours, and avoid working in bed, as this should be your safe space. Avoid social media while trying to relax. Some mobile phones, like iPhones, have features that allow you to set a reminder for yourself to get ready to go to bed and get the amount of sleep you need.

Prepare your clothes and lunch in advance for the next day instead of in the morning. This means that when you are in a rush during the morning you can just grab and go! Some teachers I know cook and prepare for the week, or have leftovers for lunch the next day.

Marking Work

Avoid correcting every single piece of work at once. This will be difficult for those of you who are incredibly detailed. Depending on the age of the class that you are teaching, sometimes it may be OK to simply give the paper a once over to check for understanding and then return it to the student.

Exercise

Have an exercise routine in place by joining a gym or doing some regular stretching or yoga. This could be in front of the TV, or using YouTube videos to direct you. Exercise helps alleviate stress, gives you energy, helps you sleep better, and is great for decompressing.

Make Time

Wake up earlier, even just 30 minutes or 1 hour early, as this will allow you to prepare for your day and could also provide you with more positive energy instead of having to rush. You may decide to stay a bit later after school to avoid the rush hour. This could allow you more time after school to prepare for the next day, which means you would have less work to do at home.

Avoid Gossip

Teachers, as much as other professions, can be rife with gossiping, complaining, and venting. Try to avoid the people that engage in this behaviour, and spend time with colleagues who inspire you and make you feel good. These individuals can lift your spirits when you really need it, and you can do the same for them. You can share ideas with them without ridicule, and confide in them.

Balance

Work on your balance between teaching and spending time with your family and friends. Find time for relaxation, such as gardening, reading, or going for walks. Learn how to turn off from being a teacher. This way you can give the best to your students, your colleagues, your family and your friends. Take time to meditate or go to a quiet place to consciously clear your mind, even for 10 minutes a day. Learn to relax every part of your body and breathe deeply.

Personal Development

Continue to develop and grow in your profession, and learn to grow personally too. Learn a new skill or hobby just for you, such as painting, playing guitar, knitting, salsa dancing, or baking.

Holidays

Plan down time for yourself and your family. Find a place to have fun, enjoy and relax.

Set Boundaries

Don't overcommit yourself. Stop volunteering for more and more committees and projects, as you may end up working yourself to the ground. So long as you know that you have tried to be the best teacher that you can be, you have done enough. Take care of yourself, and make your well-being a priority. Gain the support of a teacher trade union which may be able to offer some support.

CHAPTER 6: Performance Anxiety

"Every time I've had a bad performance at an event, I come back more determined and focused."

- Shaun White

Iszi Lawrence's Story - Television History Presenter, Comedian and Children's Author, England
(www.iszi.com)

'I have performed over 2000 gigs across Europe since 2008. There are things which make stand-up comedy more difficult, and it is already quite stressful. You stand alone on a stage while a room of strangers decide whether they find you funny or not. If they do, it becomes a lovely conversation where their laughter feeds your confidence, which in turn makes you funnier. If they don't, you are left questioning yourself. Your punchlines are either delivered as apologies, or worse, with a false bravado which makes you look crazy, like you wandered into a party and are chatting to the coat rack. Sometimes you are completely out of control of the room. On one occasion, I was faced with an audience consisting of nothing but Christmas office parties. This poses a problem for a comedian, because no-one wants to be seen laughing about being naughty at work, sex, drugs, or politics in front of the HR department or their boss. Also, unlike doing a show at an indie theatre or festival, no-one in that room is there to see you: they are there to see 'comedy.' Some people's idea of comedy is Stewart Lee and others is Mrs Brown's Boys. There are few topics or styles which are universally funny, so the chances that the entire room will find me funny is unlikely. What's worse is they were eating, and you can't listen, chew, order things, chat to your table and concentrate on jokes all at once. Comedy is not like music; you must tune in to the whole joke for it to make sense.

I was introduced without applause. I told my first joke and they stared back in confusion. Some had already turned to talk to their neighbours. It felt like waving and shouting at a group of friends from across the street, then suddenly realising that they aren't your friends. Normally at this point, I would have continued to stumble through my set, my confidence in my material dwindling as fewer and fewer people laugh. The more I'd try to control the situation, the more my voice would catch, the more my timing would be off. It would feel like trying to climb out of a muddy hole, each movement pulling me further down. Not this time though. I knew this gig was a lost cause. So, I dumped my jokes. I didn't try to be funny; I decided to work the room. I asked the first table in front of me what they did. They turned out to be estate agents, and there was another group of estate agent at the back of the room. I then got a table of mechanics to judge as I invited an estate agent from each company to the stage to sell me the most revolting houses I could imagine (with suggestions from a plumbing centre employee). It sounds rather daft now, and it wasn't the most hilarious gig I've ever done. But I worked with what I had, and the room became invested in what was happening. A group of teachers donated a mince pie to the winning table and friends were made that night. It was a fluke, but it was only able to happen because I let go of my plans and realised that the gig wasn't about me, but about everyone having fun.

I was able to recover after an awkward start because I genuinely didn't care how it went. I realised that this gig was never going to be perfect. I had to let go of my expectations as well as my ego, and once I did that, I was able to have fun with it. This experience was unbelievably valuable as it taught me that, if your initial plan does not work, you have to adapt in the moment and take a risk. I doubt anyone in that room remembers my name, or what I said. But I bet they all remember the cardboard box under the flyover as being 'unexpectedly available; a rare opportunity to own a deceptively cosy property with a minimalist open plan style, a large low-maintenance shared garden and centrally located to national transport links.'

'The Unstoppable Letty Pegg' by Iszi Lawrence is now available on Amazon, HIVE and Bloomsbury. It is 1910. Lettice Pegg's Mum is a Suffragette, and her Dad is a Policeman. In her attempt to unite her family, she bumps into Edith Garrud, a skilled jitsuka with her own secrets to hide...Will Letty find her true family in a Dojo? Or will society's constraints stop her from discovering her untapped powers?

"You're always going to be nervous teeing it up in a Major Championship. It's very natural and it's a good thing. It means that you want it."

- Rory McIlroy

Andreas Lerch's Story – Economy Specialist, Austria

'I am a 36-year-old male and have been practicing The Jiu Jitsu Foundation style of Japanese martial art for 15 years. One of the most pressured situations we face in Jiu Jitsu is a grading, which is a test for your next belt. Gradings get more gruelling as you become more advanced and can last up to 4 hours, as the grading panel wants to see whether you can handle the mental and physical pressure of multiple stressful situations to accurately simulate self-defence scenarios. I was facing my grading for 2nd degree black belt, 2nd Dan, which is one of the hardest physical gradings within our organisation, not to mention that you only get one chance at it per year, if that. However, there were also several complicating factors: I live in Vienna and am the only black belt there in our style of Jiu Jitsu. All my training peers were in the UK, which meant I had to travel to train, despite having a wife and child at home as well a busy career as an economy specialist.

The prospect of managing training, travel, family, and my full-time job (Jiu Jitsu is merely a hobby) was overwhelming. So, I decided on a plan and carved out several hours a week to develop routines and train by myself. I set aside specific weekends to travel to the UK for advanced training with peers. I invited other instructors to Vienna to help me train and relieve some of the travel burden. While doing all this, I made sure all my training weekends were spaced out in a way that left enough time with my family. This took a huge amount of effort, organisation, and support from my family which, thankfully, I received. I had to spend multiple weekends away from home, leaving my wife to work a full-time job and take care of our son by herself. Being away from family and knowing I put this strain on them for my own personal reasons was hard, and placed even more pressure on me succeeding. Which eventually led to the thought: What if I fail?

What if all of this is for naught and I have to wait another year, possibly more, to try again? What if I spent all this money on travel, time away from family and physically exerted myself, all for nothing? The thought paralysed me. I had similar fears and doubts going into my previous two black belt gradings. As they are so rare and I was already abroad for one of them, I adopted a 'now or never' mentality, which brought this fear of failure to the forefront of my mind. I ended up failing the first grading and narrowly passing the second, in each case performing way below my capabilities.

I decided I needed a new approach to help me handle the situation this time around. I started by identifying the cause of my struggles, which was fear of failure. In doing some research, I realised that this is a problem that many people struggle with, and that there are ways to overcome this. Feeling like I was not alone in this provided me with a great boost. My wife was also instrumental in helping me talk through my problems and identify new, healthier thought processes.

I came to see that fear of failure is natural. Being afraid of failing just showed that I cared and that this was important to me. My wife then turned my thinking on its head by asking me, "Well, do you think you deserve to pass?" My answer was a resounding yes. After all the hours I had invested, everything I have committed to this, I felt that I fully deserved to pass, perhaps more so than anyone else going for this grading. This helped calm my thoughts and gave me a massive confidence boost. I started telling myself, "You have done all the work. You have put everything into this. You know what you are capable of. You deserve this." Was a part of me still afraid of failing? Yes, it was. However, I was no longer overwhelmed by it. I embraced it and used it, together with my newfound confidence, to ensure that I was determined to see this through, no matter what.

On the day of the grading, I was calm and determined. I paced like a caged animal, visualised what I would do, and set my focus on this one single purpose. When I finally got to step on the mat, I was ready. I was nervous but within 5 minutes I knew that I had this, that nothing was going to deter me. My techniques flowed and everything went smoothly…until I came down awkwardly on my shoulder, almost separating my AC joint. It was a numb pain but, after making sure I could still move my arm, I was determined to carry on. At this point I had come too far to give up. I gritted my teeth through the pain, which got more intense with each movement. The fear of failure turned into grim determination and I saw the grading through until the end. At that point I was physically and emotionally exhausted, and my shoulder was almost literally connected to my arm by a thread.

A few hours later, I got the wonderful news that I had passed my grading. The joy and relief were unbelievable. It was without a doubt the hardest grading I have had to go through, and after putting all this time and effort in, I did it. I anticipate having a few more gradings over the course of my Jitsu career. However, this time I know I will not only be prepared physically, but also mentally. I hope you too can face your fears and doubts in whatever situation you face in life. Plan and balance your life, especially if you have family commitments. I was extremely fortunate that my wife and friends helped me in my journey.'

176

Tips for Performance Stress

"Every time the ball leaves my fingers, I always believe that it is going through the hoop."

- Michael Jordan

Performance stress and anxiety can happen to seasoned professionals, as well as those with less experience. You may get stage fright when presenting in front of audiences or when having to compete in sports, martial arts, or other activities. Being able to manage stress is vitally important, as it could enhance your performance or ruin it. Good athletes and those performing in public can harness nervous stressful energy to uplift themselves. On the other hand, if nerves are out of control, they can overtake your body and mind, and waste all the hard work and practice you have put in. Some players, like basketball's Michael Jordan, play their greatest games under stress. Performers such as Beyoncé also do the same on stage.

Michael Jordan famously had an amazingly high level of confidence in his own abilities. You don't have to be a world-famous athlete to be confident under stress. Learning how be calm under these circumstances is vital. It doesn't matter what level of pressure you are under, but rather how you handle the stress that counts.

Research shows that there are two effective strategies to mediate performance anxiety: these are meditation and guided imagery, which are both elements of mental rehearsal. Guided imagery involves concentrating on positive images only, and is a practice often used to relieve stress and pain. Remembering a bad past experience creates stress and anxiety, and yet by imagining the future you can dismantle the stress. In other words, your imagination can reshape your reality, so it's important to harness it to serve your purpose and goal.

You may be as scared by the possibility of success as you are by the possibility of failure. You may be frightened of losing control of your body when tired and exhausted. This can lead to self-defeating behaviours, such as inadequate or excessive warm-ups and poor training regimes. If you can control your emotional highs and lows, you can preclude the need to defend against self-defeating ways. Focusing on staying calm prepares your body and mind for a state of focused readiness.

Social Stress and Anxiety
Stage fright is a colloquial name for performance anxiety. Some people are frightened to speak or perform in public. This can cause emotional nerves, or physical symptoms like dry mouth, sweaty palms, shaking hands, an inability to make eye contact, and even vomiting. There are many ways to overcome social anxiety (Marks, 2019):

Good preparation - Regular practice with a positive mindset will help to overcome performance anxiety and stage fright. It's also important that you work through numerous worst-case scenarios. This way, if you ever encounter these situations on stage during an actual performance, you are more prepared to deal with them, and have a plan B or C as a backup. Practice your performance at home in front of a mirror.

Focus on the audience - Instead of being overly focused on yourself, focus on the audience. This way you can spend time enjoying yourself and the joy you are bringing to the audience.

Avoid stimulants - Caffeine and sugar can agitate the negative symptoms of stage fright, so it's best to avoid sugary foods or caffeinated beverages the day of your performance.

Accept the fear - Accepting that what you're feeling is a natural biological response can be incredibly freeing, and will allow you to work past your stage fright.

Other things that you could do include doing 5 to 10 full breaths and exhaling to help you relax. Entering the stage with a big smile or even listening to motivational or calming music may also help. Lastly, make sure to plan time in for a bathroom break before starting.

Tips for Public Speaking

If you struggle with speaking in public, then the following steps below are necessary to become more confident:

- Seek out and create opportunities at work or your personal life where you can speak up and be heard
- Listen to motivational videos or TED talks on YouTube
- Read books about overcoming fear and anxiety
- Learn how to relax better when having to speak in public – e.g. breathing exercises
- Prepare notes that will keep you on track
- Be passionate about your message

A useful acronym to remember is K.I.S.S., which stands for Keep It Sweet and Simple. Remember this when presenting to an audience. Start by introducing what you will be talking about to the audience, tell them briefly about your topic, and end by summarising the presentation. This keeps it simple and easy to remember.

Handling Stress when Delivering Presentations

Many students become stressed and anxious when asked to present in front of others. Ensure that you leave a good amount of time to prepare for a presentation rather than leave it to the last minute. Collect all your research for your talk into a format that you are happy with, such as on a word document, study cards or in a notebook. Organise the information into a logical manner so that the audience can understand it, and have a clear introduction and conclusion. You may want to pose an upfront question to the audience so that they feel involved.

Practice with your powerpoint or other technology, and have a back-up plan in place if technology fails on the day. Ask someone to listen to your talk who can give you honest feedback. Is your text clear enough to be read from a distance? Avoid reading the words on powerpoint slides out: instead, talk around the topic at hand and use the bullet points to emphasise a point. Keep your nerves, emotions and attitude in check so you are in the position to perform at your best. Practice delivering a confident and passionate talk with varying tones and pitch to make it more interesting.

CHAPTER 7: Home Life

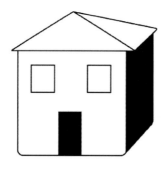

"You're braver than you believe, and stronger than you seem, and smarter than you think."

- Christopher Robin

The stress and anxiety that are experienced as a child can live with you through to adulthood, and shape how you behave in future stressful situations. These memories cannot be erased: however, with the right advice, guidance, and strategies, you can accept the past and create a stronger you. This chapter has inspirational stories of how individuals have overcome their own stressful times while growing up, and how they are managing to cope now.

7.1: Early Years to Adulthood

"The feelings that you stuff, hide and deny are running your life because feelings can never be denied. They must be faced, embraced and healed if you want to start over."

- Rhonda Britten

Karen Johnson's Story – Strategic Marketing and Commercial Leader, Canada

"'Stress is a state of mental or emotional strain and tension resulting from

180

adverse or demanding circumstances."

Reading the Oxford Dictionary definition of the word 'stress,' one would think this feeling should not manifest often. Yes, we all have times of 'adverse or demanding circumstances' but, in an average day, how many of these circumstances could one have? This definition also implies, at least to me, that all stress is negative, which we know is not always the case. Indeed, stress manifests in various ways, can be positive or negative, and different people's ability to 'handle' stress can be vastly different.

Although I did not yet know it, or indeed have a name for it, I experienced stress and anxiety at a very young age. In fact, in a therapy session in my 40's, my therapist indicated that anxiety (a way stress manifests) is inherited. Interesting. For me, stress could be a small change in my environment such as sleeping over at a friend's house. I would experience what my grandmother would call 'a nervous tummy.' It would feel like a thousand butterflies fluttering in my stomach, and would often be so debilitating that one of my parents would need to collect me. Despite feeling this way, I persisted in wanting to have sleepovers as all the other children were doing so. As I grew older, they refused to collect me and, invariably, I would be fine and have a good time.

Growing up, I spent a great deal of my time with my grandparents, as both of my parents worked full-time and there were few options for day-care. I also would spend the night at least once on the weekend. Interestingly, this did not bring out a stress response (my nervous tummy); however, I distinctly remember on one occasion my dad came to take me home and, you guessed it, I was struck down by a 'nervous tummy.' Why? I was going home. To be honest, I still don't really know why I felt that way. I guess it illustrates how unpredictable stress can be in terms of triggers.

Over the years, there have been many occasions that have brought out my stress response. Still vivid for me is my experience at sleep away camp. While I did manage to stick it out a couple of times for the full week, there was one occasion where my mom was required to collect me and take me home. The issue with this was that my mother was at summer university completing another degree. She needed to leave school to collect me and drive me 2 hours to the ferry (I lived on a small island off the coast of New Brunswick, called Grand Manan). As one can imagine, my mother was NOT pleased. Not only did my parents pay for the camp I did not attend, but my mother was also severely inconvenienced and had to miss classes.

Another incident happened when, as a family, we travelled to visit friends to stay with them for the weekend. My parents were in a curling tournament with these friends, and I was left to be minded by one of the older sons. The younger boys were around my age and played together. I was in a new environment, over-night, in a strange place with people I knew but not well. If I could not sleep over at a close friend's home, well, you likely get the picture. This is when I first recall getting resourceful. I was young enough not to know how to dial long-distance, but I was old enough to know how to dial 0 to connect with the operator and then provide my grandmother's phone number. Bless the operator as she connected me, collect of course, to my grandmother, my safety net.

Through these couple of stories, one can begin to see a pattern emerge. Anything new, unfamiliar, or uncertain would cause a stress response - my 'nervous tummy.' I mentioned earlier my therapy experience, and it was through these sessions that I would finally get a name for this response – anxiety.

When I think back over my childhood and young adult life, I experienced anxiety frequently. To this day, I still have moments of my 'nervous tummy,' but the difference is that I now have a name for it. I cannot tell you how helpful that has been for me. I read somewhere that to name something, to acknowledge it, is very powerful. This is because one can then identify why the feeling manifested, and what caused the unconscious response of anxiety. Over the years, I unknowingly developed mechanisms to manage my stress and anxiety, namely routine, exercise, and structure. Reading also helped me to calm my mind, and thus my anxiety. These strategies worked to some degree; however, I still had episodes. I remember one in particular distinctly, as it was soon after I realised that my 'nervous tummy' had been anxiety all along.

I was driving downtown in Toronto, Canada, to meet my friend. We were going to an art exhibition and then out for dinner. On the drive, I started to experience butterflies in my stomach. I was meeting one of my best friends, and we were going to experience something fun and interesting - why should this cause me stress? In thinking this through, I realised that it was the simple matter of not knowing where I was going to park and how I was going to find my friend in the crowd. It sounds silly and trivial doesn't it, and for most, this would not be a big deal or cause them any stress. For me and my nervous system, this was not the case.

Over the years, I have been able to identify the stress triggers that bring on my anxiety. One obvious response would be for me to avoid these situations; however, this is not entirely practical, and I would not be where I am in my life if I had. With that said, one can begin to understand why some individuals shut down, play it safe and, in extreme cases, isolate themselves. This can be far preferable to some than 'feeling the feeling.'

I, in a large part due to my mother, have gone the other way. She pushed me, cheered me on, and supported me to persevere - to feel the stress and anxiety, and move forward anyway. It has not always been easy for me, or for her! There have been many tears over the years, and I am grateful for her and her unconditional support (and tough love at times!).

Stress and anxiety manifests physically for me in other ways, including hives, shingles, and eye infections, to name some of the more serious. Each time, there has been a particular stressful circumstance that brought on the response. I write this to emphasise that stress and anxiety can cause serious health issues, and should not be ignored or trivialised.

Earlier, I indicated that the unknown caused me stress. My move to the UK was the unknown multiplied by 100, but it was a wonderful opportunity for me. Talk about being scared and doing it anyway! In the Spring of 2018, I accepted a long-term position in the UK. While I knew the hiring manager (we served on several global and regional teams together) and a couple of other colleagues, I can safely say I did not know anyone well. When I arrived, I did not yet have a place to live, I had to learn to drive on the 'other side of the road,' and even simply buying groceries and supplies was new. Who knew that garbage bags are called bin liners in the UK? Everything was new, strange, and unfamiliar. Cue acute stress and anxiety! I knew I would have some of this, but not nearly to the degree that it manifested. I cried easily, lost 20lbs and approximately half of my hair. About two months in, I was ready to call it quits, admit defeat, and go home. Everyone told me to give it time. I credit the support of many people, including people I had just met, who helped me not only settle in, but to seek the help I so very much needed. One individual, my dear friend Colleen, a therapist, pointed out that I needed medical help. Now the interesting part is, I am in the pharmaceutical industry and should have recognised this but did not.

To make a long story short, I sought medical help through my GP and was prescribed anti-anxiety medication. It has changed my life. Acute anxiety is caused by a chemical imbalance, and whilst everyone experiences stress, not everyone has severe manifestations of anxiety requiring medication. Stress is multifactorial and, as I mentioned earlier, not all bad. However, too much stress over a prolonged period can be. The biggest gifts I have given myself are the following:

- I sought therapy and found a name for my 'nervous tummy'
- Feeling the feelings and doing it anyway
- Seeking pharmaceutical help from a medical professional

I cannot tell you how important it is to have strong, supportive friends and family. It is in large part due to them that I am where I am in my journey. I learned perseverance, resilience and strategies to help myself, which have served me well and continue to do so. With that said, please don't continue to suffer. If you have resonated with anything I have written, talk to someone; a therapist, your GP or ask about an Employee Assistance program at your place of work. There is help.

I still experience anxiety from time to time - that 'nervous tummy' - but it is manageable and transient. As I said, stress is not bad, and it can help us to take on difficult tasks. What it shouldn't be is debilitating, paralysing, or cause one to become sick. I am grateful I have found natural remedies, like exercise, as well as pharmaceutical help, that have helped me to manage my anxiety in a much more productive manner.'

Kim Burton's Story – Lecturer, North America

'Stress is one of those difficult feelings that seems easy to apply to a variety of situations, yet hard to define. It's certainly subjective, as one person could be quite intimidated by the prospect of having a six-foot long python wrapped around their neck, whilst to another it could bring back fond childhood memories of a beloved pet - though I'll admit my childhood was perhaps odder than most. Stress can exist in the background for years on end as a near constant presence, or it can feel acute yet fleeting in moments of intense pressure. For many, stress has become so commonplace that it simply seems like an inevitable, if undesirable, part of life.

When I was younger, prior to entering high-school, I was rather unpopular, and I can vividly recall feeling a sense of unease and distress that would pique even at the mere mention of my name, having been conditioned to know that little good would follow. My father ensured that the atmosphere I could expect when I got home would be little better. It was not until my early teens that I could expect a night of restful sleep without nightmares waking me at least once.

As I got older, there came a time when stress became so commonplace that it almost seemed to disappear into the background, like a fish in water; I cannot pinpoint the exact day, but I eventually came to understand that the objects which brought out feelings of stress were not necessarily directly causing it, but it was the nature of my relationship with and attachment to them that enabled it.

I came to understand the nature of stress to be a particular kind of fear that takes the form of what can best be explained as a tension between something external and oneself. I began to draw inward and practiced a form of radical acceptance of how things were and desiring nothing to change one way or another, breaking any attachments I had to possible futures. For every attachment I severed, for every person's opinion whose worth I denied, I felt the stress dissipate. Eventually I found that, without concern or investment, even in oneself, stress disappeared.

This is of course easier said than done, and I was in the unique position of having little to lose. Yet it brought an understanding that allowed for the creation of peace and calm such as I had never known. It

185

was a welcome time of healing and discovery, much needed given the circumstances. It was only later that I realised that the same connections and investments that can cause such negative feelings in life can also cause positive meaning and worth. So, little by little, I extended threads of connection and attachment again, but this time with incredibly careful forethought and awareness. I was cautious to invest only in those people, places, or ideas which were worthwhile, and only to the extent that it had been earned.

It may sound somewhat cold or calculating, but the reality is that, as a result, the very finite energies we each must commit to people and projects in our lives are kept focused and available for those that really deserve it. The people that we love have access to the best of us, and the projects about which we are truly passionate make consistent progress.

Coming to understand stress as a tension, we can either manage that tension by using our energies to get closer to our object and alleviate the strain on the connection, or we can sever it. If we find ourselves connected to too many things, then we are sapped of our energies by attempting to manage too much, and often have too little to give to those few we genuinely care about. As with any exercise, the goal is not to avoid any stress whatsoever, but only to strain as much as we are comfortable with without hurting ourselves. In this way, we can slowly increase our inner reserves and our capacity for connection, enriching both our own lives and increasing the positive effect we can have on the lives of others.'

Ian Lambert's Story - Dean of Graduate Studies & Professor at College of Creative Studies, Detroit

'I have for many years subscribed to Nietzsche's notion that 'what doesn't kill me, only makes me stronger.' I would describe myself as having a generally robust mental resilience to external factors, although it is important to remain aware of one's own vulnerability. All humans are susceptible to stress, and there have been times when I have failed to recognise the build-up of certain factors that can accrue towards mental exhaustion. Awareness of the fabled 'straw that broke the camel's back' or 'final straw' is something we all need to keep in check.

I am fortunate to have had a stable and supportive upbringing, and recognise the privilege that has brought me to stable adulthood. I am grateful for my parents, family, and friends, and my loving and supportive wife. In addition, two important factors in my life, one bad and one good, have given me enormous strength.

First, the bad one: I did not enjoy school as a child. I hated it. I was shy and had difficulty mixing in until my mid-teens, and experienced bullying from both other boys and some teachers. I have a visual brain and a very short attention span for linear instructions. I struggled academically, and under-achieved badly. I believe that the stupid question is the one that isn't asked, but many of the teachers really didn't see it that way. School left me lacking in confidence - I flunked my exams and had low self-esteem. Teachers told me I had no future in academia, and suggested that I forget thinking about further study after school. Art college would be a waste of time, they said, and I should find a safe, sensible career. Well, thank goodness I didn't listen! My first year at art college revealed to me a love of learning, and today I have a PhD. I had planned to write to my old headmaster to tell him, but he died the year before I finished it. My negative experience in childhood has provided me with thick skin as an adult, and a mental resilience that has seen me through many challenging times. It drove me to work on myself and my own personal development.

So, to the good experience in my life: martial arts. As a child, I was terrified of confrontation and aggression. As an adult, Jiu Jitsu and Judo have provided me with enormous confidence and self-esteem. This does not mean I go in search of trouble (although I am susceptible to provocation). I have done Jiu Jitsu for almost all of my adult life. Without it, I would simply be a different person. It is not just about capability in self-defence or accomplishment in the art; the camaraderie and life-long friendships give a strong sense of belonging and being part of something big and important. Friends provide so much: love, kindness, laughter, support, reflection, and advice. And if they're good friends, they'll also give criticism.

Thick skin and confidence have given rise to what I regard as my superpower - namely, my ability to take criticism constructively in both my

187

professional and personal life. Through this, I can openly consider my weaknesses and accept when I am wrong. Criticism, however hard, is a good thing. If taken personally, it can destroy you; if taken objectively, you can only grow. If the criticism is unfair, it can be gracefully dismissed, which is a skill in itself. However, if the criticism is warranted - better still, if it is intelligent and constructive - then to heed it with humility is to learn and grow. It is something to seek throughout life. If it does not kill you, it will only make you stronger.'

Catherine Montgomery's Story – Poet and Author of '*Apple Crumble*' Children's Book, Scotland

'Stress has been with me my whole life. I was adopted as a baby by my wonderful parents when I was about 10 months old and, in recent years, I have begun to realise that I didn't have a great start in life prior to my adoption.

As a little girl, I was desperate to fit in and be part of this lovely family. I was always trying so hard with friends and my cousins, always wanting my parents to be proud of me. Looking back, I realise how exhausting this was. I remember suffering from horrible headaches and stomach pains which persisted into adulthood. I now believe these were all symptoms of stress. My father was a GP, and during the 1960's when I was small, he would go on house calls in the middle of the night. I remember lying awake till he got home, terrified that something awful might happen to him, even though it was normal for him to be out 2 or 3 times a night!

This anxiety continued into adulthood; it ebbed and flowed, but as a young woman it ultimately led me to make some horrific life choices, culminating in a hideous marriage. It is very hard to believe in yourself when you are constantly trying to please others.

After leaving the bad marriage, with help from a great manager at work and his belief in me and my 3 children, I can look back with great clarity of mind and see the lessons learnt and the strategies which helped along the way.

Firstly, a good education and my parents' example allowed me to have career choices, which ultimately meant I could make a life for my children as a single mum. This success meant that my children could have confidence in me as their mother, and I believe allowed them to flourish in friendships, in school, and ultimately with life partners.

One of my early successes as a single mother was completing a Diploma in Performance Coaching. After a difficult breakup and divorce I was very tired, but my energy was boosted by working with 2 of my colleagues who agreed to let me coach them as part of my diploma. This was mutually beneficial, as they were looking to take on more responsibilities within their roles at work, and I enjoyed helping them with strategies to achieve this. They both achieved a lot during the year we worked together, and I gained my Diploma. This helped my confidence and cemented great relationships in the team, which also brought us tremendous results and made us a top team in the company. All these positive results meant that I personally felt happier, calmer and far less stressed. Eventually, I ended up in a new team with great people, but a boss who was a bully. I had never encountered this form of bullying, and two thirds of the team went off sick within two months of joining. I did not. All the coaching work I had done on myself over the years, as well as my friends' and my children's expectations of me, meant that I had the grit to withstand, knowing this would pass - and it did.

Great friends and colleagues in my life have helped to give me courage just by being there and listening. As an adult, I learned that you don't need to try too hard; just being yourself is good enough and far less stressful!

Walking and writing have also helped me. Having no car, I now walk miles every day, and being out in nature has been great therapy. Also writing poetry, which I do every day, allows me to clear my head of gremlins - I recommend it!

Lastly, being honest with myself and asking for help when I need it has made life far less stressful. The anxiety might still be there, but it can be managed, and life can be enjoyable. Being there for friends when they need support is important to me, but you can only be that person if you are not constantly in your own head, so I think working on yourself is paramount to achieving this. I do this through my favourite coaching book and writing. Positive affirmations are also useful. During this past difficult year, there has been a lot said about getting out in nature and walking amongst trees, in parks or even urban landscapes. Listening out for birdsong on a frosty morning is a delight which I am certain alleviates stress!

Actively caring for others, listening, looking for ways you can support them and be kind all require active engagement, so you need to engage as often as possible. It has also now been proven that this helps to improve your own well-being, as well as that of the recipient, but I think we all already knew that.'

As can be seen from the above stories, experiencing stress in early life can cast a shadow over our interactions and behaviour, and can leave a scar. However, with the right amount of support, self-belief, and time, we can still achieve many personal and career goals in life, and can become stronger due to our childhood and adolescent experiences.

7.2: Resolving Conflict

"I have seen many storms in my life. Most storms have caught me by surprise, so I had to learn very quickly to look further and understand that I am not capable of controlling the weather, to exercise the art of patience, and to respect the fury of nature."

- Paulo Coehho

Bhavina Rahani's Story - Web Designer, India

'When the author asked me to contribute to this book, I knew instantly what had caused me the most stress in life, but quite frankly I really did not want to go through it again, even on paper. After some debate with myself, and the fact that I had challenged myself this year to do a few 'scary' things, here is my experience, which was one of the most stressful and terrible times of my life.

In my late 30's, I was single and still living at home. Despite it not being the 'done' thing in the Indian culture (I grew up in a time when girls only left home if you were getting married), I found myself a nice little two-bedroom semi-detached house and moved in. At first, I was happy - apart from being skint!

Problems started about a year later when a new family moved in next door. At first they were friendly, but after an incident which involved the man throwing garden waste onto my lawn, I went over and had a chat with them.

That was the first time I heard their accusations about my alleged 'night-time noises.' They said I had been running the washing machine at night which meant they could not sleep, and throwing what sounded like beads on the wall to keep them awake.

I was taken aback. I had never had any problems with anyone like that before. I said they should have told me about the washing machine, I can easily to do my washing earlier, but regarding the other noise I had no idea what it was.

This time things ended amicably, but what I did not realise was it was the start of months of harassment and stress. This included being woken at 5am with shouting and banging on my front door telling me to stop making noises. There were loud bangs on my bedroom wall at night and in the mornings. The man would sit in his car waiting and glare at me before I left the house at 7 am, and he was always outside when I arrived back, no matter what time it was.

I began to get upset and was afraid; I had no idea why it was all happening. My only thought was that perhaps it could be racially motivated.

My stress levels began to rise as time went on. I was sleeping on the floor in the spare room some nights and wearing ear plugs to get away from the banging and loud noises.

Being Hindu, I turned to my faith and started a religious fast one day a week and prayed to give my mind some peace. It felt good because it was something I could do, and the neighbour had no part in it. The stress, however, was taking its toll. I lost about a stone in weight as my anxiety levels hit the roof; I could not relax in my own home. I caught him banging my windows with his broom once, which made a shocking bang, shook the whole house, and was quite terrifying. This happened a few times. For the second time I sought help from the police, who suggested CCTV, which I had installed after a short while.

I told my family briefly what was happening, and a few close friends who gave me some support. Going to work and being away from the house gave me hours when I didn't have to think about it or him - hours when I could just be me, not be on edge constantly. The irony was that, at the time, work was more stressful than usual. A website project was going horribly wrong, the agency we had was making huge mistakes and my manager had just been sacked - but this was all still better than being at home! Keeping busy became a great distraction.

The police had suggested arbitration to resolve the issue without going to court, but the thought of being in the same room with him made me sick to my stomach. However, I was willing to give it a go. Though the arbitration brought a few months of peace, he continued to bang on the walls or drop weights on the floor in the mornings, especially at the weekend when he knew I wasn't at work. There was no relaxation in this home I had worked so hard to get.

The final straw came he started playing weird music in the early hours of the morning. This had gone on for some days. I'd already had months of not sleeping properly, and just couldn't take it anymore, not to mention him jeering and flashing his lights if our cars passed on the road.

I felt that if the situation continued, it would break me. My mind felt so fragile, and I also feared for my personal safety. I had to take back control, and the answer was to take myself out of the situation before I lost everything, including my sanity. I had to leave my lovely house. I was heartbroken, but there was no other way out.

Afterwards, I sometimes thought that perhaps I should have stayed and held on. Instead, he had won. But then I remember that I was taking care of myself. I knew my limits and I did what was right for me. If that petty little man thought he won, let him. I really didn't care.

This happened about 10 years ago, and until now I've not been able to talk about it to anyone. I hope it helps someone. Some of my main takeaways from this situation were:

- If you are facing a stressful situation, look at what you can control
- Try to tackle the source of the stress head on if possible
- Use your faith or spiritualism, it might give you some peace
- Seek external help from friends, family, or professionals
- Take up hobbies that can distract you from the stress
- Physically take yourself out of the stressful situation if you can. Flight is a natural human safety mechanism, and sometimes fight is not the answer'

Tomkin Allinson's Story - Architect, New Zealand

'I was brought up in a strict Catholic family and was expected to go to Sunday church to keep up with the practice. I did not rebel against religion like many of my friends did, but I had a lot of peer pressure to deal with and I didn't want to disappoint my parents. We never really saw eye-to-eye about anything, from the clothes I would wear and my hairstyle to what programmes or movies I wanted to watch. As I reached my mid-teens, things got more difficult as I was questioned about who my friends were, my choice of girlfriends, as well as college and university choices. This was all a stressful time for both me and my parents. I am sure that they had good intentions, but I wanted to make my own choices in life.

I went to study at university at the age of 18 to gain new experiences and give me some space from my parents. Moving away from home gave me a different outlook on life and questioned my opinions on lots of issues. It was a stressful time starting university, getting used to new surroundings, making new friends, and dealing with my own finances and self-care. I had plenty of self-doubt and asked myself if I had made the right choice of degree, if I would disappoint my parents, and if I could cope living by myself. I had my ups and downs but kept in touch with my friends through social media apps to keep me sane. Slowly but surely, I adapted and over time I settled down. I met the most amazing and diverse people, and took part in many new experiences. My circle of friends were no longer just from the catholic church, but people with different religions, beliefs, values and cultures. We all respected each other's opinions, and I learned to question what I had been taught and not always agree. When I visited home to see my parents, it usually ended up in arguments, especially with my Mum. I found it hard to cope because I could not express my opinions as freely as I could at university. It was frustrating, and I used to get terribly upset that my parents didn't agree or accept my new way of thinking and approach to life.

I had to remind myself that it was OK to have my own opinions, but also that it was OK for my parents to have their viewpoints too. After speaking to a friend, I concluded that if I wanted my parents to respect what I had to say, I had to also try and respect their viewpoint too. I made the effort to respect their values and opinions, and asked the same from them. This helped with me to get along with them more easily. We still have disagreements now and again, but they are civilised and more like debates than arguments.'

7.3: Parenting

"Parents can only give good advice or put them on the right paths, but the final forming of a person's character lies in their own hands."

- Anne Frank

Becoming a parent and raising children can be a whole new challenge in life. Emotions can fluctuate from the exhilaration of having a new-born to despair and stress because you now have the responsibility of caring for another human being. Sleepless nights with crying and ill babies can add to the stresses of being a parent. On the flip side, the joy of seeing their first steps or hearing their first words can make it all worth it. Parenting, through early school years and into teenage and college years, can bring wonderful memories, as well as some tearful days when you don't see eye-to-eye on a few aspects of life

Jyoti Soren's Story – Teaching Assistant and Author, England

'Becoming a parent and mother for the first time was a very steep learning

194

curve, like any major change in your life. The excitement of becoming a mother and having my own family was everything I wanted at this stage of my life, but daunting at the same time. No-one teaches you these skills throughout school or university, and most of the time the only thing you have to fall back on is how you were raised. Luckily for me, I had a very hands-on mother who, although working full time, was very experienced with young children.

My birth experiences were quite traumatic as I had caesarean sections for all three births. The first birth experience I had, I was in labour for 18 hours, but the baby got distressed and I had to be taken in for a C-section. The baby was OK, but I felt cheated out of the experience of a natural birth, and for a while felt very unworthy. At this stage, I was very depressed, but after talking it out with various people, I came to terms with it.

The early days of being a mother were very chaotic, trying to juggle your former life as well as looking after a baby, lack of sleep, and recovering from a major operation. Getting support wherever I could was essential, especially from my mother. It was also important to try not to be too hard on myself and take each day as it came.

I was fortunate enough to be a full-time mother with my three children, and to this day I feel it was the best decision I could have made for my family. As we had less income coming into the household, we had to adjust our spending. I did not see the point of having children only for them to be raised by someone else. I realise that this is not always possible for some families, but it is a decision we were happy with. However, at the time, I felt belittled by society for staying at home with my kids. I wanted to be there for my children when they came home from school because it was one of the best and most comforting memories I had as child when my mother was at home.

For such a long time, life was a juggling act, between school drop offs, pickups, running to after school activities and not stopping until my head hit the pillow. They then went to high school and started becoming more independent. The problems that came up were more social and emotional. Again, another steep learning curve, but with the help of my family and peers we steered through it. They grew up in a blink and now they are all grown up, high achievers and beginning their adult lives. I am an immensely proud mama.'

Terence Barkistend's Story – Engineer, Isle of Wight

'Becoming a parent was not easy for me. My girlfriend and I were surprised to find out we were going to have a baby. We were over the moon with this news, and we both decided to try our best for the new arrival of a baby girl. Parents and friends tried to give us help and advice and always seemed to think they knew better. After a difficult and long labour, we were blessed with a 7lb healthy, bouncy baby girl. Unfortunately, my girlfriend didn't take naturally to being a mother and didn't seem to bond with our daughter. We got help and advice, however I ended up doing the parenting, feeding, changing, and shopping, as well as trying to keep down a job as an electrical engineer.

Even though family and friends tried to help, I wanted to do things my own way. I was constantly stressed, cried several times (which is hard for a 6-foot 3-inch burley man to admit!), and I was no longer a good person to be around. I was angry at the world for leaving me to deal with things by myself as my girlfriend struggled with poor mental health and post-natal depression. I was coping badly, having to act like a single parent and at times regretting being a father - but that thought didn't last long, and dissipated every time I saw the beautiful eyes of my baby girl. Once I nearly fell asleep while driving because I was so tired, and luckily I bumped into the kerb which woke me up, giving me enough time to avoid hitting a tree. A few months later, my girlfriend got the help she needed for post-natal depression, and after 6 months she finally began to feel more like herself, which was a relief for both of us. We started to work together and take turns looking after our little baby girl. Only when I allowed others to help me did I realise that it takes more than one or two people to raise a child, but also extended family, friends, and neighbours. The stress of raising a young girl who is now a teenager brings its own challenges, stress and anxiety.

The only advice I can give is to take time out for yourself. Wind down, and trust others in your network of family and friends to help.

Recognise when you are struggling and let someone know – don't try to be a martyr. Enjoy and appreciate the things that are going well in your life, and you will be surprised to find that there are usually a lot more good things than bad.'

Advice for Parents

The physical, emotional, psychological, and hormonal changes that follow birth can leave mothers feeling exhausted, frustrated, worried and elated. To first time parents in particular, newborns can be quite intimidating. It is therefore essential that parents take care of themselves during those early months. Many people may believe that being a stay-at-home parent is an easy job. This is far from the truth. Managing children, cooking, cleaning, and running errands can be stressful.

One thing all mothers have in common is increased stress levels, whether you are a new mother, a working mum, a stay-at-home mum, or a single mum. The stress hormone cortisol can increase new parents' risk for both mental and physical health problems, and can impact parenting skills, patience, and ability to bond with their child.

Tips for Reducing Stress

Pam Myers has shared some helpful tips for parents to reduce stress (2014):

Planning and organising - Being organised will help to reduce stress. This can be simple things like preparing for the next day the night before.

Delegate - Rather than take on all the tasks and burdens by yourself, identify the tasks that are priorities and delegate them accordingly.

Seek support - Be it from your personal network, family, parent circle, community group or similar.

'You' time - Plan some 'you' time for self-care, such as a good book to read, a nightly bath or watching a movie. Exercise, meditation, and social outings are all important and help bring balance to a busy life.

Be kind to yourself - Avoid trying to be the perfect parent. It is not easy to have a perfectly clean house all the time, and laundry can wait. Enjoy the experience of parenthood. You may want to be a stay-at-home mom or dad rather than returning to work. Some people you know will be incredibly happy with your decisions, while others cannot understand why you have not gone back.

Additional tips:
- Listening to music can be relaxing
- Eat healthy foods and have occasional treats
- Exercising several times a week can reduce stress and tension
- Avoid watching the news before going to bed
- Take time out for a hobby or two
- Avoid too much caffeine or alcohol, as these can increase stress

Helpful Tips and Advice

Many parents try to do the best for their children, and as they grow up find their teenager's behaviour very stressful, and worrying. Teenagers can challenge even the calmest of parents. Many parents find it hard to connect to their teenagers as they can be quite independent, searching for their place in the world and defining their identity. Puberty and the circulation of more hormones can add to behaviours such as isolation and mood swings. Many teenagers prefer to spend large amounts of time on social media or with friends their own age than with parents, guardians or other family members. Some teenagers may be very well adjusted and get on happily with the family, while others may test the status quo by being rebellious, rude and seemingly inconsiderate. Often, teenagers who feel misunderstood and not listened to may think that no one cares about them, and may reject your attempts to comfort them.

If you're feeling overwhelmed, that doesn't mean you're a bad parent. You may have too much on your plate. This is important to remember, because feelings of inadequacy, defensiveness, and guilt make parenting stress worse. Try to identify specific sources of parenting stress. A family household can have many stressors at home and at work. It can feel as though the stress of parenting your teenager is too much and will push you to breaking point. Try to step back from the situation and view it objectively. Your child or teenager may be going through a personal crisis or physical health problem that you are not aware, of so it's important to give them space and seek medical or psychological support as required:

- Take time out for yourself to relax and do something just for you
- Join a support group
- Find a go-to person who can offer you help
- Find a coping strategy that will work for you

CHAPTER 8: Relationships

"The meeting of two personalities is like the contact of two chemical substances: if there is any reaction, both are transformed."

- Carl Gustav Jung

A good relationship can be a wonderful and enriching experience for both parties. The love, trust and mutual respect can sometimes turn bitter for a variety of reasons, such as poor communication, reduced quality time, infidelity, or simply growing apart and having different expectations. Finding a good partner to have a lasting relationship with is half the battle, and keeping and maintaining the relationship despite everything that life throws at you is the other half of the battle.

This chapter is about those who have found love and lost it for whatever reason, and the heart ache and struggles they have had to endure. It also looks at the coping strategies used to get through the dark clouds of emotional turmoil.

8.1: Break-Ups

"There is always room for change, but you have to be open to that change."

- Kathryn Budig

Nick Hofstead's Story – Travel Agent, Peru

'My story starts around 15 years ago, and involves the breakdown of a 2-year relationship and the dark places that can lead you. Avoiding going into detail, the relationship had deteriorated and the environment within the house had reached its most toxic. I resolved to leave and move back into my empty flat with as much as I could load into a car. This was an incredibly stressful and emotional situation for me and my partner. It was an immense burden on my mental health and well-being. Even upon reflection, it remains foggy as to where the blame resides. We now believe we both played a part in our demise.

I deployed different techniques, consciously or otherwise, during this period to help me cope with the situation and the aftershock of events. A level of depression had set in, and it's well documented that exercise can help manage this. Evenings and early mornings became the ideal time to walk out into the surrounding countryside and engage in some contemplation to clear my head. It was good for my mental and physical health, and something I still enjoy, alongside a good podcast.

I found it really helpful to have a focus and a purpose. My work was busy and a place of enjoyment, with some really great colleagues around me. They provided a distraction and, on occasion, invaluable counsel and encouragement, letting me know I was indeed coping.

Having a strong bank of friends and family is important anyway in everyday life pursuits, but when you are faced with escalating events, they are a great grounding and I remain very thankful for their support. I knew they were there for me and I could rely on them.

In my early 30's, I read *The Art of Happiness* by the Dalai Lama. I took from that text that the secret to happiness was to increase things in your life that bring you contentment. Maximising the things that brought me contentment was an invaluable lesson. Music is my favourite pastime, so I invested a lot of time in my band and in my home studio. For me, very few things can substitute the sense of achievement I get from writing, recording, and the whole creative process.

The Art of Happiness also instructs you to practice forgiveness by remaining patient and tolerant. Whilst trying to avoid clichés here, time really is a healer. Practicing tolerance helped me to appreciate everyone's motivations in the melting pot of stress and emotions. By being patient, time has passed, and it has become easier to reflect on that period without anger.

So, my coping mechanisms were many; to focus and have purpose, whether that be in work, play or mental and physical health. Always trying to see all sides of the story to moderate my actions through having patience and tolerance was key to settling matters. And last but by no means least, having a robust network of friends and family around me to support and counsel me was crucial.

In the end, my ex-girlfriend married again. As for me, I met someone 18 months later… but that's a whole new story!'

Simon Zimmer's Story – Website Designer, Indonesia

'I was in relationship with a girl for several years and things were going very well. After a period of major life changes, graduating university and moving to a new city, she decided that she wanted out of the relationship. I could not get to the bottom of the reason why as she never gave me the opportunity to fight for the relationship. Instead, she delivered all my things to my parent's house and decided that she no longer wanted to be together. This broke my heart - it was a massive shock to me and to all those around me. I did not know how to handle this loss. I felt sad, stressed out and bewildered, in addition to feeling anxious and unable sleep for many months. I even started having panic attacks.

This stress created a lot of self-doubt and was a big knock on my self-esteem. I would stay up at night and ask myself where I went wrong, what I could have done differently. Why had I not seen the signs, or were there no signs? Was it me or was it my ex-girlfriend that changed? I had imagined at one point that we were going to be together for ever, and now that dream was shattered into a million pieces. Would I ever find love again? How will I get over this? I would get stressed at work because of these emotions and thoughts running around in my head about the breakup, and had to take some sick leave to be able to cope. I remember crying in front of my managers who were surprisingly supportive as one of them had gone through a similar experience, which meant that I was not alone in this journey.

I was at breaking point, so I got help and advice from family and friends. Sadly, at the time this was not enough, and I felt my life was spiralling out of control. I had just started a new job in a new city and was making new friends. This was an exceedingly difficult time in my life, so to try and handle things I threw myself into competitive sports and my new job. This did help; however, it was not until I discovered that my ex-girlfriend had moved on to a new relationship that I felt I too could move on. I had shed many tears over this time. I was not depressed, but I was awfully close to being so if it hadn't been for the help and support of family and friends. I found that mindfulness and yoga helped me, as well as regular exercise.

The good news is I am now a lot happier and in a new relationship. Going through any breakup is always going to feel like being hit by car. It is not easy to recover from. However, I suggest you focus on your own well-being, mental health and keep close to family and friends. Focusing on my career and sports did help me. In the end, time does help to heal the blow to the heart, and sometimes it's a blessing in disguise. The relationship may not have lasted if we got married or even had children, at which point the break-up would have been more devastating. Finding a wonderful new relationship made me realise that what I had before was not what I really needed, and I was able to find my new self and have more fulfilling intimate relationships. I have learned to be kinder to myself, and use meditation as well more regular exercise and reading for self-development.'

Edward Henry Kruger's Story – Software Engineer, South Africa

'Ah, stress. Sometimes we feel doomed being tethered to its boon and curse. The problem with this wicked beast is that if you cut off its head, another one regrows in its place, much like the mythological Hydra. It feels like no matter what we do or what method we use to combat it, at some stage or another it will wear us down and take over. Don't play its game - there is more to life.

The last 3 years were, for me, an abomination. A constant dose of challenge after challenge and stress was my drug. I had previous business partners stealing from the company - which was bad, but I could deal with it. I started my own company breaking away and taking what was left, which wasn't much – again, bad, but I could deal with it. At some stage, I ended up with terrible clients who 'forgot' to pay me for months - OK, two-minute noodles this month, bad. With no safety net and no support, I was all in, all the time.

Being stressed and burned out wasn't an option: I was in my battledress wearing the hat of the undefeated champion. I felt unstoppable and had something to prove. To top it all off, I decided that dating would be a great idea. Why not? If I didn't experience the burn of being beyond tired and still convincing myself that I was fine then I wasn't living. Who hasn't heard of the mantra 'work hard party hard'? It fuelled me in my corporate days.

I was determined to live such a full life I did everything: I did advanced cooking degrees after work, I did martial arts, I did rock climbing, I went surfing, took the red eye to Cape Town before meetings, I went diving, I got a motorcycle, I collected art, I travelled the world twice a year. I was living the perfect life!

Better yet, I started seeing an incredible woman. Little did I understand that resting your soul is not the same as distracting yourself with more intensity, nor is it losing yourself in someone else.

Slowly during the last 3 years, my personal life started dwindling and my mental state started breaking down. The day-to-day constant stress of work started seeping into every part of my life. I had debriefing sessions with my girlfriend, going on and on, day after day, about how unfair these customers were. I could speak of nothing else, and on weekends made a deliberate effort to be extremely fun. My perfect woman travelled a lot and liked to party, and little did I know at the time that she was seeing someone else on the side. This was when my entire world came crashing down at Christmas. We were supposed to travel to America for a month, we were supposed to get engaged. We had even bought the ring together.

I didn't feel safe, I couldn't share my details about my day with anyone, I don't know who I could trust. I didn't know who I was anymore. It was a disaster.

To make matters worse, when I was abroad on holiday by myself, my passport got stolen. When I got back, COVID-19 struck, and I got pulled into my ex's rollercoaster of not being able to afford her apartment and she ended up living with me for a few months. After a few terrible months, her Christmas fling didn't work out and somehow it became my problem – primarily because I allowed it to be. Then, suddenly, it got worse.

My business was losing customers and contracts and I already had bad debtors: the writing was on the wall. There was nothing left to do but to shut down my dreams before I lost everything. While this was happening, my ex decided to attempt an exit stage left. The stress had made me hit rock bottom, and in the middle of this spiral my business had to sell all its stocks and assets. In my personal life, I felt responsible for it all.

The only silver lining was the fact that I could pick up the phone at any time of day to someone. I had one great friend that watched this storm and kept staying by my side, even when it was not a lot of fun or rewarding. I will always be grateful for their support.

I gave all my employees a few months' notice that I was closing the business and going to take a job. I started out angry at not being in a management position, but today I am happy knowing that my day ends at 5pm. I helped my ex-girlfriend to find her own little house and enabled her to look after herself. I am confident that she will do well, and I wish only happiness for her.

It is only today while writing this that I realise I have really started to conquer my stress, and put in the effort to do so. It is completely worth it, and to do so I had to give up control. I had to accept where I was, and start to practice gratefulness. I started a meditation practice daily, I shifted my external validation to internal processes, and I am deep in the journey of becoming my own best friend. I got to know myself, and I have realised how much of life I have missed because I was never present in the moment. Sure, I don't know what my purpose is and that is scary, but it's all about the journey now and no longer about the destination.

My wish for you is to be deliberate and present in your everyday life, be OK with what you have, learn to accept responsibility for yourself, live guilt-free and leave the world a better place than you found it.'

Relationship Advice

"Always be a first-rate version of yourself, instead of a second-rate version of somebody else."

- Judy Garland

A relationship can be like looking after a delicate flower; you must nourish it, give it water, sunlight, love, warmth and nutrients, as well as take out any weeds and remove pests that may damage its growth. Once some of the nourishment is withdrawn, then this flower slowly begins to wilt and become damaged, and may eventually die.

I know that relationships are a lot more complicated than this. Relationships can be the most fulfilling things in your life, or they can be a nightmare that keeps you up at night, and causes you stress and anxiety. It takes regular effort and work to keep a relationship flourishing (Fabrega, 2021). You will need to know how to handle the good times as well as the challenging times. You should trust, respect and love each other, and give each other space. You should also allow them to have interests, hobbies, their own friends, a job, career or business of their own. You should be able to work through life's problems together and not let differences come between you through mutual trust and respect.

However, if a relationship is not working, the important thing is for you to recognise there is a problem and look out for tell-tale signs. What can sometimes happen is that our minds, bodies, and hearts can be taken up with work and family responsibilities. We may even get involved with hobbies and other social activities that take time away from our relationships, and can add to any underlying issues. There may be money problems, a redundancy, misunderstandings that can cause stresses, or even physical or mental health problems which add to the stress load.

Communication

It's vital to have open and honest conversations in order to build a firm foundation in any relationship, however we may not have had good experiences in the past, or have had any guidance on how best to communicate. You or your partner may have had unhealthy or abusive relationships previously which didn't work out. This may mean that you naturally try to shield yourself and your heart from more hurt and anguish. Previous difficult relationships may lead to you being more cautious and not letting anyone get close to you. Trust and respect will take time to establish in any good relationship, and will take daily, weekly, monthly and even lifelong effort from both sides if you want to make things work. If you recognise that something is not right but do nothing about it for months or years, then it's going to take a longer time to close the gap.

Let's take the analogy of a doctor who has diagnosed your illness, but does not tell you about it or have a conversation about how to make you better. Instead, they wait a few years before starting treatment. This would not be acceptable: it would lead to your health ending up in a bad place, so that even the best medicine could not help you. The same goes for a relationship. It is important to let each other know what's on your mind rather than them trying to guess. It's important to find time to talk and listen to each other's day and the challenges that they have had. It's vital to really listen to your partner and not try to come up with a solution to their problems. They will let you know if they need your help. This doesn't mean that you shouldn't offer your help and support if you sense that they need it. You can go for a walk with your partner and enjoy time together, simply talking and listening to each other and enjoying each other's company. Why not surprise your partner with something nice that they would appreciate? You don't have to splash out – sometimes it's the simple gestures like making breakfast in bed for them that can make the difference.

Tell your partner that you love them on a regular basis, not just on their birthday, anniversaries or on Valentine's Day. Ensure that distractions like TV, laptops and phones don't interrupt deep meaningful conversations. It is also important to have good eye contact, to listen and be fully present, and not judge or interrupt the other person, allowing them to get things off their mind. This will help to avoid heated discussions or shouting matches.

Quality Time

Having little quality time can have a negative impact if not addressed (Bacon, 2021). It is understandable that you may be busy with your career, business, hobbies, or time taken up with raising children. You have heard the expression, 'Our relationship is like two ships passing at night.' Well, if this continues then you will be too tired to spend quality time together. Therefore, it's vital to plan and commit to spending more quality time together if you want to build a better and stronger relationship. Consider doing activities as a couple that make you smile and laugh, to enjoy doing the things that you enjoyed together when you first met. Plan for more intimacy and physical touch which will help with closeness. The more quality time you spend together, the clearer it will become if it is meant to be or not. If you genuinely love your partner, then give each other your undivided attention, and work as a team to ensure that your relationship grows stronger. Focus on what you can be doing in the present moment to create a more fulfilling future as a couple instead of dwelling on the past.

Offer More Praise and Encouragement

Another tip for dealing with stress in a relationship and to bring back the spark is to offer more praise and encouragement to one another. Let your partner know why you love them and find them attractive. You may be thinking of saying these words of appreciation, but if said with sincerity and from the heart it will take your relationship to a new and better level. Support the one you love, and reach out to let them know they're doing a great job and that you're there for them. Offer to help one another out at home or even surprise them by doing chores in the home before you see your partner struggling. Avoid undermining or belittling your partner, and also avoid trying to change them; you should appreciate them for who they are. If you do have any arguments, don't let them fester. Instead, put some time aside to talk the issue through so that you have don't both go to bed hurt and angry. Try to listen more, rather than just argue your point of view, and really seek to understand how your partner is feeling and what's on their mind.

Seek Professional Help

It's a good idea to seek professional help from a relationship counsellor, coach or therapist if you think you need it. It's an opportunity to have a better understanding of the relationship, be vulnerable and explore topics you may have been avoiding or find uncomfortable to face. Counselling can be effective, providing both partners commit both time and real focus, thus elevating your relationship so you can be together for the long-term.

Forgiveness and Second Chances

You must be willing to forgive each other for any transgressions or problems in the relationship. In life, we will be faced with the decision to forgive and start to slowly rebuild trust in order to save the relationship. For others, the betrayal and transgression will be too big to handle and forgive.

8.2: Divorce

"The only thing more unthinkable than leaving was staying; the only thing more impossible than staying was leaving. I didn't want to destroy anything or anybody. I just wanted to slip quietly out the back door, without causing any fuss or consequences, and then not stop running until I reached Greenland."

– Elizabeth Gilbert

Divorce and break-ups can be an incredibly stressful and traumatic experience in your life. There are many studies which show that stress can compromise the immune system (Morey et al., 2015). Divorce, being a major life stress, puts anyone dissolving a marriage at some risk of disease. The more stressful a divorce, the more likely it is that illness will follow. It is important to stay mentally and physically strong during these stressful life events. Marriage vows are based on several promises and commitments, both emotionally, sexually, and physically, to one another. For many, marriage is based on lifelong commitment and exclusivity. When one of more of these vows are broken, the trust and promises are also broken and shattered.

Evgenia Markova's Story – Transformational Teacher and Coach, London
(www.evgeniamarkova.com)

'Up until February 2020, I was in a toxic limbo with my ex-husband. Even though I had moved out in December 2018, I had not really moved on, and he had been persistent in trying to convince me to get back together with him. At the same time, he was also lying to me and cheating behind my back. I am a very compassionate, understanding and open-minded person, so I kept giving him the benefit of the doubt again and again. After all, I had married him!

I wasn't sure who I was. I was desperate to find out what was wrong with me. I could feel his poison running through my veins, and all the while he claimed that I was in fact poisoning him. Whatever I said was not only not heard, but also twisted and used against me. Panic attacks were my normal, and he would never support me through those episodes. I hated the complainer that I was. All the gaslighting, neglect, and mental and emotional manipulation had caused me to start losing my mind. I was feeling frustrated, embarrassed, guilty and disempowered due to being unable to handle my own emotions. The frustration of being unable to be perfect and please everyone day after day was exhausting, and I felt powerless like a trapped and wounded animal. All I got was blamed for it, just like on the night of my last panic attack. The night when, as I looked at the wound on my forehead, I swore to never ever hurt myself again. The night when I realised that if I don't put myself and my needs first, nobody else would, and that sacrificing myself never led to anything good anyway.

I have lived through so much abuse in my life, and was eventually diagnosed with Complex Post-Traumatic Stress Disorder (CPTSD). There I was in yet another toxic relationship; alone, unsupported, and sick of it all. So, I finally started to really focus on myself, putting myself and my needs first more and more, having neglected them for many years.

It became very obvious that my ex-husband had no place in my life, and I left for good just at the start of the pandemic. This was when people were terrified, the whole world was shut down, and I had nowhere to go. I was effectively homeless, jobless, with a big debt to pay off (a good chunk of which was my ex-husbands, which he refused to take responsibility for), and battling with a debilitating health condition. And still, I left. Because I was worth it.

I finally got serious with myself about who I want to be, how I want to live, what I was happy to tolerate, and what I would never again accept from both myself and others. I decided that one day I would be an epic example of self-love, confidence, peace and joy for my children, and nothing less than that. I was starting to realise my worth, and had full faith that I would get exactly what I deserve in one way or another, even if I could not see the way ahead.

I hadn't worked for the past 18 months as I couldn't handle it physically, mentally or emotionally. I managed to find a job working as a live-in carer for a couple in their nineties, both with dementia, while also looking for a place to live (which was mission impossible for a few months). With everything that was going on, I was proud to be a carer, and the clients and their family were happy with me.

That is when my life finally moved forwards and upwards. Recently, someone asked me how my PTSD was, and I realised that I cannot remember the last time I was anxious and stressed! Even after everything that I went through in the last 2 years; all the 'gifts' of 2020, my diagnosis, my financial difficulties, a brand new very demanding job, the lack of a home. I now have a home I love, and a job that I love and was born to do. I am feeling more than strong enough, and I now run a business which coaches people dealing with trauma to reconnect with themselves just as I did! And if I could do this, so can you, my friend!

You really have no idea just how powerful you are until you choose to accept this possibility and take the leap; the leap into really putting yourself first in every way, always, no matter what. No, this is not selfishness. It's taking responsibility for yourself, something that is only and entirely your obligation. Leap into recognising your own huge potential, no matter what may be going on in your life.

Please take this leap as I did, and feel free to reach out to me if you'd like my support and assistance.'

Gillian Friarsdale's Story – Air Hostess, Portugal

'It was a Friday night when I arrived back home from a training course and saw my husband sitting in the front room drinking whisky. He looked at me across the room and said, 'We need to talk.' I knew that something was up, and immediately wondered what I had done wrong. He said that we had been growing apart for some time, and that he was no longer in love with me. He then told me that he had found someone else, and that he was moving out. I was shocked: I wanted to scream and get angry at him, but I couldn't move. My body felt paralysed, and I just looked at him hopelessly. I asked him who she was, but he wouldn't tell me.

Even though I knew that our marriage wasn't going well, I didn't realise that it had gotten to this point. We had arguments like all couples do, but we had good times too. I met my husband 9 years ago whilst on holiday in Spain. We hit it off, and within 6 months we got engaged, and were married 6 months later. I question now whether this all happened too quickly. My friends told me at the time to slow down, but we were infatuated with each other.

It turned out that he was having an affair with a woman from work. Things started to add up now, and I realised that all the times he was working late or at conferences, he must have been with this other woman. I wanted to kick him out of the house right there and then, but he had already packed his bags. I was distraught, sad and stressed all at once, but I tried to keep myself together. I ran upstairs crying and punched the pillows of our bed. I later rang my best friend, and found out to my horror that she was the other woman. My husband had been having an affair with her for 6 months, after she had started working for the same company a year ago. I felt like I had been kicked in the stomach by a horse and stabbed in the back at the same time. The whole world had fallen apart around me as my husband and my best friend had both betrayed me. I was sick to my stomach and didn't know where to turn. I had seen this happening in movies, but never thought it would happen to me.

We had two young children and I was worried about how they would handle this news. I was also worried about what my family and other friends would think of me. Was I to blame? Did I push him away? How would I cope with looking after the children on my own? I wanted to make sure he wasn't taking them away from me, as they were the only good thing to come out of our marriage. Months of anguish, stress, anxiety and self-pity followed. I am so glad that I had my family there to support me through this difficult time in my life.

Dealing with separation, divorce and legal issues caused a huge knock on my mental health, as well as my confidence and self-esteem. I was at an all-time low. I wondered whether I could ever trust anyone again. Several years later, I did meet someone special, and maybe someday we may get married.

My advice to others is to keep believing in yourself and get the help you need from family and friends. Don't be afraid of counselling, and look after your body and mind.'

Patrick Waagner's Story – Software Engineer, Germany

'I met my future wife shortly after I turned 21. She was in the year above me studying a mathematics degree and I was a freshman. We were smitten with each other, and couldn't be apart from each other for more than a day. I proposed to her 5 years later: we had been living together for 2 years after graduating. We both had good jobs, salaries, and holidays, so everything was going well. She was an accountant, and I was a science teacher. We had a wonderful wedding on the beach in the Bahamas with close family and friends, were we vowed to be together forever.

Two years after the wedding, I thought our lives were going well. Then one day, a good friend of mine told me that he had seen my wife at a restaurant in the next city with another man, holding hands and kissing. I was furious at my friend, and was in total denial that she would never do something like this to me. I later confronted my wife with this information, sure that it was misunderstanding. She broke down in tears and confessed that she was seeing someone else, but it meant nothing and she loved me. As I heard the words come from her lips, I felt like I had been hit by a truck. All I could think was, 'How could you do this to me, to us?'

I was angry and disappointed (at her and myself), as we had only been married for 2 years and it was already falling apart. She said that she would end the affair, asked me for forgiveness and said that she was prepared to work things out. I blamed myself: was it my fault because I was so busy starting my teaching career that I had little time for anything else and I was always stressed? She was also busy as an accountant, but she seemed to find the time to socialise with friends. The problem was that we weren't spending quality time with each other. I felt like a failure, and my stress and anxiety levels were through the roof. I couldn't sleep, my mind raced all night, and it led me back to bad drinking habits and smoking. It was a really terrible time for me.

I wasn't good at sharing my feelings and talking to others about my problems. It was only when a friend of mine, who had already gone through a messy divorce, suggested counselling that I started to consider getting help. I felt guilty because I took my vows seriously; to me, forever meant forever, and she had broken that promise. Luckily, I had family who loved me and friends that helped me get back on my feet. Most of them had never been through a divorce and didn't really know how to help me, but they were there for me. We tried counselling for 6 months, which was difficult and stressful for both of us, but in the end, we decided to separate and file for divorce, because I felt that I could no longer trust her, nor could I forgive her. I also had therapy and took a divorce recovery class. As a result, I slowly found my way back to the land of the living.

The biggest fear I had was whether I could trust anyone again. It took time for me to start opening up to women again and dating, and I know that there is no guarantee that someone else will not break my heart again. My ex moved on - we haven't kept in touch, and I don't think about her as much as I used to.

I too have moved on. 3 years ago, I married a wonderful woman, the love of my life, and I am forever grateful for her. We also have a baby boy on the way, so life is great and back on track. My advice to you is to seek help from counselling, and to keep talking; don't hold all the hurt and anger in. Keep working on you and hang in there, as things do improve over time. The scars will heal, and your heart will mend. Most importantly of all, be kind to yourself.'

Main Causes of Divorce

"You never really know your partner until you have divorced them."

– Anonymous

There are a number of factors that can contribute to divorce, some of which include:

- Incompatibility
- Infidelity
- Emotional and physical abuse
- Unresponsive to needs
- Financial problems
- Immaturity

Incompatibility

Compatibility is the ability to live together and accept each other's similarities or differences without having to force the other to change. Once the romance and courting has taken place and the initial sexual attraction period has passed, then true characters can come out. This will test how compatible the two different individuals are; how they live and interact with each other on top of the daily stress of life. Individuals with different personalities can be very compatible, and the same is true for similar personalities. The ideal goal is a harmonious balance by both people in a relationship, which is quite rare as most relationships require work to rebalance and accept differences. When balance does not exist or dissolves over time, it fuels a reason for divorce.

Infidelity

Infidelity is the ultimate breach of the marriage or relationship promise, and it is therefore not surprising that it is one of the top reasons for getting a divorce. Infidelity can lead to feelings of mistrust, anger, and rejection by the party who was cheated on.

Emotional and Physical Abuse

Any form of emotional or physical abuse is not acceptable in society, yet it appears to be tolerated more in marriages and relationships than it should be. Emotional abuse will significantly affect the victim's self-esteem and confidence. Physical abuse and domestic violence will open the flood gates to stress, anxiety, depression, social isolation, disassociation and denial, and also affects the mental health of any children in a marriage (Hunjan, 2017).

It is important to seek help and advice if a relationship is leading to any form of mental, physical, or sexual abuse. Turn to a trusted friend and confidant. You can also talk to doctors, nurses and the police. In the UK, many pharmacies also have safe spaces where you can get information about support and make telephone calls. There are also organisations to turn to, such as domestic violence support helplines

Unresponsive to Needs

Each person enters a marriage or relationship with a certain number of preconceived ideas and expectations. The likelihood of divorce in a marriage is around 50%, and in non-married relationships the break-up rate is also remarkably similar. It would suggest that each spouse/partner has different expectations, or that those expectations have not been communicated. Expectations may include how their spouse or partner will satisfy several needs, including emotional, spiritual, physical, financial, and sexual needs. If these needs are not satisfied then feelings can be hurt, and the spouse/partner will start to think they have become less important, and that their spouse/partner is being unresponsive to their needs and denying them an important element of the relationship (Lagudu, 2021).

This can cause anger, conflict, resentment, sadness and anger, and may bring a relationship to the brink.

Financial Problems

Married couples especially are guilty of not talking much about financial expectations prior to or during a marriage, but instead argue about not having enough money or too much spending. Money problems, such as debt and borrowing money, can be a major point of conflict in relationships. Many couples will have two or more jobs just to pay the bills. If children come along in a marriage, it can add to the financial burdens, as well as meaning more responsibilities as parents. If one or more of the spouses is made redundant or furloughed, then this can be a tremendous pressure on the marriage. During lockdown, many marriages suffered due to the health and economic crisis. This stress and pressure may have exposed the cracks in an already struggling marriage and made it fall apart. For other couples, it has helped to make them stronger, having adapted and grown closer under the same set of circumstances. Financial conflicts can sometimes be remedied with conversation and counselling, but both parties must work at it.

Immaturity

One of the key ingredients for a good relationship is that both persons are on the same maturity level when they marry or start to date, and they grow together. This may change over time as individuals in a relationship may start from the same maturity level but, during their time together, one person advances in maturity. One partner may become frustrated with the other, and this frustration can lead to anger and discontentment. If not handled at the time, this can lead to another reason for getting a divorce.

Tips for Dealing with the Stress of Divorce

To deal with divorce anxiety, ask yourself what can give you back the sense of control and predictability? What makes you feel secure and supported?
Coping with divorce is a process, and the best way to handle a

divorce is to ask yourself simple questions to help you, such as, 'What am I ready to do? What do I feel I cannot do?'

Rather than overwhelming yourself, try operating at the edge of your comfort zone. As well as support from family and friends, you may need to seek counselling to support you through this difficult time. Divorce stress symptoms include:

- Crying
- Sadness
- Isolation
- Withdrawal
- Worrying
- Restless anxiety
- Irritability
- Mood swings
- Insomnia
- Decreased productivity

Find Time to Heal

Instead of focusing on whether you should feel a certain way or not, try focusing on when and how you express it. Unfortunately, divorce can lead to depression, and symptoms can include numbness, anger, disappointment, sadness, anxiety and other emotions. If you do feel like falling apart, then that's OK, just allow time to put yourself back together again. Look for healthy ways to express your feelings, such as those shown below:

1. When dealing with sadness, consider trying a new activity like painting, dancing, or playing an instrument
2. If you are dealing with disappointment, write down positive things that are going well for you and reduce negative self-talk
3. If you are dealing with anger, try doing regular cardio exercises to get your heart rate up, mindful breathing exercises, meditation, take long walks and journal your experience
4. If you are experiencing anxiety, plan relaxing activities such as listening to calming music, taking fragrance baths and booking a

massage
5. Sharing your feelings is one of the best ways of coping with divorce stress. Confide in trusted friends and family members
6. Be kind to yourself by looking after your physical and mental well-being

Practical Support

Whilst emotional support is important, it is also often necessary to seek practical support. Think about who can be there for you when you need some extra help. For example, with work commitments you can ask for help from colleagues. Ask friends for their help and support to fill out paperwork, go shopping and take care of the children as required. Coping with divorce stress means you will have less time to yourself, as you are doing everything previously done by two people. Remember that you don't have to go through this alone; there will be trustworthy people who are willing to listen to you, so don't push these important people away.

Be Aware of Children's Experiences

As a parent, it is natural to worry about your children being caught in the crossfire of divorce. It can be heart breaking to see them have to adapt, and it's understandable that they may get hurt in the process. Keep arguments private and avoid heated discussions or talking negatively about the other parent in front of your child. Do not ask your child to spy on the other parent, and keep encouraging them to talk about their feelings. Spend some quality time with your children, and be honest and open with them about what is happening. They are likely to become more upset if you don't keep them informed. Tailor your conversation to suit the age and maturity of your children. Children are quite resilient and can bounce back from these difficult times. They need to know that they are loved and cared for, and that you are there for them.

Legal Matters

Having to deal with custody, liabilities, and assets is not easy, so take your time and seek help and advice from a trusted source. These parts of the divorce process may be some of the most stressful. Try to keep calm and keep all the legal documents somewhere safe and easily accessible. There are organisations that can offer you help and support in legal matters, such as Divorce Aid. Since 1999, this organisation has been an independent group of professionals giving divorce information and advice to people based in the UK (and internationally with a UK connection).

Finances

A divorce can be quite expensive and may be a heavy drain on your finances. Even after a divorce, it can be a financial struggle to get back on your feet again. Seek finance advice from close family and friends who have gone through a similar experience, or meet with a third-party independent advisor. If your spouse is using money to start power struggles and arguments, try and keep calm - don't allow them to get to you, and focus on being positive.

Life After Divorce

"I read and walked for miles at night along the beach, writing bad blank verse and searching endlessly for someone wonderful who would step out of the darkness and change my life. It never crossed my mind that that person could be me."

- A. Quindlen

Divorce can be a very traumatic experience, and most people are likely to experience a rollercoaster of emotions. You may have days when your mood is low and you feel hopeless, sad, confused, angry or anxious. Don't despair - there is life after divorce, and millions of couples all around the world go on to lead happy and fulfilling lives. The first few weeks and months it may seem extremely frightening, and you may suffer from low self-esteem and doubt. You may never want to be married or involved in any relationship again. You may even feel that no-one else will want to marry or date a divorcee. Give yourself time to recover and take things one day at a time. Focus on yourself as an individual, deciding what you need to do to help let go of the past and look forward to the future.

Overcoming Blame and Understanding

Many couples can get involved with the blame game, and get locked into asking questions such as: 'Whose fault it is? What did I do wrong? How could they do that to me?'

Asking questions is an important step towards recovery: what you need to watch out for is becoming more angry and bitter, thus leading to more heartache.

Rather than blame yourself, focus on what the relationship was lacking and how the relationship failed to meet your or your partner's needs. The answers may be upsetting, but having a greater understanding will make it easier to let go of the past and move forward.

Self-Care

Your well-being is vital, and even more important if you have children relying on you being there for them. Really focus on looking after yourself over the coming weeks and months.

The end of a relationship can erode your confidence and self-esteem. The following tips will help you to get through this difficult time and face the future with hope:

Allow yourself time to grieve - It's perfectly normal to feel sadness and shock when a relationship finally comes to an end. Take the time for this reality to sink in, as your days will feel like a rollercoaster ride of emotions.

Keep talking - You are not alone: there are people around to help you, so stay connected to people you trust and who love you. Avoid isolating yourself. There will be victories as well as heartaches. You may want to start socialising again by going to meet friends for coffee or walks.

Plan small steps - Set small achievable goals, as this will help grow your confidence, give you a sense of control, and boost your energy. A goal may be as simple as doing basic chores, starting a new work project, helping your children, or even booking a weekend away.

Anger management - You may have pent-up anger towards your ex-partner, or you may even be angry with yourself. Holding on to this anger it is like dragging around an anchor or burden that you no longer need to carry. By still being angry, your thoughts and emotions are constantly directed towards your ex. This will slow your ability to move on with life. Find ways to reduce your anger and stress by going for a walk, having a long bath, reading, laughing with friends, gardening or going for a run. Decide what the best way to relax is as you give your body time to de-stress.

Well-being - Look after your mental and physical health by doing regular exercise and maintaining a healthy diet. It is easy to fall into comfort eating and binge drinking, which may lead to depression. Be kind to yourself and remind yourself of all the good things in your life by writing a diary or thinking back on some of the great things you have achieved. Treat yourself to things you like. Try doing yoga, mindfulness and meditation. You could even start a new hobby like painting or taking dance classes. There will be plenty of time to meet new people in your life, so don't rush – take your time to heal.

Seek help - Don't be afraid to ask for help, especially when you feel like you are struggling. It may be helpful to make an appointment to see a relationship or divorce counsellor. There will be several organisations that you can turn to for emotional support, such as Relate, who run one-day workshops for people coming out of long-term relationships.

"When two people decide to get a divorce, it isn't a sign that they 'don't understand' one other, but a sign that they have, at least, begun to."

– Helen Rowland

CHAPTER 9: Unexpected Life Changes

"Life is a series of natural and spontaneous changes. Don't resist them; that only creates sorrow. Let reality be reality. Let things flow naturally forward in whatever way they like."

- Lao Tzu

One of key facts in life is that nearly everything changes and doesn't stay the same. Life is ever-evolving - people, circumstances, environments, opportunities, problems and challenges change. The quicker we realise this then the quicker we can adapt. The challenge we have is that we are creatures of habit, and any small or major changes can be a catalyst for stress. If not well-managed, they can manifest as anxiety and impact on your health and well-being.

This chapter is about some of those life changes and how individuals have coped with them in their own unique way.

9.1: Moving Home

"I believe that one can never truly leave home. I believe that one carries the shadows, the dreams, the fears, and the dragons of home under one's skin, at the extreme corners of one's eyes, and possibly in the gristle of the earlobe."

- Maya Angelou

Amanda Plumb's Story - Holiday Cottage and Hotel Business Owner, France
(www.combrailleurs.com)

'When I was asked to write about stress and how I deal with it, I thought it was going to be difficult. On reflection, the answers came easily. I am lucky enough to have not had to deal with the impact of massive loss, trauma or tragedy in my life so far, but I have had a number of relatively small stressful events which have given me practice for the big ones, like when I recently gave up my stable job, sold my home and left my birth country in England to start a new life and business in France with my husband.

We were turning our lives upside down, and all the time wondering if we were really doing the right thing. When the house purchase in France looked like it was about to fall through after we'd already sold our UK home, we were suddenly faced with the prospect of being homeless with no income. The brave face never slipped, but underneath it all we were not sleeping, constantly bickering, my husband's eczema and asthma got worse, I was getting headaches and we were both feeling more fearful than excited about our plans. The first step in dealing with stress is recognising it, and there came a moment of realisation around the time we were heading over to France to sign the contracts. We had a £25,000 bridging loan hanging in the balance and so much at risk; we could have lost everything.

As we drove through France, we did not speak, both locked in our own little worlds. This wasn't like us. We decided we needed a night off to re-group. We booked into a hotel and made a plan. The first thing we had to get back on track with was our health, which was mainly deteriorating due to lack of sleep. Our brains were too busy to shut off, so I brought into play a tool I had used many a time on my numerous trips away with work – write a list of the things you are thinking about or need to do before you go to bed. This offloads the burden, and you know you can pick it up again in the morning. Then I made sure, and still do, that I went to sleep using meditation and breathing exercises. My husband taught me this, as it was how he overcame his eczema itching to get to sleep as a kid.

Work life has also taught me that preparation and organisation are important in order to feel in control. I hated standing up in front of my colleagues to speak at work, but being always ahead of myself and preparing in case I hit an unexpected obstacle took away a lot of the anxiety. So, writing a list and keeping on top of the tasks we needed to do each day helped with the preparation and organisation. We also made a commitment to communicate, and not just by bickering; if one of us had a worry or an issue we would settle down and talk it out, no matter how trivial it may seem.

My husband and I talked our way through the move, and from then on, we became a team. I have always been a very open person, and during my divorce and the death of my grandmother, I learned to be upfront and speak to people about what I was dealing with. This is a very cathartic process, and the value of talking things through or writing them down should never be overlooked. We also set out a mission statement, so that we could stay focused on our long-term goal. This reassured us about our plans and the steps we were taking. Keeping this in mind convinced us that we were going to be OK. We eventually made it to France and have faced many challenges in the two and a half years since, but looking after our mental health with sleep, organisation, meditation, and communication have continued to be paramount.

Lastly, an extra tool that we have learned along the way is space. We make sure we both have time to ourselves, whether that is walking, gardening, exercise, or hobbies in which we can lose ourselves from time to time, to be reminded of the success we have had. It has been an intense time, but ultimately, we made it and now happily run a thriving business in the heart of the French countryside.'

Moving Home Advice

Moving home or emigrating is one of the top 10 stresses for an individual and family to experience because it involves having to cope with immense change. Most of us do not like change as we are creatures of habit, familiarity, routine and order. When you move homes, there are many knock-on effects which send out ripples throughout your life. This is because your whole surroundings are changing, as well as the interactions and touch points in your community and work. You are familiarising yourself with your new home and possibly a new area, city, or country. You may have to find new schools for your children, plan a new commute to work, find a new doctor, dentist, hairdresser. In your previous home, you would have built up rapport and trust with local shops and medical service providers in and around your old home. Now in your new location and home, there is no set order or routine in place. This lack of routine and order as well as uncertainty and upheaval can trigger underlying mental health conditions such as anxiety, obsessive compulsive disorder (OCD) and even depression.

Be Organised

Forward planning is your key to moving, and you should ideally start the process as early as you can. You will need to invest a good amount of time to declutter your existing home. You can donate to charity, give way, or sell things that you have stopped using, otherwise this same clutter will follow you to your new home. This may mean a delay in moving, but it will help to reduce your stress. Once decluttered, you can start to sort out your possessions into categories, such as items for each room in the new home, food stuffs, electrical items, furniture, clothes, office contents, personal items, garden, and garage stuff etc. If you can use a removal company, then they can provide you with boxes, however you may need to buy additional boxes and wrapping, foam, or bubble wrap for delicate possessions. Buy sticky labels or use a marker pen to write on your boxes so you know what is in them. You may also like to number the boxes so you know how many you brought.

Store important documents, jewellery, computers, and cameras in a lockable box and take them with you in your own vehicle for safe keeping in case you need easy access to them. You will need a bag for any medications and a change of clothes so that you can have easy access to them if you need them. You may need to organise a disposal skip or van to get rid of items that cannot be sold or given away.

Allow a good chunk of time every day for planning and preparing, as well as resting in between. Also ensure that you book time off work after your move to unpack, organise and settle into your new home and

226

surroundings. This extra time also helps with recovering from exhaustion.

Register with Local Doctors and Schools

You should register with your new doctor, dentist and local schools if you have children. Find out about local restaurants and bars for socialising and enjoying evenings and weekends. You could even organise a local online delivery of food to cover you for your first few days in a new home. Find out about shopping, banking, and local conveniences. Also consider where your local fuel station and 24-hour chemists is located. You may like to find out about sports facilities, swimming pool, local clubs and associations, such as martial arts, football, hockey, athletics, ballet, and yoga classes. If you are religious, consider finding out about your local church, mosque, synagogue, and other spiritual places for non-religious individuals.

Be Kind to Yourself

Moving homes is very tiring and can cause anxiety and stress, so it is important to look after your health and well-being by eating and getting a good night's sleep. You could even consider going to a sauna, booking a massage, having your nails manicured or whatever makes you feel good after you have moved home. Book a table at a local restaurant, go to the cinema, go bowling or treat everyone that helped you to a take-away or whatever is in your budget. If it helps, try going for a walk, meditating or spend time with friends. These things can help to reduce stress and anxiety.

Ask for Help

Ask family and friends for help and do not try and do everything by yourself. Do accept offers of help to clean, cook, pack, unpack and carry boxes. If you do have the money its worthwhile considering getting professionals to do the packing for you.

Comfort Box

Prepare a box of items for the whole family that will help them to feel better. This could include, favourite blankets, toys for small children, favourite jumper, slippers, scented candle, a special mug or chocolates. Whatever will help you settle and relax in your new home will be comforting.

Prepare a Checklist

The following checklists have been adapted from BBC advice on moving home (2014).

Six to eight weeks before the move:
- Get quotes from removal firms
- Confirm moving date
- Book pets into kennels
- Notify your landlord if you are renting
- Check home insurance
- Order boxes and packing cases
- Start to declutter
- Organise phone redirection
- Order new furniture or carpets for new house
- Check flights and visas are all confirmed if going abroad

Two weeks before the move:
- Start packing
- Notify utility firms
- Arrange for post to be redirected
- Cancel milk/newspapers
- Tell the council
- Tell your insurance company
- Run down the freezer
- Arrange to collect keys
- Inform your bank
- Tell your GP and dentist you are going

- Make a list of people to be told
- Finalise removal plans

All these useful tips should help you ease the burden and stress of the move or emigration.

9.2: Redundancy and Furlough

"Everyone has the right to work, to free choice of employment, to just and favourable conditions of work and to protection against unemployment."

- Eleanor Roosevelt

Joe Pritchard's Story - Unemployed, Ireland

'I had lost my job through redundancy and company downsizing. I had extraordinarily little savings across my bank accounts, as was the case for my wife. I am a father to two young children, and my wife was fortunately still in employment as a nurse. I was on a reasonable salary of £50,000 plus annual bonuses and my wife was on £25,000, so together we seemed to be earning a good salary. Sadly, the bonuses started to become less frequent and smaller. Unfortunately, I was only robbing one bank account to pay another, and only paying off the minimum monthly payment at a time. I had no choice but to re-mortgage our property and borrow more money to buy a car and pay off mounting bills. This was short lived as we had already re-mortgaged 5 years earlier and we were back to square one.

We were addicted to spending more money than we earned and didn't know where to turn for help. My wife was not much better than me at saving money. We liked spending money on holidays in the sun, buying nice Christmas presents, quality cars, clothes, and throwing big lavish parties, but we were out of control. I would get up in the middle of the night stressed and anxious. How had I let my credit card bills mount up over the years so much that I owed nearly £25,000? This was an extremely worrying time for us. Once one credit card reached its credit limit, I would get another one and another one. The final straw was when we found out that there was another baby on the way, and we wanted to make sure we could provide for the new arrival. We were both excited about the news that my wife was pregnant, but at the same time we knew that having a new baby would be an additional cost. I had to borrow money from family and friends which was embarrassing, but we appreciated the help.

I told my sister who advised I speak to the citizens advice bureau. I am so glad for the advice as I finally got a chance to jump off the treadmill of debt. I was advised to write down all my spending and outgoings as well as income coming into the home. I moved my credit cards from high interest to zero interest rate, which helped me save hundreds of pounds each month. I was able to negotiate with my bank to allow me a 3 months payment holiday on my mortgage. I rang all the companies such as car insurance, broadband and telephone providers to explain my situation or threatened to leave them. They all gave a reduced rate, plus I stopped paying for movies and sports which saved a lot of money. I changed my gas and electric providers which saved £100 month, so my bills were further reduced.

We agreed to live within our means, which may seem obvious to others, but we had gotten into bad habits over the years and had to create new ones. We started budgeting for the first time in our lives and started to buy non-branded products from supermarkets. I was fortunate to receive 3 months salary as part of my redundancy which was blessing, and I managed to find another job within 6 weeks paying a similar salary, which meant that I still had some money left from my redundancy pay out. This time I didn't take a company car, and instead took the car allowance and downsized my car. I started to sell my expensive shoes, clothes and jewellery online, most of which we didn't wear, and we raised £1500 by doing this. Holidays were put on hold, as was my big 40th birthday party, for which we would normally spend a lot of money on alcohol and going to an expensive restaurant. We stopped having takeaway food each week and cut down to once a month. Once we applied these cost-saving measures, our outgoings went down by 30% within 3 months. My wife and I asked for overtime at work, which boosted our salary by 25%. This money we saved in a high interest savings account, which we didn't touch for 5 years. We used the money we saved by reducing our outgoings to clear our debts and pay our family back. We now only have one credit card for emergencies.

I can now sleep easier and have less stress due to having regular savings. We don't spend money on fancy holidays, clothes or jewellery anymore, but we are a lot happier and we don't have heated arguments about money anymore either. We had healthy baby boy who is now 4 years old. My advice to you is to really think if you need to buy that expensive holiday, car, or item of clothing. Only spend what you can afford to pay without a credit card, seek help with your debt early on and if you must, consolidate debts so you are only paying off one payment per month. Talk to your creditors and explain how you will pay off the loans and debt, as most are very reasonable. Avoid loan sharks and high interest pay day loans. Don't let money and possessions be your master; be in charge by budgeting properly. I had to change my relationship with and perspective on money.'

Dave Gardner's Story - IT Manager, England

'When we were first told about the likelihood of redundancy, there was resentment from some. However, given the economic climate, if we were totally honest with ourselves, it was not a total surprise. The worst part for most of us was not knowing the scale of it and what opportunities might be left, and it was not until over a year that a more detailed picture was given.

The employees with young families and mortgages had different worries to the older ones like me, but we had worries too, especially as the thought of looking for a new job was a gaze into the relative unknown. During this period, talking to each other and being open and honest with the facts was the best way to get everyone through it. Some colleagues seemed in denial of the situation, but time ticked on regardless.

At the end of October 2020, I left the company that had been my employer for 33 years, 20 of which were spent as a manager in the IT Department. I had never been unemployed before, and while some of my colleagues saw it as an opportunity for some time off, I wanted to find a new job as soon as I could. Financially, we were probably OK, but I was not yet ready to retire, as my wife still worked and all our friends were working too.

Of course, with COVID-19 and Brexit around, I realised that the job market was difficult, but told myself to just do my best, and if that fits well with a company, great. I felt I had good experience and, despite my age, I had more left in the tank. This was an opportunity for me, and I had a mix of feelings, as with any unknown situation.

I wasn't exactly sure what I wanted to do; I was experienced in several areas, had broad management skills and was happy to turn my hand to most things. Financially, I was not under pressure to get a package that was like my last role, so I was in a good position and was confident I would get some interviews soon.

I started applying, often for jobs I knew I was more than qualified to do, and either heard nothing back or received an, "I'm sorry but on this occasion..." email. Each time I got one of these, it chipped away at my confidence, no matter how much I told myself not to let it.

Now, I am lucky - I wake up and for me it's a new day, and I have a positive outlook, but I can understand how people can get very down during this process. I had seen the impact on the mental health of colleagues over the years, and knew it could creep up on you without you or anyone else realising, so I kept this in my head. I think exercising and getting outside really helped to relieve the situation and keep any potential stress at bay. I started going on walks and found footpaths locally that I never knew even existed.

I am a social person who enjoys interaction with others, and I would recommend keeping in touch with people, either virtually or face-to-face if you can. If you have someone you can confide in then do so, as that really helps too.

Limit your time searching for jobs, too - do it every day, but not all day! I found a couple of hours in the morning and an hour or so in the afternoon or evening worked best for me.

If things don't work out, you must not take it personally. Brush yourself off and keep going. Don't put pressure on yourself to get a job within a certain time, or else you will set yourself up for failure. Just believe the right job and the right company will come along if you keep going and applying. My future was uncertain, but I kept thinking that others were in a far worse position than me, so kept I busy and kept applying.

As time moved on, I learned to modify my CV for each application, sometimes even dumbing it down to prevent the comment that you are 'overqualified' for the role. I also brushed up on some skills and did training, either with an outplacement company or via YouTube. I felt this reminded me how much I knew, and it made me feel more confident in my abilities and therefore more marketable.

After 4 months of trying and 2 months out of work, I had completed over 100 applications and began to wonder if life was trying to tell this 56-year-old he was not wanted any more.

Then, I suddenly got some interest from a company which caught my eye. They saw my experience as a real asset and not a hindrance. To cut a long story short, I was offered a role and accepted; my rollercoaster ride was complete!

Now, I know others have had to try for a lot longer than I did, but whatever time it takes, there will be a company out there that value what you can bring to them, so stick with it and you will find each other if you haven't done so yet.

Try to keep positive. Perhaps use the time to train up and learn new skills as well as building up your network of connections on LinkedIn. Finally, keep talking to people and don't let your uncertainty build into something that could impact your health. Good luck, believe in yourself and stick with it.'

Kent Splawn's Story – Temporarily Retired, USA

'A few years ago, I was offered a new job which required a move from Germany to Israel. We were excited about the prospects of a new position. Another cross-cultural adventure, another new language (never easy for me) and a new baby - what's not to like? It started well, but unfortunately, just a year into the job, a restructuring took place, and I was made unemployed, with no prospects and 4,000 miles from home in the USA. My wife and I were shocked and wondered what was next. Do we return to the States, with no work? Stay, and look for work locally? We had envisioned working in this country for years and didn't think our time in Israel had ended. We had to decide quickly as we needed income, plus we had to find a new place to stay, as our apartment was part of the job package. No job, no home, no pressure. Right. Stress? Absolutely.

At this point, let me say that we are committed followers of Jesus Christ. In fact, he was the reason we were in this country in the first place. The job had come to us. We had not applied for it. That offer came through God, and it closed the same way. Yes, there was still stress, but in dealing with it, we had help. Two verses from the Bible gave us a lot of peace.

Proverbs 3:5, 6 says: *'Trust in the Lord with all your heart, and don't rely on your own opinions. With all your heart, trust Him to guide you, and he will lead you in every decision you make.'* Another promise comes directly from Jesus in John 14:27: *'I leave you the gift of peace - my peace. Not the kind of fragile peace the world gives, but my perfect peace. Do not give in to fear or be troubled in your hearts. Instead, be courageous!'*

Trust in Jesus is a characteristic which defines the life of a serious Christian, but that kind of trust does not come without challenges, and we were about to run into a string of tests.

I found some freelance work, but it was inconsistent. We stayed at a friend's place for a few weeks, then camped out with a young couple for a while with our toddler in tow (whose personal needs pay no attention to the clock). This stressful, uncertain life went on for several months. You can imagine the tension around the house. We were praying and trying to trust the Lord, sometimes not so successfully!

Finally, I was offered a job. The company was a couple of hours north, meaning another move, but there was one slight hitch. The job would represent only 65% of my previous position which meant a major cut in pay. This took me by surprise. Usually, this offer would have been rejected immediately, but after briefly shouting 'No way!' at each other, my wife and I stopped. Did God open this door too? If so, he knew how much the position paid. We did the maths anyway, and calculated that the paycheck would be gone by the 21st of every month. Three weeks of pay for four weeks of living. God did know about this, right?

We kept praying. Jesus reminded us of his promises. Would we trust him completely? Could we let his peace become our peace? Continuing in prayer, we accepted the job with a small knot in our stomachs. Sure enough, three weeks into the job, we had no money, and truly little food. The next day, as I opened the door to go to work, there was a big bag of food on the step. No note. Just food. Jesus was backing up his promise. The next month however, on the 21st day we were back in the same situation. With faith though, I headed out the next morning, expecting more groceries. Nothing! A bit discouraged, I finished work, walked to the car, and found an envelope inside with enough money to carry us through to the end of the month.

This went on for 11 months. Sometimes we knew who gifted us, more often it was anonymous. In my 12th month, I received a raise, which meant I was finally earning enough to cover a full month of expenses. Never again did we receive any 'surprise' gifts. Jesus asked that if we would trust him, he would take care of us. And he has fulfilled that promise (and controlled our stress levels!) for more than 33 years.'

This Christian story is heart-warming. I know this wonderful couple well as they are long-term family friends who live a deeply religious life and have faith in God and Jesus Christ to carry them through life's stresses. Many will relate to this story, while others may not as you may not be a religious person. It takes all sorts of people to keep this world going. Kent's message is to keep the faith and believe that things will get better, and not to take on all of the burden yourself. They sent a message out to the world by regular steadfast prayer, and their prayers were indeed answered.

Advice for Redundancy and Furlough

The coronavirus pandemic has created huge financial pressures on our workforce across many industries and organisations. This has led to staff being furloughed or made redundant, despite support from the Government, such as the Job Retention Scheme. Very sadly, some industries have ceased operations entirely. All this financial pressure leads to a heavy stress load for individuals who no longer know if there is enough money coming into the household to pay for bills, mortgage, rent, gas, electricity, new clothes or even food. We may have strong feelings such as shock, anger, resentment, relief and much more all in a short period of time if we lose our jobs. Some companies and organisations may offer support and counselling after redundancies or furloughing. Give yourself a period of time to adjust and adapt. Make sure you give yourself space and time to express your feelings as you process them. Keep talking to other people about what you are experiencing, and also to others experiencing the same feelings and emotions. Being made redundant is nothing to be ashamed of, so do not blame yourself.

Being out of work can have a dramatic effect on your self-esteem, self-worth and sense of identity. It's important to be kind to yourself during this change. You will be used to your routine revolving around your job, and its loss will have a big impact on your day-to-day life. Use this opportunity to reflect on what types of activities make you feel happy and fulfilled. Start collating a list of all the skills and qualities you have that could help you in your next role. You may be struggling with feelings of uncertainty, so try to focus on the things you can control. You may not be able to get your old job back, but you can spend some time polishing your CV and reaching out to your old contacts. By accepting the things we can't control, we can start to focus our energy on the things we can.

Update Your Resume

This is a good opportunity to update your CV and adapt it to suit the needs of the company or job that you are looking for. The jobs and industries that you have previously worked in will determine your search parameters. You may need to widen your net and look for jobs where you can transfer your range of skills, and demonstrate your adaptability and flexibility. You may be able to attend training courses to learn a new skill, or even go to college or university. Some companies and organisations may offer counselling, advice or courses on finding jobs and updating your CV, so take the opportunities available to you and accept help where offered. If you had a large redundancy pay-out or if you are due a good pension, then you may like to consider following your dreams and venture into starting a business - just make sure you do your research and due diligence. You may even want to retire early, play golf, go on holiday, start a new hobby or do charity work.

Money Management

Your financial state after being made redundant can be a big cause of stress, and can affect your physical and mental health. Money worries will also impact your sleep and you may become extremely restless. Unless you have managed to save a good sum of money, it's important to review your spending on a regular basis and put together a budget, only withdrawing the cash amount that you have planned to spend. If you have a partner, then find time to plan together, and if you have children, be honest with them and explain that things may get tight on spending until you find another job. Work out how much you are spending on areas such as:

- Mortgage or rent
- Household bills
- Living costs
- Finances and insurance (e.g. credit cards)
- Travel
- Leisure
- Shopping
- Meals out
- Mobile and internet
- Other

Once you work out your outgoings, you can start to plan and organise your spending. If you are struggling with debt, then seek advice from family and friends, local debt charities or speak to a friendly bank manager and credit card companies who may be willing to give you payment breaks.

Keep Busy

It's likely you'll be spending a lot more time at home, so consider stimulating your brain by reading personal development books, listening to podcasts or watching TED talks. Relax and enjoy watching films or doing puzzles and quizzes. You could also consider volunteering or learning a new skill.

Take a Break

Take time off to rest and relax if you know that you have enough money in the bank. You may need time to think about planning your future and your next steps. Use this time period as an opportunity to prioritise self-care. Things like going for park or county walks, doing yoga, painting, gardening or even starting DIY projects could be beneficial for your mental health during this period. Consider doing jobs that you have put off, such as tidying the garden, car, or garage. Remember to take it easy, and don't make yourself so busy that you are too tired and stressed.

CHAPTER 10: Illness

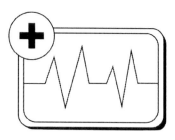

"If I feel depressed, I will sing. If I feel sad, I will laugh. If I feel ill, I will double my labour. If I feel fear, I will plunge ahead. If I feel inferior, I will wear new garments. If I feel uncertain, I will raise my voice. If I feel poverty, I will think of wealth to come. If I feel incompetent, I will think of past success. If I feel insignificant, I will remember my goals. Today I will be the master of my emotions."

- Og Mandino

Christy Bischoff's Story – Community Development Worker, England

'The diagnosis hit me hard. In the midst of the pandemic and the grief of losing my brother, to find out I had breast cancer felt like too much for me to hold. I could feel the stress weighing on my body and mind.

On the morning the Doctor was to call me with the results of my biopsy, I took my daughter to school and walked back through the woods. I came to a place on the path where there is a steep drop off. When the kids were little and they would run past this place, my stomach would drop with fear that they might tumble over. Today, I stood looking over the steep edge. If I fell, I would be really hurt. I could feel the pull, and felt like I already was falling down this edge. I looked back towards the path, so flat and wide. I made a conscious choice to look away from the edge and keep walking on the wide path.

As I walked, I breathed in the trees and I tried talking to my brother. He died only 5 months previous of brain cancer. Since then, I had spent a lot of time coming to the woods and talking to him. He was the one person in my life who seemed to really understand me, and I missed him a lot. The woods provided the stillness my soul needed.

As I walked, I felt my brother's presence, as if he were walking behind me on this path, and then my phone rang. It was the Doctor's office; they wanted me to come in and meet the consultant. I felt my world shift. I knew something big was happening, and I also knew that I was not alone.

The Doctor said that I was lucky, that they had found the cancer early. They recommended a mastectomy. If, after the surgery, it looked like it had not spread, then I would need no further treatment. However, it was possible the surgery could show something else.

The next weeks were a mix of fear, love, and anxiety. When my brother was diagnosed with brain cancer, he immediately started a blog about his 'health adventures.' At the time I thought he was crazy, and yet I saw how he reached out in his vulnerability and found so much love, connection, and healing. My brother is 6 years older than me, and I have spent much of my life learning from him and copying aspects of his life. Cancer was not one area that I was hoping to copy, however I did want to learn from his approach to healing. I went to the same blog site he used and wrote my own entry, asking for support. I felt nervous to share and ask so directly, yet I so desperately needed to not be alone in this. As I pressed send, I felt sick. I had what I have heard called a 'vulnerability hangover.' I did not look at my phone after that for fear that I may be rejected, that I did not deserve love. When I finally found the courage to check my messages, I was overwhelmed with the love that we were receiving through prayers, words of encouragement, and offers of practical help. I was not alone.

Over the next few weeks, I went to the woods every day, knowing that the exercise, fresh air and wisdom of the woods was what I needed. Every afternoon, my husband helped me with a guided meditation to prepare for surgery, and I soaked in the love from friends near and far.

Two weeks after my surgery, I went back for the results. I was terrified. I felt like I had managed the surgery, but the idea of chemotherapy and radiation scared me. The Doctor told us that although the tumour was 7.7 cm long, the cancer had not spread, and I needed no further treatment. I did not get the instant rush of relief that I was hoping for because the last year had left my body and mind so full of stress, but I could start to feel a glimmer of easing in my body.

There is still much more healing I must do, but I have made it through this part. I know that reaching out to connect with my brother, my faith, my family and friends are what got me through. We are not alone.'

Terry Chittock's Story - Business Owner, England (www.thorsonnsworkshop.co.uk)

'When I was 14 years old, I was diagnosed with kidney disease. It was out of the blue and a complete shock, but at that young age I never really understood the situation. For me it meant a slightly different childhood, one with medication and regular hospital visits.

As I grew older, I began to comprehend the severity of my illness - the possibility of having dialysis treatment, the inevitable need for a transplant at some far-off point in my future.

At 26 I was really struggling to work, being physically ill on a daily basis and battling just to get dressed in the morning. One day I was violently ill to the point I couldn't even hold down water. I called my medical team, and they explained that my kidneys were almost completely shut down and it was time to begin dialysis treatment. My body could no longer function on its own. Four days later I went to hospital for my first treatment session. It was a heart-breaking time to realise that my body had finally failed me, a matter of weeks before my wedding.

In the years since then I have experienced a multitude of traumas. I have been critically ill, teetering on the edge of life several times. I experienced the total joy of receiving a transplant, and then the gut-wrenching pain of my body rejecting it to the point of losing the organ and having to go back onto dialysis treatment once more, only 18 months after my transplant surgery. I have dealt with anxiety, depression and stress, and

I have come out the other side.

One thing I have to be grateful for is the perspective that these tests have given me. I have learned how to deal with stress and anxiety, and with this new perspective I have become more focused on the positives in life. Although I am back on dialysis and awaiting a second transplant, I am fortunate. I am happily married, and I run a successful business, which I have used as a platform to spread awareness and offer support for others who may be going through what I have experienced. I have held charity fundraisers and campaigns through my work to help those that have helped me.

I have dealt with a huge amount of stress in my life due to my ongoing illness and the challenges it brings, but I am proud to say I can now use those experiences, having come out the other side stronger, to help make a positive change. I also hold talks on Facebook to help others struggling to deal with stress and anxiety.'

Sue Duncombe's Story - Cancer Campaign Ambassador, England

'At age 52, my husband Philip, who appeared extremely fit and healthy, was diagnosed with prostate cancer. He had surgery, which was initially successful, but after a year, routine tests showed that the aggressive cancer had spread. For a couple of years, he had various treatments, his quality of life was generally good, and he remained active. 3 years later, Philip became really unwell, and the dreaded day came when he was told that the chemo was being stopped and there was no other licensed drug available. However, he was lucky to participate in a clinical trial of a new drug which extended his life by about a year. This drug also had a huge impact on Philip's quality of life, and so my life improved too. Unfortunately, eventually the drug stopped working, and Philip died on Christmas Day that year.

Before Philip's diagnosis, we had no significant stress in our lives. We were both employed in jobs we enjoyed - jobs which created pressure but not stress - we were reasonably financially secure, we were fit and healthy (or so we thought) and had a circle of loving friends and family.

Following Philip's diagnosis, we endured the rollercoaster journey

242

that many families of cancer patients undergo. The highs, like when tests show that a drug is working; you feel physically better and psychologically it has a really positive impact. The lows, like when a drug stops working and you worry about how much time you have left.

So, how did we deal with the emotional rollercoaster journey for those 5 years?

It sounds clichéd, but we tried to take control of things we did have control over. One example is that, before clinic visits, we'd agree what our objectives were; what information we wanted, what scenarios were possible, what the next steps could be. This made us feel prepared, and also that we were facing up to the situation.

In the latter stages of Philip's life, I was his carer, and knew that I had to stay healthy as he was dependent on me. I hated running, but forced myself out on a 2-mile circuit early in the morning each day to keep fit. As well as staying physically strong, this also allowed me to deal with the mental stresses and strains of the day. I never did get to enjoy running – the best bit of it was getting in the shower at the end!

Our friends were keen to provide support, so we accepted offers of help. This included chats over a cup of tea, but also practical support. Our GP was surprised when he came to visit us a week before Philip died that one friend was in the bathroom doing some plumbing work, another in the garden getting unruly bushes under control, and then a third walked in with the weekly shopping. We learnt that when people offer to help, they really do mean it.

We tried to make the most of the time we had left together. This included enjoying golf when Philip was well enough, spending precious time with family and friends, and sometimes taking risks on overseas holidays, which our insurance policy wouldn't cover!

We always maintained hope, but planned for reality too. This doesn't mean that life was perfect whilst Philip was ill. There were many times when one or both of us was in tears as the harsh reality of Philip's disease and his prognosis hit us.

When Philip died, things were tough. However, I was determined to make the most of my life. Whilst there was the huge gap of that very special person being with me to enjoy things with together, I had many other things to be thankful for – I particularly made the most of my supportive group of friends.

I began fundraising by doing some sponsored physical challenges for Cancer Research UK, the second biggest funder of cancer research in the world. I wanted to do my small bit to improve the lives of other cancer patients and their families. The fundraising led to other volunteering opportunities with the charity, which has provided some personal benefits to me – I have a real purpose in life, I feel part of a community of like-minded people and that together we are making a difference.

Whilst I would have done anything for Philip to have never been diagnosed with cancer, I do feel that the experience has made me stronger, more able to deal with the stress that life will always create, and I now make the most of every day.'

Radhia Tarafder's Story – Governance Professional, England

'Imbalance: too much of a good thing, too much of a bad thing.

Modern day life, with all its advantages and demands, can be a brainwashing prison for us. I feel stress is a side effect to a life filled with blessings, with hiccups along the way to help us work out the growth and healing that your body, mind, and soul needs at that moment. How to manage our own stress and be sensitive to others' stress is vital emotional intelligence work that needs to be shared. I hope my own story can help others. Trust that you can and will be OK.

I do believe that the same trigger resurfaces until you have learned the lesson that it serves to bring. Unresolved it recurs, wearing you out until breakdown occurs. My breakdown consisted of increasing symptoms, one after the other over a period of 15 years or so, until I was no longer able to function. I had, amongst other things, irritable bowel syndrome (IBS), depression, insomnia, chronic pain, and chronic fatigue. Chronic is defined as that which lasts over 6 weeks despite rest and medication. It took two years after my breakdown to be diagnosed with fibromyalgia 7 years ago, having 15 out of 17 markers (symptoms) for the condition. My doctor said he had never seen someone so happy to be diagnosed with it, but for me it meant ruling out various cancers and other diseases.

I began my healing journey, beginning with thanking God. I thanked God for the wake-up call to work out how I got there, and then set to work on the symptoms one by one. I knew that stress was the root of it all - I had been in a bad marriage and I struggled as a single parent, financially and emotionally. Other than my immediate family, the outside world got my happy face, and when it was just me and four walls, I just could not escape from the anger and self-pity.

Mindfulness was all the rage, and my birthday was coming up, so I planned a month of it. I chose a set activity for a small amount of time where I had to just concentrate on the experience of it, not think of what I had to do next or even what it meant to me. I discovered that feelings were only ever momentary. Even in the depths of sadness, a conversation, thought, or memory can take you out of it for a moment. This paradigm shift has been the most powerful of all. I was able to mobilise and get other areas of my life in order, refusing to remain a victim of circumstance. It also finally showed me how to be grateful, especially for the little things. I had previously failed on the gratitude journey, but a new light was emerging. I would try to find 3 things to be grateful for each day, even if to start with I could only find one thing for a few weeks. Like mindfulness and meditation, gratitude is a muscle that needs exercising. Build the habit and eventually (however annoying it is to those uninitiated!) you can find gratitude even in the midst of tragedy.

The other area of my life I set to work on was my diet. The gut is your second brain, and studies have shown that even depression is linked to your gut health. Pain and fatigue are inflammation related, as are most illnesses today. Rather than increase my medications and doses, I studied how to reduce inflammation through my diet. Thanks to God and my transformative journey, I have been medication free for four years so far, and have better health now in my 50s than I did in my 40s and even my 30s.

I no longer feel bitter and angry, but grateful for the journey and wish my former husband well. If ever I recognise stress in myself, I go through a bit of an integrity checklist, practice mindfulness, gratitude, and self-care. I also have a prayer, which I would like to share in case it helps you. For those of no faith, substitute 'God' for 'Universe,' or whatever suits you:

'Oh God, thank you for your infinite wisdom, the life you have given me and the multitude of blessings you have showered upon me.

Thank you for my past (the particular challenge, its journey and all its impact/elements).

Thank you for my present (the current situation you find yourself in, knowing there must be a good reason for it and a lesson to be learned from it, and the fact you had the wherewithal to ask God for help right now).

And thank you for my future (trust that God has your back and if you work on yourself/the issue, you will find yourself precisely where you need to be).''

Katy Deacon's Story – Information Governance Manager, England

'I was diagnosed with Multiple Sclerosis (MS) in 2012, which was an extremely stressful time for me and my family. I was shocked at the time and very scared. One Neurologist said, 'I don't know why I am seeing you as you have secondary progressive MS, and nothing can be done about that.'

My symptoms began the year before with the failure of my bladder and bowel, followed soon after by difficulty with my legs. Now I am considered doubly incontinent. By 2017, I was unable to balance and had to walk with two crutches for short distances inside, and use a mobility scooter for anything more than 10m outside because clonus (a type of neurological condition that creates involuntary muscle contractions) would take over and knock me down. However, a Magnetic Resonance Image (MRI) in 2016 showed that, whilst I had additional lesions from my 2012 scan, they were very old, and I had absolutely no new activity in any of the layers of the MRI scan. My neurologist suggested I should consider myself as having a spinal cord injury rather than having multiple sclerosis. So, by managing my MS and following the Overcoming Multiple Sclerosis

(OMS) pillars, I've managed to successfully put my MS to sleep.

That's all well and good, but it doesn't help the clonus in my legs or my ability to walk. I eventually got to a point where I was damaging my arms and wrists because of the pressure I was putting them under with my crutches. The whole situation was causing considerable stress and anxiety, especially as my main concern was always whether I could get to the toilet in time. I was extremely limited by the distance I could walk, which meant missing out on activities with my family. With hindsight, I can see that I needed a different perspective, but I just did not want to let go of my ability to walk.

I am mother of two young, lively children and wife to a wonderful man. We all live in West Yorkshire, a very hilly and fairly inaccessible part of the world. I am heading into my tenth year diagnosed with MS and I have been very up and very down throughout my experience. In March 2020, we went into lockdown and everyone's world changed. I decided that in this scary situation I needed to be brave. I had a wheelchair which sat in the garage, to aid me getting from the house to the car on a bad day. I decided to bite the bullet and see what could come of being in a wheelchair throughout the day. I felt it was important to get out of the house and interact with people, as I could no longer rely on the therapeutic effects of seeing people at work.

Whilst this could be looked at as a step backwards, it actually was a mighty leap forward. In the breaks between lockdowns, because I was in my chair, I was able to go out with my family! We had days out to theme parks, to the cinema and to the local park every weekend to see family members and I was able to be with them. It was such a special time and really helped me realise that my wheelchair gives me a new ability and a tremendous amount of liberty.

As I don't actually have a spinal cord injury, I don't qualify for NHS support. So, I researched the support that I can access. There are some fantastic websites out there and brilliant charities. The training that is provided on the Back Up app is wonderful and really helped me.

In post-lockdown world, I can now make a cup of tea for myself and my husband and take it into the living room by myself, which I hadn't been able to do for all of the years I had to use crutches. I am able to do physical activities which I have missed for so long and I feel fantastic for it. I still do mindful physio with my legs every night, and I make sure I am using my standing frame to maintain my leg strength as much as I can. I am now looking forward to the adventures that our vaccinated world will bring, with additional mountain bike style wheels to my wheelchair which will allow me to go off road!

I held on to my walking ability for so long, but I eventually realised it was limiting my actual ability to live. I really miss being able to skip down the road with my children, but those times have gone now, and I need to look at what opportunities my wonderful, wheeled world can provide. My message to you is that even with MS I have a full-time job and have a family: life is too valuable to throw away! Live for each day and face the challenges as they come along. I was a high achiever before MS, and I am still a high achiever. I am fortunate to have a loving and supportive family to keep me going, which I really appreciate.'

Ingrid Walker's Story - Business Owner, Wales
(www.pyramidstainedglass.co.uk)

'I was surprised when I first saw the physio at the hospital to be asked if, leading up to the collapse of my spine, I had the support I needed. The answer was a resounding '*No*,' but I had not expected the mainstream NHS to have this holistic approach. The initial stress had come from my usual work and family commitments, as well as trying to look after my mum who broke her hip at 89 and was suffering with vascular dementia, which of course we only realised along the way. Supporting my mum and getting her needs met would have been a privilege had it not been for the difficulties of dealing with my dad as well. It was after I saw that he could not care for my mum and she was settled in a nursing home that my slipped discs and trapped sciatic nerve occurred.

The anxiety I suffered was all encompassing. I woke up in the early morning struggling to breathe, shaky, and so tired, hardly able to sit up against the pillows. I felt sick, I was constantly yawning and barely able to speak, or concentrate on anything. I couldn't eat breakfast. Then I couldn't eat lunch. If the anxiety did not reduce by the evening, I could not eat dinner. I saw a counsellor, who explained that the pain I had felt had brought about a fight or flight response, but as I could not take flight or fight, I was left in that extreme state with all the adrenaline and cortisol running around my body. My muscles were poisoned by stress, and so of course I couldn't concentrate on everyday things such as eating, sleeping and usual interests. Although she gave me exercises to do, there was no clear path forward to bring my mind back to health. The strange thing was that with the anxiety, I felt guilty - guilty for feeling like this. I felt I was a failure for feeling so ill. I can only think that this is something that is caused by societal norms, as it doesn't actually make sense to me. Sometimes though, my son (who still lived at home) would give me permission to lie and rest. He would tuck me up on the sofa, and only then did I feel safe, because he had given me 'permission' to just be.

A helpful technique to push away the anxiety was to clean. I think that because it was something physical which also took a certain level of concentration, the anxiety retreated. I gradually worked more, listening to the radio when there was something on which was not too distressing. Books and television were helpful in taking me out of my anxiety, but only if they were not about trauma - not an easy ask. If I could find a series to listen to on the radio that was wonderful, and if I found a book I could enjoy, I dreaded finishing it. Walking was not enough to make me feel better, but I found having to breathe deeply and regularly whilst swimming made a huge difference. I would go in the pool a shaking wreck and come out a fairly balanced individual. Going twice a week with the same two friends gave me the knowledge that I would feel reasonably OK for periods of the week, and I felt that my friends accepted how I felt without judgement and cared enough for me to want to spend time with me. I joined a yoga class with another friend, which really helped, and I not only felt relaxed when I came out but started to look forward to those days.

I think the final way I overcame the anxiety was to confront these feelings. Even if I felt relaxed by the evening, I would have bad dreams and wake up the next morning anxious again. This led me to dread the morning. I decided to confront it, so that rather than trying to get away from it I would let myself feel it and know that nothing worse was going to come. If it made me shiver and shake, so be it, I accepted it. I do think, however, that I had to get to the stage of finding some peace, dialling the feelings down a bit so that the day wasn't so painful, before I could do this final step.'

Sara Jackson's Story - Senior Talent Resource Manager, England

'From a very young age, I have always done some form of exercise. At school, it was gymnastics, netball and cross country. I swam for the county as a teenager, and in my adult years I would run regularly, compete in the odd triathlon or half marathon, and aim to get away snowboarding as often as I could.

I felt strong, healthy, flexible, and stress-free. That was until July 2013, when things started to change. Intermittently, my left knee would flare up and, believing it was just a sporting injury, I would stop exercising and use crutches to help the situation. These flare ups, however, became a regular occurrence and started to affect my mood increasingly.

X-rays and scans did not show any real damage, so it was categorised as 'wear and tear' by the doctors I saw. At times it would be both knees and I would stop exercising, which made me feel even lower as I wasn't getting the endorphins I needed. The problem progressed to other areas of my body, where I would experience flares and chronic pain. At times, my wrists and forearms felt like knives were driving into them, and I would wake up in agony in the middle of the night.

On one occasion, my physiotherapist noted that my neck's stiffness was terrible, almost as if I had been in a car accident. During this period, I had been jointly visiting both an osteoporosis consultant and a rheumatology consultant to find the cause. I received a test for rheumatoid arthritis (RA), but my markers showed negative.

Eventually, in April of 2014, I was booked to have a minor knee operation. However, I was so debilitated (so much so that I could not hold a cup of tea or a kettle) that I booked an emergency appointment to visit my RA consultant, who confirmed that I did in fact have a positive diagnosis for RA. This was a stressful time for me both mentally and physically.

RA is an auto-immune disease that attacks the linings of your joints and wears them away. I was relieved to have the diagnosis, but by this point my body was under so much stress I had to stop working for three months. My stress and anxiety were triggered by the constant pain, inability to exercise and fear from not knowing what was happening to me. The combination of all of these gradually made me feel quite down. I was brought to tears more easily, wondered why it had happened to me and what the cause was. Unfortunately, with this disease, there is no explanation as to why it occurs. Experts say a combination of factors at a certain point in time causes your body's immune system to go into overdrive, and is then unable to turn this immune response off.

Thankfully, I had such incredible support during this time from my husband, family and friends. It was still a long nine months to find the right medication. I trialled several different drugs, but I was still in chronic pain and also had chronic fatigue, which is another side effect of the disease.

After trying many different options, I was finally prescribed an injectable drug, administered weekly. I can honestly say that since the first injection, my life has changed for the better. Gradually, through less pain and fatigue, learning from other people's experiences and a positive mindset, I have come through the other side.

Looking back, I realise how much stress my body and mind were under, and that keeping focused on the positives was essential. Since then, I have made a full recovery. I am an active member of CrossFit Nottingham where I train most days. I also maintain a healthy nutrition plan and focus on a positive mindset. When I have a flare up, I listen to my body and relax until the inflammation settles.

Having a chronic disease means that stress can manifest itself in many ways, and just when you least expect it. I have learned that if you listen to your body and learn to manage your symptoms in the best way possible, you can get through it.'

Advice on Medical Stress

Each person reacts differently when first being informed by their doctor about a new medical diagnosis or long-term condition. You may be in shock, feel dizzy, frightened, disorientated, your heart racing or even feeling faint. It will take time to come to terms with this information, so it's important to learn how to cope with this illness and the vulnerability and stress which comes along with it. The following advice is taken from Robinson, Segal and Smith (2021).

Depending on the type of illness and long-term prognosis, the levels of stress will vary. You may have to deal with stressors such as:

- Feelings and emotions such as frustration, despair, sadness, self-isolation, and feeling overwhelmed
- Pain management or discomfort from your symptoms
- Disability and quality of life adjustments
- Getting to know and trust new medical staff and carers
- Loss of memory or clear rational thinking
- Taking steps to manage your condition and practice self-care
- Dealing with financial burdens and managing increased financial pressures

How you deal with these factors will depend on the illness or longer-term condition, which could be one or more condition. These may be cancer, stroke, Multiple Sclerosis, Parkinson's, rheumatic problems, recovering from an accident or injury, diabetes, epilepsy, heart conditions, mental health issues or others that have not been listed above. You may even have an addiction which requires medical guidance and support.

You can plan and take steps to maximise your quality of life with the support of family, friends, and medical professionals to minimise the challenges you will be living with. The massive shock and upheaval may make it difficult to think, adapt and function. You may also feel powerless and out of control. However, with the right coping tools you can navigate this new and challenging chapter in your life.

Managing Emotions and Feelings

You may be asking yourself, 'Why me? What have I done wrong to be punished in this way?'

These questions and thoughts are normal, so allow yourself time to come to terms with your condition. It's OK to become angry, cry and be frustrated. You are at a crisis point in your life and trying to face up to your own fragile mortality. You may start to worry and lose sleep, grieving the demise of your health.

Trying to ignore your feelings will only increase stress and maybe even delay recovery, so allow yourself to feel what you feel. This will be a difficult as it can mean intense feelings initially, but it will pass, and you can start to destress. Be patient with yourself and others around you. You may spend anxious hours on the internet looking for a cure or help: instead, have faith in your doctors and nurses, and remember that you have the choice to seek a second opinion if you are worried.

Self-Care

Eat and sleep well. Pursue those relationships and activities that bring you joy. Be open minded to change and adapt to new ways of living. Cultivating positive thoughts will help to motivate you to meet treatment and health goals. Choose the support that's right for you and people you can confide in, lean on. These individuals could be friends and loved ones who are good listeners and who will listen attentively and compassionately without being distracted, judging you, or trying to tell you how you should think or feel.

Find time for face-to-face support, not just over the telephone or through social media - that is unless, you have no other choice. Connecting in this way plays a huge role in relieving stress and boosting your mood.

Support Group

A support group is a good way to keep connected with others who are going through the same or similar experiences. These groups can help you to share your thoughts and burdens, and are safe places to talk about what you're going through. You may be able get coping tips from others who attend these groups. It may take several visits to the support group before you feel comfortable to open up so you can gain the support you need, and you may make new friends in the process. If the first group is not right for you, then find one that is.

Talk to someone you trust - Talking face-to-face with a friend or loved one will keep you connected with people you love and who care for your well-being.

Quality sleep - Sleep can help to reduce stress, and helps the body to deal with health issues. You can modify your daytime habits and develop a peaceful bedtime routine.

Relaxation - Activities that can help reduce stress and lower blood pressure include mindfulness and deep breathing meditation. Progressive Muscle Relaxation (PMR) is a natural way of relaxing the body and mind (Axe, 2020).

Keep active - Regular exercise can burn calories, as well as help dissipate tension and relieve stress. Only attempt to do what you can manage without over-exerting your body. Exercise can boost your endorphins and help to keep you more positive throughout the day.

10.1: COVID-19 and Lockdown

"It is not the strongest of the species that survives, nor the most intelligent; it is the one most adaptable to change."

- Charles Darwin

People initially thought lockdown was a novelty and hoped it would soon pass, but as it went on, they started to worry that it was beginning to affect their daily life. The most vulnerable groups were elderly people and those who were stranded away from home, without work, wages and support networks. Governments stepped in across the globe to return stranded citizens and to provide meals for less fortunate people, including those living in isolated villages. COVID-19 started to spread, killing many people. A sense of panic ensued, and people were afraid to go out, prisoners in their own homes. Globally, we felt the impact of the COVID-19 pandemic on our stress levels. These and other stories in this book discuss the impact of COVID-19 on the stress and well-being of those affected.

When COVID-19 hit the world in early 2020, the disease swiftly started to spread, killing millions around the world and making many lives miserable. This pandemic forced people out of their comfort zones, and to adapt to new ways of living and interacting. Social distancing laws were put in place, and large fines introduced for law breakers. Masks had to be worn in public spaces. Hugs and physical contact were an exceedingly rare experience, and families were isolated for months on end. There was a sense of panic and people were afraid to go out, instead remaining prisoners in their own homes.

You may have had little choice but to use Zoom, WhatsApp, Facebook, Instagram, and other social media platforms to communicate over the lockdown period. New businesses, such as Quarantine Buddy (Qbuddy), which was founded by a team of Cornell University students, were formed over lockdown. Qbuddy, according to their website, are passionate about empowering people to socialise from their homes. Their machine-learning algorithm strategically ranks and outputs the best possible buddy for you based on your background and what you are looking for. Their slogan is, 'Empowering people to socialise from home.' I have personally taken part in a Qbuddy 'guitar group jamming session' with people from all around the world that I had not met before. It was initially a stressful experience, but I did enjoy it and took part on several occasions.

Many people lost jobs, were given pay cuts, or furloughed. All these drastic changes had a major impact on our nation's health, well-being and finances. We also had to adapt to social distancing measures, and to work from home for months on end.

Like many sales managers, I had to manage a team of a dozen sales representatives in the pharmaceutical industry who would normally visit doctors, nurses, pharmacists, and other health care professionals face-to-face. National lockdown measures meant that they were no longer able to engage face-to-face. Many of their meetings and appointments had to be online or rearranged. Most interactions then had to move to remote calling via Zoom, Microsoft Teams, or just over the telephone.

This meant having to adapt to new ways of working. This was quite a stressful time for me, the team and the company, as it was a major change in the way we all worked. Some individuals adapted quicker than others, whilst others struggled and required extra support. The lack of face-to-face interaction during our daily lives due to lockdown and having to continually social distance meant that the normal things we used to do, such as attending birthday parties, seeing family, friends, and work colleagues, could no longer happen. Our normal social experiences such as going to pubs and restaurants, football, rugby, baseball, athletics, and other sports were closed to us. Music concerts could no longer take place, and Eid, Holi (the Hindu festival of light), Christmas, Hanukka and other religious gatherings were restricted.

My Story: Raj Soren – Area Sale's Manager and Martial Artist, UK

'Little did I know that, while writing this book on stress and collating wonderfully inspiring stories, my wife Jyoti, daughter Lukhi and I would all would test positive for COVID-19. As for many of us, lockdown has had a major impact on my business and personal life.

This has been quite a stressful year, and to catch COVID-19 at the tail end of it was very unfortunate. The process of taking a COVID-19 test swab was an unpleasant one. You are asked to swab deep in your throat for 15- 20 seconds then use the same swab up one of your nostrils, swabbing vigorously before placing it back in the sample tube. We were both gagging and felt like being sick. It would look very amusing if it wasn't so unpleasant! We found out the next day that we were positive for COVID-19, and that we had most likely caught it from my wife who was a key worker in a school. The good news is that my wife and daughter managed to recover from COVID-19 far quicker than me. They did suffer several symptoms, but their bodies seemed to have been better at defending themselves.

The fear and anxiety of COVID-19 suddenly became real for me. I had been working from home for the last 8 months doing everything possible to avoid catching the virus. I am a relatively fit individual who has regularly trained in martial arts for 40 years. Unfortunately, research has shown that Black, Indian and Bengali men above age 50 and who are bald

256

were statistically 2-4 times more likely to die from COVID-19 than their white counterparts. All these facts in themselves were worrying, as I had known friends and acquaintances who died or struggled to recover, resulting in long-term complications. I already had a lot of stress from adapting to the new lockdown and managing a team of 12 sales representatives. I also had the added stress of trying to keep my Jiu Jitsu and Aikido martial arts classes together, as I formerly ran 6 classes a week. There was the loss of revenue as we stopped our regular classes, and unfortunately bills mounted up for hall hire and loss of students, as many of them did not want to attend virtual classes. Fortunately, my sons Suraj and Chandni, who are both black belts, helped by covering my online classes to keep the Jiu Jitsu club going. I am very thankful for their help and support. My Aikido instructor Alex also covered my sessions, and I am very much appreciative of their support.

I did not have any major underlying health conditions, apart from high cholesterol. However, the first 3 weeks of contracting COVID-19 were the most stressful, being both physically and mentally draining in a way that I had never experienced. It was so bad that I was not sure if I was going to wake up each day. Each day I would suffer from a cocktail of symptoms, including headaches, shortness of breath, loss of voice and appetite, low energy and mood, brain fog, poor memory, and being unable to have a conversation for more than a few seconds without getting breathless. I also had weak muscles and limbs, stomach-ache, constipation, lack of sleep and hot and cold fevers that meant me changing my clothes each morning because my clothes would be soaked with sweat.

I could no longer go to work to support my team, or teach Jiu Jitsu or Aikido due to lockdown restrictions. I was ill for 6 plus months with long-term COVID-19 health issues.

I was worried about what would happen to my family if I did not recover from COVID-19, leaving them to pick up the broken pieces. Sadly, a good friend of mine died suddenly in his sleep, which was devastating news to his family to all that knew him. His death was always in the back of my mind, and I prayed even more than usual that I would get through this for my family. I have a wonderful wife, family and friends who showed great patience and loving support to get me through this difficult time. Work colleagues would send me get well messages, and my workload was being shared amongst my colleague and my boss, who was also incredibly supportive. Prayer, meditation, breathing exercises, and plenty of paracetamol and fluids helped to mend my body and mind.

The good news is that after week three, I started to make steady progress towards better health. I was on the journey to recovery, but also unsure of the long-term effects of COVID-19. I remained off work for 6 weeks. I have learned to appreciate taking each healthy breath, walking, and just spending quality time with family and friends when the opportunity arises.

This stressful time helped to make me more mentally focused, and helped me to believe in myself and that things would improve for me and my family. I was fortunate to be one of the survivors, taking small steps in my recovery and connecting with loved ones in the aftermath of the virus. I just hope you do not suffer like I did, but wish you strength and perseverance to get through the tough times, no matter what they are for you.'

Tina Masson's Story – Senior Sales Representative, England

'2020 was supposed to be a great year. A year full of promise, full of weddings, my 40th birthday, a chance to take time to spend with my ageing parents who have waited many years to be able to stop hearing, "Sorry, I have work!" or, "I can't spend more time with you as the kids are driving me insane!"

What instead occurred was that we were forced to embrace rapid changes to a world that became full of fear, apathy, and division. In other ways, we also became more considerate, more aware of our surroundings and had a chance to connect with the people who are a part of our day-to-day lives. For many, it meant embracing local communities and banding together.

The start of the pandemic was indeed the scariest place to be, and what is even more scary is how quickly people forget what it was like back in March. I have suffered great losses as many have, but I have learnt to embrace the positives and count my blessings through journaling every day.

My father-in-law was the second General Practitioner (GP) to die in Essex from COVID-19 after battling for more than 35 days. My husband, myself, family and friends were all called upon to analyse data, make calls for his care, and try to pull every string to make sure he got the care and consideration he should have. Sadly, the NHS care he received mostly led to his untimely demise. We had a tough time dealing with the hospital, fighting for oxygen and against early discharge when the hospital did not seem to realise how unwell he was. The system I had invested my time, energy, and career in for the past 18 years had let my father-in-law down.

He passed away on April 16th, and both what preceded and followed was unprecedented. Just 5 days earlier, my father-in-law's only remaining brother passed away with no explanation, and 5 days after my mother was diagnosed with Stage 4 pancreatic cancer. As there were no oncology services running, we had to accept the inevitable, and she passed away on the 25th of July.

This came at a time when I was home-schooling 3 kids, looking after a dog, fighting for care for my mother, and making sure my dad, mother-in-law and husband had the emotional support they needed. I was exhausted!

Without realising it, I found that support was everywhere if I just took a second to look up. I felt alone, desperate, and full of more sorrow than I thought I would ever be able to deal with - I couldn't breathe. It was at this point that I learned what 'community' means – it's people! The last 20 years of my adult life had been spent slowly and unconsciously building different communities who were there for me when I needed it. My local village, friends, family, work colleagues and complete strangers all got in touch to make sure I did not get lost in the cracks. Until this point, I never knew just how many people I had in my life and how my small part over the years had led to a community wanting to look out for me.

Work had supported me through all my trials and tribulations, my team were tirelessly making sure I was on track and that my career did not suffer and, more importantly, I didn't give up. As the news spread around our local community, people whom I had never even met started to get in touch. This meant I had to learn how to process our tragedies and to talk to people about how these events really affected us.

What I learned is that people matter. Having someone in your life who is there to support you when you are not at your strongest can mean the difference between surviving and struggling. It is OK to accept that you cannot be everything to everyone, and that does not make you a failure. I learned that you need a range of ways to deal with emotions, and that writing down your feelings, screaming into a pillow and eating your way through a whole bar of chocolate are all OK tools. The key goal is to identify the point in a situation where you need to stop, process, and find a way to deal with it. I learned that hearing my children laugh was a privilege I should cherish every day and that mess, dirt and not having the most presentable home 24 hours a day was a sign of the beautiful life Harish and I have built.

I finally learned that, whether you have 5 minutes or many hours in the day spare, you should volunteer in the community. Helping one other person contributes to that bigger picture; a world where people talk to each other and learn to look after each other.

Life is about making the most of everything you are handed and striving to achieve more than was afforded to you.

During the second and third waves of the lockdown, I learned to forgive; to accept my father-in-law's fate and make sure I was donating food, making masks, getting local businesses to support our hospitals, GP practices and vulnerable families that needed more food, support, and heat in what was a chaotic and isolating time.

What I know is that people bring hope; together, we will keep progressing and accepting each daily challenge with certainty and optimism.

Finally, and most importantly, human nature means we are creatures who hold on to emotions - positive or negative. By embracing the idea that we need to 'let go' of the pain and upset of this pandemic and stop dwelling on what cannot be changed, we will all come out stronger, more connected, and ready to build a community that enriches our lives.'

Dr. Reena Murmu Nielsen's Story - Neuroscientist, Researcher and Fitness/Health Activist, Demark

'Life without stress is unimaginable. Stress is an important part of being human; a common biological reaction that is essential for 'flight or fight' responses. Stress, however painful it may seem, is a natural part of life, that when present can motivate us and help us get things done. However, chronic stress can have severe consequences on our bodies and brain. High levels of chronic stress, if left untreated, can negatively impact our psychology, leading to depression, high levels of anxiety, boredom, fear, loneliness, confusion, anger, and uncertainty (which are all signs of psychological stress).

Last year, the COVID-19 pandemic caused significant psychological stress on everyone, including me. I was beginning to feel the negative impact of the pandemic on my well-being. I have always been a physically active person; I go to the gym at least 5 times a week, and I particularly love Zumba and strength training. It relaxes my mind, keeps me fit, and improves my sleep and mood. Although I love exercising, I only like working out in the gym. I am not an outdoor person, and therefore I hate jogging or taking long walks. Last spring, when COVID-19 hit Europe, several countries went on a complete lockdown, and it goes without saying that all the gyms were closed. I immediately felt unhappy and depressed because I could no longer exercise. I started feeling all those physical problems (back pain, neck pain, and more) that until now were foreign to me. I quickly realised that, if I were to cope with the stress of the pandemic in a healthier manner, I had to make some lifestyle changes that could be inconvenient to me. I felt lucky that I was able to notice the psychological stress of the COVID-19 pandemic early enough.

Fortunately, the gym is not the only place for physical activity, and there are several other ways to stay fit. A great deal of scientific research has shown that any form of physical activity, even 15 minutes of walking or dancing, is beneficial for our physical and mental well-being. At first, I started taking slow walks, followed by 20-30 minutes of Zumba-style, home-based dance workouts After a month or so, I started to love these walks, and before I realised it I was already running 5Ks. In addition to the physical activities, I also started eating a regular and healthy balanced diet, with meals full of whole grains, vegetables, fruits, and lean proteins which strengthened my immune system. And when things became extremely stressful, I took a break and performed deep breathing exercises, which took the pressure off straight away.

What I have learned from being in extremely stressful situations is that it is important to recognise the 'stress signals' that our body is sending us, and do something about it before it is too late. There is no singular way to combat stress, but any form of physical activity, together with a healthy and balanced diet, helps us cope with stress in a healthier manner.'

Daniel Fahy's Story – Director of Dads and Kids and Healthy Mind, Games Community Investment Company, England (www.dadsandkids.net)

'I remember staring at a roof tile that was on the ground when I was a child. I was hypnotised by a drip that was falling on it; each time it fell through a hole exactly the right size. There was something about the perfect fit of the drip to the hole and the speed it shot through the tile that entranced me. My dad came along and explained that the reason the hole was the perfect size for the drip was because the drip had worn a hole in the tile. One by one each drip had taken a tiny piece of the tile away in that spot until there was no more, and the drip could pass through. That was the thought that occupied me for hours from that day on.

In 2019, I had a severe bought of anxiety. I managed to get on top of it after about a year. Then in March 2020, I got COVID-19 during the first week of lockdown. This was the start of an ongoing battle with Long COVID. Long COVID is a nasty illness, the main symptoms being significant pain, reduced cognitive functioning or brain fog, and fatigue, but it also has over 200 other associated symptoms.

The thing about Long COVID is that it is (at the time of writing) unpredictable. Doctors, despite various potential theories, are still utterly baffled by the cause and have no treatment. It is prone to sudden and unprompted relapses, and random fleeting symptoms (I lost the power to form words for a morning - just one morning - during a 9-month illness).

The fatigue is crippling. I heard someone say, 'It's not just being tired, it's like being hit by a truck and then being attacked with chloroform.' This is as good as any description.

This was an incredibly stressful time for me as I am the main carer for 3 children, and was responsible for getting them through the lockdown happily and educated. I also had 2 not-for-profit businesses I was trying to get off the ground, as well as another business opportunity I was considering. I am an extrovert who was no longer able to meet with people, which was a pretty frustrating situation for me. I felt pressure to get the businesses up and running, because when lockdown ended we would need the income.

I was trying to manage multiple project goals while physically unwell. I knew what anxiety felt like and I didn't want to go there again. There were so many demands on my energy, and I didn't have nearly as much as I needed.

At some stage shortly before lockdown, I heard a phrase that was attributed to Bill Gates: 'People vastly overestimate what they can achieve in one year, and they vastly underestimate what they can achieve in ten years.'

If I was to identify the one driving thought that got me through this time, it would be that phrase above. I would ask myself each day, 'Have you progressed today in the slightest?'

Yes, the kids are slightly more into their school routine, yes, I answered one of their maths questions so now they understand it a little bit better, yes, I thought of a routine which helps keep the kitchen a little tidier.

Are things today better than yesterday? Yes - great, well done! No - well, was today better than yesterday? Last week? Did I get a little bit more done this week? Have I been a little bit more consistent than last week? Is there any aspect of my life this month that I can say has moved forward?

Inch by inch, I moved forward, and fought hard to hold on to where I was, whilst fighting to make the tiniest bit more progress. I spent time looking into how to get more out of each minute, little habits that would help. Of course, I had help from friends and family too, but a lot of things

I did for myself.

Two steps forward one step back is definitely still one forward. Just trying to put one foot in the right place each day is enough. Remember that backward steps are an unavoidable part of every story. Expect them, because, let's face it, who did I think I was trying to manage all those challenges without making a mistake? So, when they happened, there was no surprise or defeat, just acknowledgement. If today is going to be a backwards day, that's OK, because my goal to keep going is still achievable.

I made my progress inch by inch. These thoughts of pride in tiny, tiny victories became the drip, drip, drip that helped me burrow my way through my anxieties and through the tough days of Long COVID. Just like the drip, it was a very tight fit - only just big enough to get through - but that's all you need. Just like the drip, each thought seemed to make no difference; but it did, and together they were powerful. My anxiety is well under control despite Long COVID, and my health has been improving steadily for over 3 months now. I'm getting there, drip by drip.

I would like to point out though that this isn't how I would have thought of myself, as slowly ploddingly relentlessly. Yes, I probably had some resilient qualities, but discipline and routine weren't ones I was conscious of. The relentlessness of these thoughts was a skill I practiced and acquired over time, and got better at. We change over time - not instantly but drip by drip, each positive thought a victory.

So, whatever challenge you are facing, set tough goals, but always remember that progress, any progress whatsoever, should be acknowledged by you and be a point of pride no matter how miniscule. Seriously, life is tough, sometimes it's the smallest progress that's the hardest to achieve.'

Tips to Reduce COVID-19 Anxiety and Stress

The World Health Organisation (WHO) has termed COVID-19 stress 'pandemic fatigue.' Here are some tips to reduce stress:

- Breathe deeply – Take a few deep, long breaths in and out. Count to four as you breathe in through your nose, and six as you breathe out through your mouth. Repeat for about a minute

- Focus on what you can control and set small goals
- Cold water - Splashing your face and skin with cold water can help to reduce stress
- Have a healthy routine – Eating healthily and exercising, even if it's cleaning, gardening, or walking, can help to reduce stress and improve overall well-being
- Do one thing every day that makes you smile
- Get a good night's sleep
- Accept the situation
- Be kind to yourself
- Accept change and be prepared to adapt - learn something new or get creative
- Reach out for help from family and friends
- Keep a daily diary - Write down what you feel and think. Try not to re-read what you have written until long after the stressful period has passed
- TV and social media overload - Choose one trusted source of information to keep up with news

10.2: Grief

"Everyone must leave something behind when he dies, my grandfather said. A child or a book or a painting or a house or a wall built or a pair of shoes made. Or a garden planted. Something your hand touches some way, so your soul has somewhere to go when you die, and when people look at that tree or that flower you planted, you're there."

- Ray Bradbury

Muhammad Mustaqeem-Shah's Story - Independent Arbitrator, England

'Life is fragile and must be handled with care. We hear this vital saying often but, unfortunately, not many people seem to be able to manage it successfully. People stress out, put themselves under immense pressure, and go on to take antidepressants or even become dependent on alcohol or other forms of dangerous recreational drugs. It may well be that not everyone is properly equipped with the skills to overcome the tough situations they are faced with.

However, we also know that humans have built-in survival mechanisms, and that throughout history they have magnificently managed to overcome numerous existential threats, including pandemics, plagues, natural disasters and so on.

Personally speaking, being a Muslim (believer in the Islamic faith), I find my spiritual relationship and connection with my Creator and the Creator of this whole universe extremely supportive when I am stressed.

My wife and I have personally witnessed that it is this spiritual connection with God that makes us, otherwise weak and fragile, strong and determined to move on in life after having three miscarriages and three new-born infant babies passing away, all within the first eight years of our marital life, as well as many other complications during each pregnancy.

I remember the first gorgeous smile of our daughter Marwah, but little did we know that this precious life was going to leave this world after only forty-one days in our lives. Had I known what tragedy was to unfold, I would have held Marwah on my lap all the time and not left her for one second. The tragic time of our young daughter falling ill and then leaving us behind took three days, and my wife said it felt like dream. Soon after her sad departure, we both prayed to God, sobbing and shedding tears while her body was still resting there. This connection with God gave us some short relief and strength at the time that we never expected we would have that soon. Sadly, we faced the same tragedy for our other daughter, Du'a, who passed away after only three days while we were living in London. Again, we turned to God with more prayers. Every time we faced a stressful and difficult event in our lives and thought we would not be able to cope with it, we found amazing peace of mind when we turned to God. We realised that we were being tested, and as a result we have become even closer and have a stronger relationship.

After eight years, we were finally blessed with our four lovely children, two boys and two girls. On one hand, God says He loves us seventy times more than our own mothers; while on the other, He says He is closer to us than our own jugular vein. So, He is all-aware of what we are going through. In fact, any good or bad circumstances we face come from Him.

God says, 'Perhaps you dislike something which is good for you and like something which is bad for you. Allah knows and you do not know.' (Quran 2.216)

I feel that He is always there for me. To reinforce this incredible feeling, I try to read the Quran (Muslims' holy scripture), the final message from God to humanity, every day. He talks to me personally, and when I want to talk to Him I do so by my prayers (Muslims pray five times a day). 'Whoever puts his trust in Allah, then He alone is sufficient for them. Certainly, Allah achieves His will. Allah has already set a destiny for everything,' says Allah.' (Quran 65:3)

The Quran also mentions five tests and trials that we will go through as human beings during our lifetime:
'And certainly, we shall test you with something of **fear**, **hunger**, loss of **properties** and **lives** and **fruits**. Give glad tidings to those who shall remain patient during these tribulations.' (Quran 2:155)
I hope my story can help others come to terms with the difficult situations they are in and find their solace and peace in life, for God is merciful, forgiving, caring and certainly loves those who are grateful to Him.'

Anna Gorst's Story - Children and Young People's Psychological Well-being Practitioner, England

'Speak to me and tell me, was it all lies?

I believed I was safe, that you held me, that I was part of you. I never doubted you, even when the raging teenage maelstrom of my troubled years was screaming; even when you sucked the disappointment from the air around me and blew it out in great, exasperated breaths.

You will forever be scrubbed clean, pink from a hot bath, ironed blue and white check shirt, sitting agile on the rug at my mother's feet, throwing a log on the fire. Puccini. Good wine, always from decent glasses. The softest fingertips. Piano. Up early don't waste the day, cup of tea by the bed way, way before I'm ready to be conscious. Mountains. Belief in kindness, in people, whoever they might be.

I believed in you. And now, halfway down my first gin and tonic, no signal in the basement bar – I have to run up the stairs past the bouncers to take the call. My brother's voice.

Then screaming, screaming and silence together inside my head, and blackness, and it's too bright and I can't breathe, and I can't move but I need to find a taxi get home get in my car get to you.

Taxi isn't moving. Traffic. Teeth are chattering. Trying to smile and talk to the driver. Trying not to throw up, not to scream.

In my car. Begging him to drive faster. I must get to you.

Another phone call.

Pull over here. I can't breathe - am I screaming? This lay-by next to a chip shop is now burned into my mind. I'll never pass it again without falling.

You have died. You're dead. You can't be dead. You're my world. I can't breathe. I'm freezing. I'm high. I need sugar. We're driving again. I need to be there. The journey takes hours. It takes seconds.

Out of the car. Into arms. So many people. I need to throw up. I need to empty my whole body of everything inside.

I'm being taken in to see you. Your dead body. Your hair is all wrong – sticking up, shocked by the machines that didn't work they didn't save you. I know this because I have to kiss your rigid forehead and tell you I love you, you're a silly old man, how can you do this to me? You can't die you're the core of who I am.

And that was just the start.

Days and nights of drinking whisky, nibbling bananas, sleeping in half hour bursts just to try and wake up to it not being true. Waves of adrenaline and disbelief crashing over and through. Sometimes hours between them, sometimes seconds.

Then weeks of talking, of doing, everyone propping everyone up, finding distraction where we can.

Then months of nothing. Numbness. Lying in bed, on the left side and then the right. Blankness. When the blankness breaks, the terror is so overwhelming I can't accept it: I'm dropping from the top of a rollercoaster, tripping over the edge of a cliff, falling through space, dizzy and frightened, and no air in my lungs, gasping and grasping and just trying to hold on takes everything I've got, so how on earth could I be expected to get up or get dressed or go to bloody work?

I trusted you to be there, and you stopped existing with no warning. Nothing. And I simply didn't know how to be, without my Dad.

***

That was then. How long has it been? Years now and I can think of you with love, with gratitude and laughter.

How have I got here? Avoiding that stretch of motorway where my brother and CPR lost the fight. The terror pushed into a locked filling cabinet, preventing it from burning me to the ground.

How do you learn to trust in life again when it was ripped away with no warning? How do you trust in anything with the shadow of the fear always hovering inside your head?

Time plays a part, it's true. Twelve years, therapy, friends, family.

Something offered up by a counsellor – undiagnosed PTSD?

This makes sense. We come back to trauma. Trauma causes the body to experience stress – a tsunami of stress hormones imprinting on the brain. Any trauma, big or small, triggers a stress response. Mine is not to fight, but to freeze – or fly.

Knowing this is helpful. Locked filing cabinet will be opened again. And again. To understand our stress response is to give us back some control.

In the end it really doesn't matter what the trigger is. All the soul searching in the world won't bring back my Dad. But the impact of the stress – now that you can influence.

Breathe.

Breathe deep.

Exhale.

Exhale slowly.

Notice the painful thought – it's a memory from the filing cabinet. Notice it and let it go. Let it go and adjust your focus.

The here and now is yours. And nothing can take away what you had, before the loss.'

Gordon Gibb's Story – Author of '*Fifth Season*,' Canada

'Stress has been part of my life since I was 11 years of age, when my family pulled up our roots in Canada and moved to the U.S. Up until then, my life was an idyllic existence, with regular contact from treasured grandparents, friends close at hand to the only home I ever knew in a Toronto suburb, and summers spent at the family cottage in the Kawarthas. My life was structured and familiar. I had roots.

And then, in the summer of 1968, we moved to a new country without the sense of community I had come to cherish. My parents drifted apart, and Dad went on long business trips. In his absence, my mother struggled and we suffered. Our parents eventually split up for good. Our mother moved us back to Canada and we endured one winter of extreme hardship before splintering, including my siblings. I stumbled into a career and also married young. The struggles to provide for my family started when I was still a teen.

Aside from the first 11 years of my life, stress has been a constant. At times, it has been intense.

So, how have I managed? The honest answer is that I don't know. I have never sought professional guidance – but more on that in a moment.

I think that for me, the fact that I am stoic by nature pulls me through. I am also not one to panic unless I am faced with an imminent danger or risk. When faced with a challenge – which is another constant of my life - I usually bull ahead and face it head-on, something for which I have probably become conditioned. Stubbornness helps.

When faced with a formidable challenge or crisis (and if the situation allows), I'll sit quietly and go through the particular issue in my mind, perhaps mapping out a strategy and making a plan to follow. I benefit from both a penchant for acting in the spur-of-the-moment in some situations and the need to plan within others. In the end, I think what has saved me is my capacity to roll with the punches through stoicism and the outright shutting down of my emotions to get through.

There have only been a handful of situations which have left me so overwhelmed that I was unable to cope. When that happens, I either remove myself from the situation, find someone else to do it, or find someone with whom to share the load.

The one stressful situation I can isolate that is fairly recent was the death of my father in August 2018. I was named Trustee of his Canadian estate, and I knew that it would be complex going in. As the oldest of four siblings, I also knew that I would be running both his Canadian funeral and a similar undertaking in the U.S., where he continued to live in the winter months. Once interred, I began making plans for dealing with a vastly disheveled situation involving property and possessions, not to mention the legal ramifications of an estate lacking any forethought on my father's part - his Will aside - prior to his death. There were hornet nests at every turn as I proceeded to map out a strategy for vending the property, handling the sale, and dealing with his scattered possessions. Summarising the challenges I faced would fill the pages of a book. True to form, I proceeded stoically and stubbornly. Luckily, among the many hands available to help me was a surprise hero who swooped in and served as a conduit for clearing his property in time for the sale to close.

But there is more to this story. Three weeks after his death, I received notification that I had been named Trustee for his U.S. estate as well as his Canadian one, which I had yet to begin to tackle. There was no one to pass this on to. I was backed into a corner.

My response was to map out a strategy for both estates, then park the U.S. matter until January 2019. I would focus on the Canadian estate in the fall, which we wrapped successfully. I would turn my attention to the U.S. estate in the New Year – a situation which involved an even greater number of minefields than the first.

I was also working full time, running a side business, and doing volunteer work. I don't know how I made it through, but I did.

There was only one time in my life when I sought professional help for stress involving a particular situation, following strong recommendations from a friend, and it did prove helpful. However, by and large, I have relied on myself for stress management. There is no question I've been lucky and blessed with a stoicism that gets me through. I might have serious health problems, otherwise. I have also learned only recently that asking for help is a sign of strength, not weakness. All this time, I've been looking at it backwards…'

Subhash Jogia's Story - Non-Executive Director and Entrepreneur, England

'Ever since my early teens, I have been seen by others as the thoughtful, self-sufficient, get-it-done, go-to guy amongst my family, friends, and colleagues; someone who keeps their cool under pressure. This has, for the most part, held me in good stead through the many roles I have at home and at work.

However, pressure came with the expectation that I could take on burdens from anybody who came knocking on the door. Who does the Mentor turn to when they themselves need support? Leadership, surprisingly, can be a lonely path, but wise counsel can ensure that it is still a rewarding one.

As an IT executive in global investment for over 20 years, I was fortunate to be afforded opportunities for personal growth and reward. This of course came alongside the stress that comes with managing large organisations across different time zones, where 9-to-5 was more like 7-to-

7, including weekends.

When I look back at how I have coped with stressful situations, I realise that I accumulated (inadvertently) many coping tools, as well as much emotional baggage. Here are a few tools that I wish I had used more often than I did. They are actually more like a football medic's magic sponge and bucket: one swish of the sponge instantly makes the pain go away. Magic!

Be kind to yourself. Mentors or leaders at home and work do not need to have all the answers. Saying to yourself and others that you do not have the answers is incredibly liberating. As a young adult, I could only watch helplessly as my Mum succumbed to a two-year battle with breast cancer. The prodigal son did not know how to save her from pain, nor the words to soothe her last days. Over many years, I channelled that burden into helping my brother, sister and Dad, as well as counselling Mums and Dads whose children were fighting cancer. Finding greater meaning in the challenges we face can really help us tap into the inner strength within all of us, and change our perspective of stressful situations.

Roll with the punches. Not everything is going to go as planned. Have a plan, but write it in pencil and be ready to change it. The ability to adapt to circumstances is far more valuable than a perfectly executed plan. On more than one occasion, I have invested in business ventures that, despite brilliant ideas, exciting technology and a driven management team, just did not deliver. Recognise and respect that there are greater natural forces in play that cannot be planned for. There is incredible strength in softness. Give yourself a break - perfection is not the objective.

Take small steps. One thing that is empowering, energising, and lights a fire to keep going is simply taking the first step, then the next, towards a goal. Overthinking all possibilities and permutations just causes more stress – just go for it! I often draw from my experience of running a high-altitude ultramarathon in the Himalayas: I learned to keep going, and find the joy in each step.

Trust your instinct. As an engineer, I take great satisfaction in analysing, solving problems and taking action. Big projects inevitably involve organisations, committees, and lots of well-meaning but often divergent opinions. Amongst all the mentors I have had the good fortune to have, meditation has proven to be my best friend, especially in the aftermath of coping with my wife's recent sudden heart attack. I do not know if one can be prepared for such an event, but entering a semi-meditative state helped me stay calm, focused, and maintain situational awareness that probably saved her from long-lasting effects or worse. Find a meditation technique that can help you quickly detach from the noise and listen to your inner voice and instincts.'

Earl Lynch's Story – Business Coach, Facilitator and Keynote Speaker, UK
(www.thekairosexperience.com)

'On August 2nd 2019 at 7pm, I was driving to the final wedding rehearsal of my friends Bobby and Nisha, who were getting married on Saturday 3rd. I was their Master of Ceremonies, and I was really looking forward to the event. As I drove towards the church, a phone call came through on the car speaker system. The call that informed my wife and I that my elderly, treasured Dad had just passed away. The pain in that few seconds was excruciating. The days, weeks and months afterwards were extremely hard.

We immediately changed direction and went to the hospital to meet with other members of the family and say our final goodbyes to Dad, who looked so at peace. Almost as if he were fast asleep, he was no longer in that vacant state that dementia affords people of his age. My 89-year-old Dad had gone, and in my heart I felt relieved.

The question then was, what do I do now? Go home and ponder what happened? Or call on a higher power for strength to continue, for strength to fulfil my commitment to a couple who were very much alive and ready to commit their lives to each other?

I decided to go to the church, clicked into 'MC mode' and fulfilled my obligations to Bobby and Nisha. I didn't tell anyone as I did not want to draw attention to my situation, but just before I was about to leave my

Pastor, Bishop T.A. McCalla asked me, 'How's your Father?' I told him, 'He just passed away a few hours ago,' and he replied, 'I'm sorry son.' I said, 'I guess you'll have to be my Dad now,' and there are 101 stories that come from this single statement, but now is not the time.

I did my duty as a Master of Ceremonies. Nisha and Bobby's wedding was a fabulous occasion and it will live in my heart forever, remembering the smiles, the laughter, the love and the joy the whole occasion provided us.

As we fast forward to the end of 2019 and the beginning of 2020, I have achieved a lot as a husband, father of 4, eldest brother, son, Learning and Development Consultant, Master Facilitator, Business Coach, mentor, employer, Men's Ministry Leader, Public Relations Director, musician, basketball enthusiast and friend. I reviewed my entire year, my roles, my goals. It was a tough year, but I enjoyed some very good successes, such as winning some major accounts in business, losing over a stone in weight and appearing on How to Lose Weight Well on Channel 4. I have also built an even stronger, deeper, closer relationship with my wife and family. However, as we careered into March 2020, I was going to need to draw on all my reserves - physical, social, emotional, developmental, and spiritual.

How do I go from 100 days on the road delivering exceptional courses and events to staying at home, in 'lockdown,' still trying to inform, inspire and drive people to take great actions in their lives? Part of me felt like an imposter; however, another part of me said, 'This is what you were put here to do.' This was my purpose; this is what I was created for. Scriptures came to my mind and reassured me of my worth:

'Who of you by worrying can add a single hour to his life? So if you cannot do such a small thing, why do you worry about the rest? Consider how the lilies grow: they do not labour or spin. Yet I tell you, not even Solomon in all his glory was adorned like one of these…. If that is how God clothes the grass of the field, which is here today and tomorrow is thrown into the furnace, how much more will He clothe you, O you of little faith! And do not be concerned about what you will eat or drink. Do not worry about it….' (Luke 12: 25-29)

This will not go down well with everyone - many will stop reading and believe this is just a bible basher, spouting Christian claptrap! However, for me it works, and I have proved it over and over again. Sometimes you think you are in control of your situation and how you overcome stress; I would invite you to think about how to best handle these situations.

How do I cope with my stress? I talk to my heavenly Father every day; I reflect on His word in my bible and I listen for advice and guidance: *'We are hard pressed on all sides, but not crushed; perplexed, but not in despair; persecuted, but not forsaken; struck down, but not destroyed .We always carry around in our body the death of Jesus, so that the life of Jesus may also be revealed in our body....'* (Corinthians 4: 8-9)

Stress and Grief

"Where you used to be, there is a hole in the world, which I find myself constantly walking around in the daytime and falling in at night. I miss you like hell."

- Edna St. Vincent Millay

The stress of dealing with the death of a loved one can be an extremely difficult and heart-breaking experience. It can also quite different from normal, everyday stress. There are several different challenges that need to be faced when one is dealing with grief (Whalley & Kaur, 2020):

Emotions

Grief can evoke similar stressful emotions to trauma, and we may not have the mental capacity or tools to deal with this level of intensity. Many people believe that they lack the resources to cope with grief. Internal conflict is also a common source of stress.

Change

Many people will find that, after the death of their loved one, they may struggle to adjust to a life without that person. Everything may feel and look different. Like one domino knocking down the next, the death of a loved one can cause secondary loss after secondary loss, which means an immense amount of change.

Pressure of Life

The pressure of normal life, work, or running a business can be overwhelming. Ideally, it would be wonderful if after the death of a loved one, people were able to adjust and given a grace period to grieve. The time to grieve will vary from person to person, however it needs to be long enough to allow you to process your emotions, cope with logistical issues, and rebuild your life.

CHAPTER 11: Managing Stress

"There are times when we stop, we sit still. We listen and breezes from a whole other world begin to whisper."

— James Carroll

Throughout this book there have been real-life stories about stress and how the authors have dealt with it. You may relate to some stories more so than others. What have you learned from each story about how you can cope with your own stresses and challenges? First, try to identify the aspects of your life that are causing you stress.

Ideally, in any scenario, a person will choose constructive coping, but people are especially susceptible to negative coping when feeling overwhelmed, confused, stressed-out, or exhausted.

Not so constructive ways to cope with stress include:
- Giving up
- Blaming others
- Defensive coping
- Striking out at others
- Substance abuse
- Avoidance
- Isolating

Stress has been linked to several mental and physical health problems, including cancer, diabetes, heart disease, headaches, ulcers, hypertension, migraine, sleep problems, anxiety and depression. Therefore, those that are stressed should seek out constructive ways to cope.

Some constructive ways to cope with stress include:

Healthy Habits	Time Management	Setting Boundaries	Perspective changes
Keep a stress journal	Say no to tasks you cannot afford to take on	Avoid people who stress you out and create problems	Avoid unnecessary stress
Eat well			Express your feelings
Exercise	Prioritise tasks	Eliminate unnecessary tasks	
Talk to someone	Make manageable to-do lists and stick to them		Put problems into perspective
Meditate or practice yoga		Ask for help and accept it	Practice gratitude
	Plan ahead		
Practice breathing exercises	Take things on one at a time	Seek support	Don't try to control what you cannot
		Process feelings that are holding you back, like anger, shame etc.	
Reduce substance use	Separate your home and work life		Do something you enjoy every day
Get a good night's sleep			Don't catastrophise
Take up a new hobby		Be proactive about dealing with stress	Congratulate yourself for little wins throughout the day
		Disconnect from electronics	

11.1: Coping Strategies

"In all planning, you make a list and set priorities."

- Alan Lakein

This may well be dependent on how you have dealt with stress in the past, and whether these coping strategies have worked or not. Some suggested coping strategies are presented within this section. Your mindset and the kind of lifestyle you live will also determine what works best for you.

Lifestyle adjustments may include:
- Exercising more
- Adopting a better diet
- Meditating regularly
- Sleeping better

Don't Think of Pink Elephants

In 1987, Professor Daniel Wegner from Harvard University found that, when we try to not think of a particular thought, one part of our mind will avoid the thought but another part will keep checking to make sure the thought is not being thought about. It is quite interesting that our minds work in this way. Trying not to think about something makes us focus on it more. This is called Ironic Process Theory (Wegner, 1994). Professor Wegner's work found that the inability to inhibit certain thoughts could be worsened during times of stress, particularly in those who are prone to anxious or obsessive thoughts. For certain individuals, ironic mental processes can result in intrusive thoughts about doing something immoral or out of character, which can be disturbing.

Consider the following exercise. For the next 30 seconds, think about anything that you want to think about. You can think about the most recent movie that you have watched, a funny Instagram post you have seen, a conversation you recently had with your best friend, or what you are going to have for lunch. However, whatever you do, DO NOT think about a pink elephant. DO NOT think of a pink elephant with big ears, a large pink moustache, sunglasses, a fluffy coat, and shiny stockings. Seriously!

Stop! I said DO NOT think of a pink elephant. Have you stopped thinking of a pink elephant yet? You know, the ones in the pink stockings? OK, now 30 seconds is over. How long did you make it without thinking of a pink elephant? I would guess less than 5-10 seconds. You might be wondering how that happened. I mean, when is the last time you have thought about a pink elephant?

Now think of a yellow hippopotamus. Imagine a big, fluffy, yellow, and friendly hippo splashing in the water. Imagine a huge, yellow, custard-eating hippo, laughing, and jumping, and floating into the sky like a yellow cloud. What has happened to your pink elephant now? Your mind could not really think of the pink elephant anymore as it was replaced by a yellow hippopotamus.

People may try and offer help when you are anxious and stressed by suggesting not thinking about the problem, however this does not usually help. Instead, a good idea is to fool your mind by a diversion or distraction technique by giving yourself something else to do and think about, just like the scenario of thinking about the yellow hippopotamus to distract from thinking about the pink elephant. This can be effective, and the more involved the idea or task is the better, because your brain will be more engaged and focused. So, go play a new game on your phone, practice your guitar, take up a new hobby, or help someone else with their own problems.

Reframing Words to Achieve a Better Result

When we communicate with others and ask them to stop doing something ("Don't talk back at me," "Don't drop the plate," "Don't fall"), we often make them do it more. Instead, tell the person what you *do* want them to do. It is much easier for a person to process a positive statement and to understand what they need to do when told specifically.

Brain Wiring

Each time we have a thought or take some form of action, a new neural pathway is created in our brain (The Human Memory, 2020). These neural pathways become stronger when thoughts and actions are repeated, which can then lead to these neural pathways being strengthened or substantiated, almost like motorway routes in your brain. By increasing the strength of these pathways, thoughts and behaviours are magnified.

An idea would be to utilise positive affirmations throughout your life, which will help to help develop more positive and robust neural pathways in your brain when dealing with stress.

Examples of positive self-affirmations are:

- 'I can cope with this situation and I will be strong'
- 'I am brave, and I can cope with challenges and problems'
- 'I am healthy and I have a strong immune system'
- 'I am calm and I come up with solutions'
- 'I have a brighter future ahead'
- 'I am in control of my thoughts and feelings'

Positive thoughts and affirmations can lead to brave behavior; similarly, calm thoughts can also lead to calm behaviour. Focusing on your breathing while retraining your brain using these positive self-affirmations can also help stop the stress response in its tracks. This can help stop the never-ending cycle of negative thinking. The brain cannot differentiate between what is actually real and taking place and what we are thinking about, so if we are reliving a bad memory or focusing on something negative that happened in the past, then we will experience a stress response in our bodies.

Examples of Coping Strategies

The examples listed below are just a few methods to consider. The methods you choose will depend on your circumstances:

- Talking to close friends or family and sharing your thoughts and fears
- Plan your time more effectively
- Delegate or share your responsibilities at work
- Learn to be more assertive
- Never take on more than you can cope with
- Regular exercise

282

- Practice yoga, Tai Chi or any other relaxing meditation
- Avoid using alcohol or drugs as a coping strategy
- Eat a healthy and balanced diet, rich in fruits and vegetables
- Go to a sauna
- Have a massage
- Take a long bath and indulge yourself with scented candles
- Find humour, positivity or absurdity in stressful situations
- Tensing and then relaxing your muscles, starting at the toes, and working up to the neck and head
- Listening to music or relaxing tapes

Music and Therapy

Many people are moved emotionally and physically by music, and it is a wonderful experience for our ears. Music can have an immediate, significant impact on the brain and body, as well as the emotions of a person. When you hear a recognisable song or piece of music, you may become aware of good or bad memories and experiences associated with it. You may sing or cry because of music, or even start dancing. Movies are full of music and songs, which adds to the storytelling or scene. Similarly, you may have a music playlist you listen to for motivation. My go-to motivational tracks personally are '*The Eye of the Tiger*' by Survivor! and the theme song of the 1982 Rocky III movie. You will have your own personal choice of songs that will move you emotionally, and listening to music can help you reduce stress.

Music therapy is classed as a psychological clinical intervention and is usually offered by registered music therapists. Music therapists are able to help individuals and families that are coping with some form of disability, physical or mental injury, or even illness (Dean, 2018). Music therapy is said to be able to "decrease various symptoms of depression, stress, anxiety, Schizophrenia and even Parkinson's, and helps in igniting creativity and improving communication between patient and caregiver." It has also been known to help manage pain symptoms. You do not need to have any experience of playing instruments or creating music to participate; one can simply benefit from listening to music or singing as well. Music therapy can be done one-to-one or in small to medium-sized groups. Simply the act of participating and allowing yourself to express your inner thoughts in an alternative way can benefit you more than you would originally realise.

Art Therapy

Art therapy utilises art media as a form of expression and communication. Art therapy involves a variety of art skills such as drawing, painting, collage, colouring, or sculpting. The good thing is that clients can benefit without having a particularly creative or artistic background. Art therapy can help those that have poor self-esteem, are experiencing stress, anxiety, depression, or fatigue (Fader, 2021). Art therapy can allow you to express your feelings without having to talk it out with a stranger.

Faith and Spirituality

Experiences with faith and spirituality are different for everyone. It can be as simple as a connection with yourself, others and the universe, as well as the meaning of life. Alternatively, it can take the form of religious observance, prayer, meditation, or belief in a higher power. For others, spirituality can be found in mother nature, and for others in a love of music or art. Connecting with faith and spirituality can help reduce stress, and help you deal with the troubles and challenges in your life. Some will state that faith and spirituality has increased their mood, mental health, and well-being, backed by scientific research which demonstrates modest yet promising connections between religiousness and improved mental health. For some, the act of relying on something bigger than yourself, such as God or the universe, can provide comfort in knowing that you are not on your own to handle whatever life throws at you. Some religious practices, such as the washing of hands and feet, prayer or confession, can serve a cleansing and detoxing role on the worries and stresses of each day.

Those that follow a faith or class themselves as spiritual feel a sense of purpose and meaning. This gives them clarity to focus on the most important things in life, like God, family, friends, prayer service and looking after nature and the community. This way of looking at life helps people to focus less on the unimportant things and to eliminate stress. You may also feel more of a connection to the world and an added sense of purpose. You may also feel less isolated and solitary when you're alone, which helps with inner peace through good and hard times. When you pass on control to a higher power you feel a connection to a greater whole, be it the natural world, humankind, God, or the universe (Weyant, 2021). In a sense, you come to accept that you aren't responsible for everything that happens in life. There is a huge burden taken from your mind, as now you can share the burden and enjoy with gratitude all of life's blessings. By being part of spirituality in a church, mosque, synagogue, or temple, you instantly have a network of people around you who you can turn to for support. You will have regular gatherings throughout the year, and be in the company of like-minded people alongside your friends and family. This sharing of spiritual expression can help build strong trusting relationships. People who consider themselves spiritual may be better able to cope with stress and may experience health benefits.

Types of Activity That Can Help to Reduce Stress

Some of the activities that have been shown to reduce stress include:
- Prayer
- Attending communal services
- Reading religious texts
- Listening to inspirational talks
- Incantations
- Incense burning
- Meditation
- Using prayer beads
- Trust in God
- Asking for forgiveness
- Connecting with nature

Using Nature to Help Reduce Stress and Anxiety

We are more familiar with reading and hearing about the harmful effect of too much sun on your skin. But did you know that the right balance can have lots of mood-lifting benefits?

There are several health benefits associated with catching moderate amounts of rays, including:

- Boosts immunity
- Rejuvenates aging eyes
- Improves metabolism
- Boosts vitamin D levels
- Helps metabolism

Both sunlight and darkness can impact on the level of certain hormones in your brain, such as serotonin. Serotonin helps people keep calm, boosts mood, and enhances focus. In contrast, darkness stimulates melatonin which aids rest and sleep. This is the reason why it's so important to have the right balance of both. Too much melatonin or serotonin is not good for you.

A prison in Bueno Aires called Cárcel de Caseros was infamous for only allowing 1 hour of sunlight per day for prisoners. Its construction was under the governance of the radical politician Arturo Frondizi in the late 1970s, during the reign of the dictator Jorge Rafael Videla. It was initially designed as a remand centre for inmates who were awaiting trial, however its purpose was changed and Caseros Prison became a place for locking up political prisoners. The lack of sunlight had a major and detrimental impact on the well-being of the individuals incarcerated there. A similar impact could be seen in individuals who were self-isolating and living in a home with little natural sunlight during the COVID-19 pandemic.

Lack of sunlight will reduce the levels of serotonin, which in turn can lower mood and even lead to depression. You may be aware that, as the days become shorter in the winter, this will mean reduced sunlight and a greater likelihood of seasonal depression as a result. Some therapists recommend the use of phototherapy by purchasing a relatively inexpensive light box (APA, 2021). These boxes radiate light similar to that produced by the sun, which can stimulate the brain to make serotonin and reduce excess melatonin.

11.2: Procrastination

"Habitual procrastinators will readily testify to all the lost opportunities, missed deadlines, failed relationships and even monetary losses incurred just because of one nasty habit of putting things off until it is often too late."

- Stephen Richards

Focus on your 'why.' It is important to keep in mind your reasons for why you are going to undertake any task. It is also important to have a clear insight into and understanding of what you and others will gain from completing the task at hand. If there is no real reason and benefit to complete the task, then there is little motivation, drive, energy or sense of urgency to start.

Stop Catastrophising and Start Visualising the Benefits

An article written on procrastination suggests that one of the biggest reasons some people procrastinate is because they have catastrophising thoughts (BetterLyf, 2021). Some people may make a small concern about a task into something large and overwhelming. This could be because the task is something that they don't usually like to do, such as tax returns or tidying the garage. This then gives the person a reason not to start the task as it could be quite mundane or challenging, so instead they procrastinate. The mere act of putting off the task can markedly increase your stress. It is important to try and keep things in perspective, as the task is unlikely to be as unpleasant as you envision, and you may even start to enjoy doing the task. You will gain more energy and motivation by imagining the benefits of a tidy and organised garage, or take comfort in knowing that your tax returns are complete and no-one can charge you for late submission. These actions can boost self-esteem, and help you to act as a role model for family and friends.

Plan in Your Diary or Calendar

Projects and tasks are more likely to get started and completed if you make a conscious decision to commit to them. This can be as simple as adding them to your weekly or monthly plan of action. These days we have electronic diaries on our mobile phones, so we can easily set regular reminders in our phones or add tasks to a paper diary or calendar. The mere fact of committing it to a certain date or time in a diary helps to inspire action. Tasks and projects may take longer than planned, so allow some flexibility with your timeline. It is also important for keeping focused on the benefits of completing the task, and the consequences of not finishing it by a certain time. This will give you the motivation you need to act.

Create a Compatible Work Space

Your surroundings need to be conducive to a working atmosphere and add to your productivity, not reduce it. Try to distance yourself from distractions such as phones, emails, pets, children or social media. You can add a 'do not disturb' sign on your door, or an out of office message to your email and phone.

Rewards

Reward yourself with a relevant treat that will boost your spirts and cheer you up (such as nice food or watching a film) after you have completed your task. Importantly, make the level of the reward match the gravity of the task.

Decision Making

"To think too long about doing a thing often becomes its undoing."

- Eva Young

The ability to make simple and important decisions will help to reduce stress. We all tend to put things off and say that we will get round to it eventually. We procrastinate for different reasons, possibly because we may fear the impact of the task or be overwhelmed by it. Procrastination can lead to health problems, reduced performance, low self-esteem, and more guilty thoughts that can result from putting off tasks (Lombardo,

2021). Procrastinators can have more sleep issues and experience greater stressful regret than non-procrastinators.

Below are a few of the things that people like you and me may procrastinate about. You can create your own list or start with this one. It's vital to complete this task below or you will find it is just another task that you did not complete.

Hard Tasks	Feelings	Benefits	Easy Tasks	Feelings	Benefits
Paperwork			Feeding yourself		
Expenses			Having a bath		
Cutting the lawn			Brushing your teeth		
Having difficult chats with friends and colleagues			Going to work		
Reading mail or emails			Going to sleep		
Doing tax returns			Doing the laundry		
Exercising			Taking a walk		

Make a note of the thoughts and emotions that you go through next to each task. Once you have completed that, write down what the benefits of completing the task would be. The next column is the no procrastination list, or the list of tasks that you complete without thinking too much about. Once you have completed this exercise, you will become more familiar with the reasons why you may be procrastinating. It will also help you realise the benefits of completing a task, which may help you make quicker and better decisions. You need a good reason to take the actions needed to complete the task, and it needs to be big enough to motivate you to take decisive action.

"My advice is never do tomorrow what you can do today. Procrastination is the thief of time. Collar him!"

- Charles Dickens

Make a Start

For many of us, if we focus on finishing a task then it can slow us down. It could be too far off to think about, so your attention is elsewhere, or the task can seem over-whelming and depressing. At the same time, visualising a finished project can be motivating for other people. Forget about completing the task, just focus on taking the first few steps. Bringing your focus from the future to what can be done right now will help you to eventually finish the task. Start with small tasks at first, then move on to medium sized and bigger ones when you have gained more confidence. This will allow you to build a habit and gain more energy to continue with the task at hand.

Chunking

If you are setting a long-term goal, it is far more manageable to set smaller goals along the way in order to reach it. When you do something in bite-sized chunks, it allows you to have small wins and a greater sense of accomplishment. This helps with positive reinforcement that then motivates you to continue to complete your long-term goal. Chunking a goal down into small bitesize pieces will also help you feel less overwhelmed. For example, when I was writing this book, I did not just attempt to write the whole thing straight away. I first started with an outline, then identified each chapter, figured out the sections within each chapter, and then committed to writing one segment at a time until the book's completion.

A big task can be frightening, which is why so many of us may put them off. By taking that large task and breaking it down into a few small tasks, you can reduce your fear and help yourself get started. So instead of thinking of completing a big project all in one go, think of doing small steps. If you have a task like having to tidy up the yard or garden, plan to start with one corner and collect your tools to do the job. Just focus on the task for 30 minutes, and soon you will get engrossed and want to complete the task. Even if you do not complete it that day, come back to it to the day after. Make the rewards of taking action more immediate, and make the consequences more immediate.

Zeigarnik Effect

The effect was named after a Lithuanian psychologist named Bluma Zeigarnik. This was back in 1927 when she was working with Professor Kurt Lewin (Cherry, 2021). They both noticed the behaviour of waiters in their local café. These waiters remembered incomplete tabs more efficiently than those that had been paid for and were complete. This suggested to them that our brains will continue to hold on to incomplete tasks until they cease to be relevant. This is why to-do list items continually pop up in your head until you write them down. A to-do list appears to calm the Zeigarnik effect by taking some of the pressure off our memory to continually keep tabs on things we should be doing.

The Ivy Lee Method

Ivy Lee was a well-known business consultant. In 1918, a wealthy corporation owner called Charles M. Schwab requested Mr. Lee's help to increase the efficiency of his team and discover better ways to get things done. Schwab asked Lee for a new way of getting more things done in less time.

Lee responded by requesting 15 minutes with each of his senior executives. Mr. Schwab enquired about the cost of his consultancy. Lee responded saying that he would not charge a penny if his idea did not work: however, if the idea was a success, he asked Mr. Schwab to send him a cheque for what he felt his work was worth.

These are the ideas that Lee shared with the executives in order to be a lot more productive, and which may also help you (Peatman, 2021):

1. At the end of each working day, think carefully and make a note of the six most important things you need to complete the next day.
2. Prioritise the items in terms of importance.
3. The next day, focus on the first important task and only move on to the next one once it is complete.
4. If any tasks are not finished, move them to the list for the next day.
5. For each working day for the next 90 days, use this same method.

The method sounded too simple, but Schwab and his executive team at Bethlehem Steel gave it a try. Schwab and his executives were initially very skeptical. However, after 90 days, Schwab was so impressed with the progress his company had made in such a short time that he invited Lee into his office and wrote him a cheque for $25,000, which was an enormous sum of money in 1918 (this is equivalent to $500,000 in 2021).

Ask A Friend for Support and Advice

Having a close, trustworthy friend (other than your partner) who can act as a sounding board is very important for your well-being. You can learn from each other, whether you have a similar goal or not. This way when you get together, you can both support each other as well as hold each other accountable for your goals and plans. Your friend should be able to offer you regular and honest feedback, and you should talk with one another about how you have both been making progress. This will help to motivate you to act on your task.

Ask For Help from Someone Who Has Already Completed This Type of Task

You may be wanting to start a do-it-yourself (DIY) task such as fixing a leak in a pipe that has been dripping for some time and you haven't got round to it. Asking a friend for help and advice can help as you can learn from them or do the task together. Ask yourself what it is that you want to accomplish, and who has accomplished this already? I wanted to write book for many years, but never got around to it. I asked a friend for help and advice who had written several books, and he helped me out. I also reached out on social media, and people were more than happy to offer help and advice. This gave me some energy and focus to make a start, first just writing a sentence, then a paragraph, then a few pages, which then led to a chapter, followed by a few chapters. This then led to editing and proofreading, and eventually to publisher and printers to be sold online. It is important to seek advice and help from others, and build connections through this. Your goals are achievable if you act.

Share Your Goals with Others

Tell colleagues, acquaintances, family and friends about your projects. This way, whenever you see them, they are likely to ask you how you are getting on with your project. Only use this method if you know that this will help you make progress towards your task. You may want to share your task on Facebook, or other social media platforms like Twitter and Instagram. Now that your goal is in the public eye, it will create some pressure to complete your task and ideally give you some encouragement by well-wishers urging you on to complete your task.

Be Kind to Yourself

Rather than beating yourself up for not completing all the tasks on your list, appreciate the fact that you have made a start and give yourself a pat on the back for moving in the right direction.

Find Your Why

It is important to have a strong purpose or reason for why you want to do any task. This way it will be far easier to motivate yourself to take action to do the thing that is important to you and that you value. Find a big enough reason that will motivate and enthuse you to act.

Do Not Seek Perfection

Some people may only start a task when circumstances are perfect. Most of the time in life, situations are not going to be perfect, so be mindful of this type of thinking, and don't let the fear of failure hold you back.

"The mind can go either direction under stress - toward positive or toward negative: on or off. Think of it as a spectrum whose extremes are unconsciousness at the negative end and hyperconsciousness at the positive end. The way the mind will lean under stress is strongly influenced by training."

- Frank Herbert

11.3: Mindfulness

"We use mindfulness to observe the way we cling to pleasant experiences and push away unpleasant ones."

- Sharon Salzberg

Mindfulness is a technique you can learn which involves noticing what is happening in the present moment within your body, mind and surroundings. The key is to notice and appreciate these things without judging anything. You don't have to be spiritual or have any particular beliefs to benefit from mindfulness.

It is important that you allow yourself to be open to mindfulness in order for it to truly work after proper evaluation and a trial period. Once you have done this, you can then decide whether it is suitable for you, or you can go on to try something else more in balance with your personal requirements. Some benefits of mindfulness include:

- Mindfulness aims to help people reduce the chatter of the mind and become more self-aware, feel calmer and less stressed.
- Mindfulness can help you cope with difficult or unhelpful thoughts.
- Mindfulness also asks that you be kinder towards yourself. We can sometimes be our own worst critic and task master.

Headspace is a global leader in mindfulness and meditation, and there is an app as well as online content offerings to support people throughout their day.

Mindfulness requires work like any therapy and practice like any skill. There are several mindful exercises that you can do for yourself and with others, including those described below (Jenita, 2021; Thompson, 2020).

Mindful Breathing

This exercise can be done sitting down or standing up, and anywhere at any time once you have practiced it (Degrandpre, 2021). Choose a comfortable position that you are happy with.

Start by slowly breathing in and out. Each breath should last for approximately 5-6 seconds. Breathe in through your nose and out through your mouth. Do not force the breath, but instead let it flow effortlessly in and out of your body. Allow thoughts to rise and fall of their own accord, and be at one with your breath. Focus on your breathing and push away any other thoughts, such as your to-do list, family, or work projects on your mind. You can use mindfulness apps to guide you through this process, or put on some calming music.

Have a sense of awareness of your breath and how air enters your body and fill your lungs. Listen and appreciate your breathing and how it enters your body as air that sustains your life. Then focus on how the air works work its way up and out of your mouth and its energy is released into the world. This is the early stages of meditation, so enjoy the experience for a minute and continue for two or three more minutes to calm your mind.

Mindful Listening

This exercise involves listening to sounds in a non-judgmental way. This will help train your mind to be less influenced by past experiences and preconceptions. The words and sounds that we hear can have a big impact on how we feel, as they may be associated with past good or bad memories. For example, we may not like a song because it reminds of us of a sad or emotional time in our lives, such as a divorce, a breakup or a bad memory from youth. The same song may have a positive effect on others. The sound of a person's voice, such as a work colleague, boss, or family member, can have a positive or negative influence in your life. The idea of this exercise is to listen with a neutral mind to some music, being fully aware and unhindered by preconceptions.

Ask a friend to share their favourite song or music collection and find one that you are unfamiliar with. Once you have chosen a piece, find a quiet room or put on some earphones on. Now, the challenge is not to judge the music, but allow yourself to get absorbed in it. Listen to the end and give yourself the permission to enjoy it. Pay attention to the melody the variety of instruments as well as any rhythm and tones. If there is more than one voice, try to separate them out, listening intently and becoming fully immersed in the composition. Don't think - just listen with your ears and let the music flow into your whole body. Mindful listening will open you up to enjoying music even more, as well as enjoying the sounds of nature such as birds singing, waterfalls flowing, the voice of a loved one and many more sounds. Many more mindful listening exercises can be found online.

Mindful Observation

This exercise very is simple yet effective and powerful because it helps you appreciate and notice your surroundings, and perhaps see things that you may not have been aware of before. Most days we are busy rushing around trying to get from A to B and back to A again, either at work or at home.

This exercise will help you to be aware of and connect with the beauty of your surroundings, and what nature has offered to you all this while. Focus on a natural object in your immediate vicinity and look at it carefully for a minute or two. This could be a flower, a tree, an insect, clouds, or the sunset. Immerse yourself in the beauty of the natural object - notice the shape, colour, and size. Simply relax into watching for as long as your concentration allows. Allow yourself to be part of the energy that emanates from its beauty and its purpose within the natural world. This level of detailed observation is what helps your mind to relax. Many prophets, saints, spiritual people, artists, and scientists have benefited from this level of mindful observation.

Mindful Awareness

This entails being fully aware of the trivial tasks and rituals that we perform every day such as brushing your teeth and putting your clothes on. Rather than be on auto pilot, be mindful of what you are doing as soon as you pick up your toothbrush or put on your socks and appreciate the simple moment and task.

Mindful Immersion

The objective of this exercise is contentment in the moment, rather than mindlessly completing tasks and achieving goals. For example, if you are cleaning your desk or car, pay attention to every detail of the activity. This can be further enhanced by being fully aware of how your body is able to do the task. Think about oxygen moving from your lungs to the muscles which then move the joints that help you do your task.

Mindful Appreciation

In this exercise, all you have to do is notice 5 things in your day that usually go unappreciated, such as objects or people. Make a note on your phone or diary to check off 5 things by the end of the day. Once you have identified your 5 things, make it your duty to find out everything you can about their creation and purpose, in order to deeply appreciate the way in which they support your life. The purpose of this exercise is to express gratitude, give thanks and appreciate things in your life which were previously insignificant (Furman, 2020).

This may be:

- The road that you use to go to work
- The electricity that charges your mobile phone
- The gardener in the park who cuts the grass
- The warm clothes that you are wearing
- Your muscles that enable you do things and get to places
- Your nose that smells the flowers
- Your ears that hear the birds singing in the park

This will give you an opportunity to think about the relationships between these things and how they play a part in our universe and on planet earth (Thompson, 2020):

- Have you stopped and thought about how different things would be if you didn't have these things?
- Next time, pay attention to the beauty of intricate details which originated from a spark of inspiration from someone else
- How often do you pause to notice and appreciate?
- How do these things benefit you and those around you?

Mindful Eating and Drinking

"Whenever we eat or drink, we can engage all our senses in the eating and drinking experience. Eating and drinking like this, we not only feed our bodies and safeguard our physical health, but also nurture our feelings, our mind, and our consciousness."

- Thich Nhat Hanh

Mindful eating is being fully aware of the food and drink you put into your body, and accepting the taste, sensations, feelings, and thoughts associated with eating (Swartzendruber, 2017). This awareness can extend to the process of purchasing, preparing, as well as serving food. It is important to enjoy and observe how the food makes you feel, as well as the signals your taste buds send to your body, satisfaction, and fullness.

Studies have found that mindful eating can help with your health and well-being. It will help to reduce weight, overeating and binge eating, as well as reduce your body mass index (BMI). Mindful eating and drinking will help you deal with eating problems, reduce anxious thoughts about food, and improve the symptoms of Type 2 diabetes. It can also help deal with anorexia and bulimia.

Mindful Walking

This is being more aware when walking down a familiar street. Look around you and take in the sights, smells and sounds. Do this without judgment and make a note of your thoughts and emotions. If you see someone you know, wave and smile and appreciate what you see.

Mindful Listening

Mindful listening works well by yourself and in a group setting (Ackerman, 2021). Listen to someone with more than your ears - involve your whole body. Open your heart and soul and remove the habit of judging what you hear. We all have internal voices and thoughts, but try to silence them and create inner calm and peace. Listen with real empathy and depth of understanding. Once you have carried out this type of listening for 5 minutes swap roles with your partner and you talk so others can listen.

11.4: Meditation

"A flower does not think of competing to the flower next to it. It just blooms."

- Zen Shin

Meditation is a form of exercise that focuses on relaxation and greater self-awareness. Its purpose is to silence or dampen one's reactions to negative thoughts and feelings (Psychology Today, 2021). The practice is usually done individually, in a still seated position, and with eyes closed.

People who meditate are happier, healthier, and more successful than those who don't. The amazing benefits of practicing meditation and mindfulness are available to everyone who has the time to practice these skills:

- Reduces stress
- Controls anxiety
- Improves sleep
- Promotes better emotional health
- Enhances self-awareness
- Increases attention span
- Lowers blood pressure
- Helps manage pain
- May help with age-related memory
- Can generate kindness
- May help combat addiction

Types of Meditation

The following are six popular types of meditation practice:

- Mindfulness meditation
- Spiritual meditation
- Focused meditation
- Movement meditation
- Mantra meditation
- Transcendental meditation

A mantra mediation is when a syllable, word, or phrase is repeated during meditation. Mantras can be chanted, spoken, whispered, or repeated in the mind (Sen, 2020).

Transcendental Meditation (TM) refers to a specific form of silent mantra meditation. Maharishi Mahesh Yogi created and introduced the TM technique and TM movement in the mid-1950s in India. The TM organisation claim that the technique helps to reduce stress and promote relaxation, awareness, and higher states of consciousness (Transcendental Meditation, 2022).

11.5: Yoga

"Yoga means addition – addition of energy, strength and beauty to body, mind and soul."

- Amit Ray

Yoga is an ancient form of exercise which originated in India over 5000 years ago. Yoga focuses on breathing, strength, and flexibility. Improving breathing techniques boosts physical and mental well-being. The main components of yoga are posture and breathing. Yoga is now commonplace in leisure centres, health clubs, schools, hospitals and in medical practices, but can also be learned at home. Yoga is the practice that aims to join the mind, body and spirit. The word yoga comes from the Sanskrit yuj, which means 'to yoke' or 'unite.'

There are many different styles of yoga, so look for one that will suit you. There are many forms, and so do your own local research and ask family and friends for recommendations (Pizer, 2020). If you are not up for attending a class in person, there are videos on YouTube and Amazon prime, or you can purchase a DVD and learn from books.

Yoga has many health benefits, and can help to (Woodyard, 2011):
- Reduce stress
- Increase muscle tone
- Improve confidence
- Improve breathing
- Build core strength
- Improve flexibility
- Prevent back pain
- Improve posture
- Improve balance
- Improve mental health
- Boost memory
- Improve concentration

Reduce Stress

Any form of physical activity is good for relieving stress. This is especially

301

true for yoga, the reason being that yoga requires concentration, which means less time to worry about daily problems. This helps to lift the burden from our minds. Yoga places importance on focusing on the present moment, and not dwelling on past uncomfortable memories or worries about the future. Yoga helps to put your problems into perspective, and will leave you feeling less stressed than when you started.

Increase Muscle Tone

Regular yoga practice makes you stronger and will also increase muscle tone in your legs, arms, back, and abdomen.

Improve Confidence

Yoga improves awareness of your own body and mind as you learn to accept your body without judgment. Yoga teaches you to make subtle movements to improve your alignment, putting you in better physical and mental well-being. Over time, this leads to feeling more comfortable in your own body, boosting your self-confidence.

Improve Breathing

Yoga focuses on how to take deeper breaths, which benefits the entire body. Many of us take shallow breaths and don't realise that this is not the best way to benefit the body and mind. Certain types of breath can also help calm the nervous system, clear nasal passages, and have physical and mental benefits.

Build Core Strength

Yoga poses can require you to hold your body weight in new ways, such as balancing on one leg or supporting yourself with your arms. Holding these poses and breathing exercises helps build muscular strength.

Improve Flexibility

Regular yoga helps improve the range of motion to tight areas of your body, including your back, shoulders, hips, and hamstrings. Yoga can help with the effects of aging because as we age, our flexibility usually decreases. This is especially true if you spend a lot of time sitting, which leads to pain and immobility.

Prevents Back Pain

Increased flexibility and strength can help prevent the causes of some types of back pain. Many people who have back pain spend a lot of time sitting at a computer or driving a car, which causes tightness throughout the body and spinal compression. Yoga counteracts these conditions.

Improve Balance

Balance is especially important as we become older and muscles and joints stop working as effectively. Improved balance is one of the most important benefits of yoga. Poses where you stand on one leg and inversions are great ways to build the core strength that keeps you upright. Yoga improves balance by strengthening your lower body – particularly your ankles and knees – thereby reducing your chances of falling.

Improve Mental Health

Yoga asana practice is intensely physical. Concentrating intently on what your body is doing has the effect of bringing calmness to your mind. Yoga also introduces you to meditation techniques, such as how to focus on your breath and disengage from your thoughts. These skills can prove to be very valuable in intense situations off the mat, like childbirth, a bout of insomnia, or when having an anxiety attack.

Improve Joint Health

Yoga also helps strengthen the muscles around the joints, lessening their load on the body. The movements and postures in yoga are low impact, allowing you to use your joints without injuring them. Some people with arthritis have experienced improvement in their pain and mobility with regular gentle yoga practice.

Boosts Memory

When you push away stressful thoughts and internal chatter in your head and focus your mind, you'll find that you're able to remember things, concentrate, and perform much better.

Improve Concentration

When you are tired and overworked, you may find it difficult to concentrate on your day-to-day tasks. Yoga has been proven effective at improving your concentration. The practice of yoga helps to clear your mind and calm your senses.

Author's Parting Words

Congratulations! You have reached the end of the book, and read and digested many stories, as well as reviewed some of the psychology and science of stress. You have also discovered how many different people across the world manage stress in a multitude of ways. If stress is still causing you upset, irritability, anguish and anxiety, then this is your opportunity to change how you view stress. Managing stress is a matter of practice. If you stop exercising, you will gain weight and become unfit. The same is true if you stop managing your stress; you will become unfit and out of practice to combat it.

Choose the coping methods that suit your character and find ways of relaxing more often. This new way of coping can reduce your stress burden so you can have a calmer life, which will also benefit family, friends, co-workers, managers, and employees alike.

Managing stress is a day-to-day, minute-by-minute, second-by-second decision. This is your opportunity to take control of the stress, rather than letting stress control you. I know that the journey you are facing may not be easy, and life keeps throwing you lemons. Why not start making lemonade instead of having a sour face of stress? I wish you all the absolute best for your future, no matter what it holds. I know you can handle it.

About the Author

Raj Soren was born in India in a town called Jamtara in the state of Bihar in the early 1960s. Raj and his brother moved to the UK in the 1970 to be with his parents, Dr Dhuni and Mrs. Bhagwati Soren. His father, Dr Dhuni Soren, is a retired General Practitioner and much respected elder statesman from Jharkhand state, and an author himself in Santhal history.

Raj graduated from Manchester with a BSc Honours in Biology and Chemistry, and later gained a Master's in Business and Social Entrepreneurship. Raj is an author of several books, including *Handbook of Medical Sales* and *Little Pocket of Confidence: Ten Golden Steps*. Raj has also co-authored a children's self-help book with his wife, Jyoti, called *Pengin and the Bullies*. Raj also gained a diploma in Life Coaching and has been a sales trainer as well as a manager for top pharmaceutical companies. Raj has over 30 years coaching and examining experience for The Jiu Jitsu Foundation in the UK, and has taught in countries such as Canada, USA, South Africa, Scotland, Austria, Wales, India, Fiji and Russia. Raj has helped thousands of individuals gain confidence through his martial arts coaching, running personal safety and anti-bullying courses with Mind, a mental health charity.

Raj resides in England with his wife Jyoti who is also a Life coach, and their three talented children. Suraj is an Industrial Designer and has worked with Mind, Chandni is an Artist and Graphic Designer, and Lukhi is Fashion Designer and the founder of UnLukhi, a sustainable fashion brand.

Raj believes that having a resilient and adaptable mind helps when dealing with stressful situations in life. Stress is important to help drive us towards our goals, but having too much stress can be debilitating if not recognised and managed before it escalates into anxiety and depression.

This book will help you gain greater confidence to deal with stress and overcome anchors that may be holding you down. This book encourages you to venture out of your comfort zone, and to try ideas shared throughout the book from real life stories.

REFERENCES

Ackerman, C. E. (2021). 22 Mindfulness Exercises, Techniques & Activities for Adults. *Positive Psychology* [Online]. Retrieved from https://positivepsychology.com/mindfulness-exercises-techniques-activities/.

ACO Staff Writers. (2021). Cause of Stress in College Students Guide. *Affordable Colleges Online* [Online]. Retrieved from https://www.affordablecollegesonline.org/balancing-student-stress/.

Active Minds. (2020). Student Mental Health Survey (September 2020). *Active Minds* [Online]. Retrieved from https://www.activeminds.org/wp-content/uploads/2020/10/Student-Mental-Health-Data-Sheet-Fall-2020-1.pdf.

Aldana, S. (2021). 24 Ways Employers Can Manage Stress at Work. *WellSteps* [Online]. Retrieved from https://www.wellsteps.com/blog/2020/01/02/manage-stress-at-work/.

APA. (2021). Seasonal Affective Disorder (SAD). *American Psychiatric Association* [Online]. Retrieved from https://www.psychiatry.org/patients-families/depression/seasonal-affective-disorder.

Axe, J. (2020). How to Practice Progressive Muscle Relaxation for Stress & Pain Relief. *Dr Axe* [Online]. Retrieved from https://draxe.com/health/progressive-muscle-relaxation/.

Bacon, D. (2021). How to Spend Quality Time With Your Wife or Girlfriend. *The Modern Man* [Online]. Retrieved from https://www.themodernman.com/dating/relationships/how-to-spend-quality-time-with-your-wife-or-girlfriend.html.

BBC. (2014). Moving Checklist. *BBC Homes* [Online]. Retrieved from https://www.bbc.co.uk/homes/property/moving_checklist.shtml.

BetterLyf. (2021). How to Deal with Procrastination? 5 Ways to Stop Procrastinating. *BetterLyf* [Online]. Retrieved from https://www.betterlyf.com/articles/stress-and-anxiety/5-ways-to-deal-with-procrastination/.

Career Cast. (2019). 2019 Most Stressful Jobs. *Career Cast* [Online]. Retrieved from https://www.careercast.com/jobs-rated/most-stressful-jobs-2019.

--------- (2012). The 10 Most Stressful Jobs of 2012. *Career Cast* [Online]. Retrieved from https://www.careercast.com/jobs-rated/10-most-stressful-jobs-2012.

Cartridge People. (2019). Workplace Stress Study 2019: The Reasons UK Workers are Stressed and What They're Doing to Cope. *Cartridge People Stress Study* [Online]. Retrieved from https://www.cartridgepeople.com/info/download_file/force/778/618.

Cherry, K. (2021). An Overview of the Zeigarnik Effect and Memory. *Very Well Mind* [Online]. Retrieved from https://www.verywellmind.com/zeigarnik-effect-memory-overview-4175150

--------- (2019). How the Fight-or-Flight Response Works. *Very Well Mind* [Online]. Retrieved from https://www.verywellmind.com.

CIPD. (2021). Stress in the Workplace. *CIPD* [Online]. Retrieved from https://www.cipd.co.uk/knowledge/culture/well-being/stress-factsheet.

Cooks-Campbell, A. (2021). Signs of burnout at work — and what to do about it. *Better Up* [Online]. Retrieved from https://www.betterup.com/blog/signs-of-burnout-at-work.

Curl, I. (2016). 10 tips for writing a PhD thesis. *Time Higher Education* [Online]. Retrieved from https://www.timeshighereducation.com/blog/10-tips-writing-phd-thesis.

Daff, D. (2021). Does your organisation consider mental health and psychological safety a thing? (Part 2). *Zyrous* [Online]. Retrieved from https://www.zyrous.com/blog/does-your-organisation-consider-mental-health-and-psychological-safety-thing-part-2

Dean, C. (2018). Music Therapy Can Reduce Stress and Anxiety. *The Epoch Times* [Online]. Retrieved from https://www.theepochtimes.com/music-therapy-can-reduce-stress-and-anxiety_2713664.html.

Degrandpre, Z. (2021). How to Do Breathing Exercises. *WikiHow* [Online]. Retrieved from https://www.wikihow.com/Do-Breathing-Exercises.

Dias, L.P. (2012). Human Relations. *Saylor Foundation* [Online]. Retrieved from https://saylordotorg.github.io/text_human-relations/s07-01-types-of-stress.html.

EduGeeksClub. (2020). How to Write Your Best Dissertation: Step-by-

Step Guide. *EduGeeksClub* [Online]. Retrieved from https://www.edugeeksclub.com/blog/How_to_Write_Your_Best_Dissertation/.

Eulenstein, E. (2021). How to calm your monkey mind to create the work life you want. *Eulenstein Coaching* [Online]. Retrieved from https://www.eulenstein-coaching.com/post/how-to-calm-your-monkey-mind-to-create-the-work-life-you-want.

Fabrega, M. (2021). 18 Ways to Keep Your Relationship Strong. *Daring to Live Fully* [Online]. Retrieved from https://daringtolivefully.com/keep-your-relationship-strong.

Fader, S. (2021). How Counselling Websites Differ from Traditional Therapy. *BetterHelp* [Online]. Retrieved from https://www.betterhelp.com/advice/counseling/how-counseling-websites-differ-from-traditional-therapy/.

Flavin, B. (2018). Police Stress: 9 Tips for Avoiding Officer Burnout. *Rasmussen University* [Online]. Retrieved from https://www.rasmussen.edu/degrees/justice-studies/blog/police-stress/.

Freudenberger, H. J. (1975). The staff burn-out syndrome in alternative institutions. *Psychotherapy: Theory, Research & Practice*, 12: 73-82.

Furman,G. (2020). Enjoying The Small Things to Improve Your Life In A Big Way. *Live Bold and Bloom* [Online]. Retrieved from https://liveboldandbloom.com/09/self-improvement/enjoying-the-small-things.

Gallup. (2019). Gallup Global Emotions Report 2019. *Gallup* [Online]. Retrieved from https://www.gallup.com/analytics/349280/gallup-global-emotions-report.aspx.

Gregory, C. (2021). Post-Traumatic Stress Disorder (PTSD): Understanding PTSD Symptoms and Causes. *Remedy Health Media* [Online]. Retrieved from https://www.psycom.net/post-traumatic-stress-disorder/.

Hansen, F. (2015). How Do Airline Pilots Cope With Stress?, *The Adrenal Fatigue Solution* [Online]. Retrieved from https://adrenalfatiguesolution.com/pilots-and-stress/.

Harvard Health Publishing. (2020). Understanding the stress response. *Harvard Health* [Online]. Retrieved from https://www.health.harvard.edu/staying-healthy/understanding-the-stress-response.

Higginbotham, D. (2021). Saving money as a student. *Prospects* [Online]. Retrieved from https://www.prospects.ac.uk/applying-for-university/university-life/saving-money-as-a-student.

Hooke, R. (1678). De Potentia Restitutiva, or of Spring. Explaining the Power of Springing Bodies. Printed for John Martyn Printer to the Royal Society, London.

HSE. (2020). Health and Safety at Work: Summary Statistics for Great Britain 2020. *Healthy and Safety Executive* [Online]. Retrieved from https://www.hse.gov.uk/statistics/overall/hssh1920.pdf.

Hunjan, B. (2017). Emotional, psychological abuse – How your self-esteem can be affected. *Counselling Directory* [Online]. Retrieved from https://www.counselling-directory.org.uk/memberarticles/emotional-psychological-abuse-how-your-self-esteem-can-be-affected.

Jenita, T.J. (2021). 8 Simple Yet Effective Mindfulness Exercises for You. *Icy Health* [Online]. Retrieved from https://icyhealth.com/mindfulness-exercises/.

Jones, E. (2012). 'The gut war': Functional somatic disorders in the UK during the Second World War. *History of Human Science*, 25(5): 30–48.

Lagudu, S. (2021). 15 Things That Are Most Important in A Relationship. *Mom Junction* [Online]. Retrieved from https://www.momjunction.com/articles/most-important-thing-in-a-relationship_00497027/

Lanese, N. & Dutfield, S. (2021). Fight or flight: The sympathetic nervous system. *Live Science* [Online]. Retrieved from https://www.livescience.com/65446-sympathetic-nervous-system.html.

LFS. (2020). National Statistics Overview: Labour Force Survey Annual Report Summary 2019. *Northern Ireland Statistics and Research Agency*.

Li, Y., Li, Y. & Castaño, G. (2019). 'The impact of teaching-research conflict on job burnout among university teachers.' *International Journal of Conflict Management*, 31(1): 76–90.

Lombardo, E. (2021). 11 Tips To Overcome Procrastination. *The Minds Journal* [Online]. Retrieved from https://themindsjournal.com/overcome-procrastination/.

Marks, H. (2019). Stage Fright (Performance Anxiety). *WebMD* [Online]. Retrieved from https://www.webmd.com/anxiety-panic/guide/stage-fright-performance-anxiety.

Mayo Clinic. (2021). Job burnout: How to spot it and take action. *Healthy Lifestyle: Adult Health* [Online]. Retrieved from https://www.mayoclinic.org/healthy-lifestyle/adult-health/in-depth/burnout/art-20046642.

Middleton, T. (2019). Burnout is real – here's how to avoid it. *Productivity* [Online]. Retrieved from https://www.atlassian.com/blog/productivity/work-burnout-symptoms-and-prevention.

Miller, I. (2010). The Mind and Stomach at War: Stress and Abdominal Illness in Britain c 1939–1945. *Medical History,* 54: 95–110.

MindTools. (2021). Avoiding Burnout: Maintaining a Healthy, Successful Career. *MindTools* [Online]. Retrieved from https://www.mindtools.com/pages/article/avoiding-burnout.htm.

Ministry of Defence. (2013). Treating PTSD in the Armed Forces: How eye pupil movement is helping Service personnel fight the symptoms of post-traumatic stress disorder (PTSD). *GOV.UK* [Online]. Retrieved from https://www.gov.uk/government/news/treating-ptsd-in-the-armed-forces

Myers, P. (2014). Five Tips, Ideas, and Strategies to Reduce Mom Stress. *Child Development Institute* [Online]. Retrieved from https://childdevelopmentinfo.com/parenting/five-tips-ideas-strategies-reduce-mom-stress/#gs.gk9wsl.

Peatman, B. (2021). How To Be More Productive by Using the Ivy Lee Method. *Prialto* [Online]. Retrieved from https://www.prialto.com/blog/ivy-lee-method.

Pereira, S., Bottell, J., Walker, L., Dzikiti, C., & Platt, C. (2017). The Insight Network and Dig-In: University Mental Health Survey 2017. *The Insight Network and Dig-in* [Online]. Retrieved from https://uploads-ssl.webflow.com/561110743bc7e45e78292140/5adf5c4ce5bf338853d75086_DigIn-Insight-Mental-Health-Survey.pdf.

Perkbox. (2020). 2020 Workplace Stress Survey. *Perkbox* [Online]. Retrieved from https://www.perkbox.com/uk/resources/library/2020-workplace-stress-survey.

Pizer, A. (2020). Most Popular Types of Yoga Explained. *Very Well Fit* [Online]. Retrieved from https://www.verywellfit.com/types-of-yoga-cheat-sheet-3566894.

Pratt, N.D. (2012). Stress in Aviation. *Aviation Knowledge* [Online]. Retrieved from http://aviationknowledge.wikidot.com/aviation:stress-in-aviation.

Psychology Today. (2021). Meditation, *Psychology Today* [Online]. Retrieved from https://www.psychologytoday.com/gb/basics/meditation.

RABI. (2021). The Big Farming Survey: The Health and Well-being of the Farming Community in England and Wales in the 2020s. *The Royal Agricultural Benevolent Institution* [Online]. Retrieved from https://rabi.org.uk/wp-content/uploads/2021/10/RABI-Big-Farming-Survey-FINAL-single-pages-No-embargo-APP-min.pdf

Reynolds, S. (2013). 6 Ways to Reduce Business Stress. *Forbes* [Online]. Retrieved from https://www.forbes.com/sites/siimonreynolds/2013/03/25/6-ways-to-reduce-business-stress/?sh=498ba9806f99.

Robinson, L., Segal, J. & Smith, M. (2021). Coping with a Life-Threatening Illness or Serious Health Event. *Help Guide* [Online]. Retrieved from https://www.helpguide.org/articles/depression/depression-symptoms-and-warning-signs.htm.

Robinson, L. & Smith, M. (2021). Dealing with Uncertainty. *Help Guide* [Online]. Retrieved from https://www.helpguide.org/articles/anxiety/dealing-with-uncertainty.htm.

Scott, E. (2020). What is Chronic Stress? *Very Well Mind* [Online]. Retrieved from https://www.verywellmind.com/chronic-stress-3145104.

Seligman, M.E. & Maier, S.F. (1967) Failure to escape traumatic shock. *Journal of Experimental Psychology*, 74(1): 1-9.

Selye, H. (1965). The Stress of Life: New Focal Point for Understanding Accidents. *Nursing Forum*, 4(1): 28-38. doi:10.1111/j.1744-6198.1965.tb01011.x.

Sen, P. (2020). 5 Benefits of Mantra for Good Health of Child. *The Sound of Silence* [Online]. Retrieved from https://themeditationguides.com/benefits/5-benefits-of-mantra-for-good-health-of-child/

Shadowfax, MD. (2013). Dealing with psychological stress of being a doctor. *Kevin MD* [Online] Retrieved from https://www.kevinmd.com/blog/2013/01/dealing-psychological-stress-doctor.html.

Shanafelt, T.D., Boone, S., Tan, L., et al. (2012) Burnout and satisfaction with work-life balance among US physicians relative to the general US population. *Archives of Internal Medicine*, 172: 1377–1385. doi:10.1001/archinternmed.2012.3199.

Swartzendruber, K. (2017). The health benefits of mindful eating, *Michigan State University* [Online]. Retrieved from https://www.canr.msu.edu/news/the_health_benefits_of_mindful_eating.

Tedeschi, R.G. & Calhoun, L.G. (1996). The Post-traumatic Growth Inventory: measuring the positive legacy of trauma. *Journal of Trauma and Stress*, 9(3):455-471.

The Human Memory. (2020). Neural Pathways. *The Human Memory* [Online]. Retrieved from https://human-memory.net/neural-pathways/.

Thompson, O. (2020). Move From Stress into Mindful Awareness with These Six Simple Techniques. *Oliver Thompson Training* [Online]. Retrieved from https://www.oliverthompsontraining.co.uk/post/move-from-stress-into-mindful-awareness-with-these-six-simple-techniques.

Transcendental Meditation. (2022). Benefits of Meditation. *Transcendental Meditation* [Online]. Retrieved from https://uk.tm.org/benefits-of-meditation.

University at Buffalo. (2008). Impact Of Stress on Police Officers' Physical And Mental Health. *ScienceDaily* [Online]. Retrieved from www.sciencedaily.com/releases/2008/09/080926105029.htm.

Volodina, E.V. (2010). Metamotivation and burnout. *Young Scientist*, 8 (19): 113-115. Retrieved from https://moluch.ru/archive/19/1939/.

WebMD. (2020). What Does Stress Do to the Body? *WebMD* [Online]. Retrieved from https://www.webmd.com/balance/stress-management/stress-and-the-body.

Wegner, D. M. (1994). Ironic Processes of Mental Control. *Psychological Review*, 101(1): 34-52.

Weyant, D. (2021). Aligning Your Higher Power to Connect with The Universe. *Meditation Life Skills* [Online]. Retrieved from https://www.meditationlifeskills.com/higher-power/.

Whalley, M. & Kaur, H. (2020). Grief, Loss, and Bereavement. *Psychology Tools* [Online]. Retrieved from https://www.psychologytools.com/self-help/grief-loss-and-bereavement/.

Woodyard, C. (2011). Exploring the therapeutic effects of yoga and its ability to increase quality of life. *International Journal of Yoga*, 4(2): 49–54.

FURTHER RESOURCES

Below are some helpful resources for the reader if they wish for more information or support regarding a particular issue.

PTSD

Seek out local support services in your country if you are suffering from PTSD:

Victim Support – providing support and information to victims or witnesses of crime (www.victimsupport.org.uk/)

Rape Crisis – a UK charity providing a range of services for women and girls who have experienced abuse, domestic violence and sexual assault (www.rapecrisis.org.uk/)

Combat Stress – a military charity specialising in helping ex-service men and women (www.combatstress.org.uk/)

Relationships

Relationship Advice Websites:

Relate (www.relate.org.uk/) - Relate are said to be the UK's largest provider of relationship support, helping people of all ages, backgrounds, sexual orientations and gender identities to strengthen their relationships.

7 Cups (www.7cups.com/) - 7 Cups is an on-demand emotional health service and online therapy provider that anonymously and securely connects real people to real listeners in one-on-one chats. Anyone who wants to talk about whatever is on their mind can quickly reach out to a trained, compassionate listener through their network.

Family Lives (www.familylives.org.uk/advice/divorce-and-separation/) - Offers core family support services through a helpline, live chat and email support. They offer tailored support around issues such as bullying, special educational needs, and support for specific communities.

Divorce Aid (www.divorceaid.co.uk/) - Established in 1999, this is an independent organisation of professionals giving divorce information and advice to people based in the UK and internationally with a UK connection. They offer legal, family and financial advice.

Domestic Abuse Support in the UK:

Women can call The Freephone National Domestic Abuse Helpline, run by Refuge, on 0808 2000 247 for free at any time, day or night. The staff will offer confidential, non-judgemental information and support. You can also talk to a doctor, health visitor or midwife.

Men can call Men's Advice Line on 0808 8010 327 (Monday and Wednesday - 9am to 8pm, and Tuesday, Thursday and Friday - 9am to 5pm) for non-judgemental information and support.

Men can also call ManKind on 0182 3334 244 (Monday to Friday - 10am to 4pm).

If you identify as LGBTQ+, you can call Galop on 0800 999 5428 for emotional and practical support.

Anyone can call Karma Nirvana on 0800 5999 247 (Monday to Friday - 9am to 5pm) for forced marriage and honour crimes.

You can also call 020 7008 0151 to speak to the GOV.UK Forced Marriage Unit (www.gov.uk/stop-forced-marriage). In an emergency, call 999 (911 in the US).

You can also email for support. It is important that you specify when and if it is safe to respond and to which email address:

Women can email helpline@womensaid.org.uk. Staff will respond to your email within 5 working days

Men can email info@mensadviceline.org.uk

LGBTQ+ people can email help@galop.org.uk

The Survivor's Handbook (www.womensaid.org.uk/the-survivors-handbook/) from the charity Women's Aid is free, and provides information for women on a wide range of issues, such as housing, money, helping your children, and your legal rights.

If you are worried that you are abusive, you can contact the free Respect helpline on 0808 802 4040, or visit www.respectphoneline.org.uk/

Farmers

The Royal Agricultural Benevolent Institution (RABI – www.rabi.org.uk/mental-health-support/) - A national charity that provides local support to the farming community across England and Wales.

Farming Health (www.farminghealth.co.uk/) - This organisation offers support, advice, and information, and contact details for key agriculture charities and other organisations providing crucial support to farming families.

Grief

CRUSE – a UK charity providing support and information for people who have experienced bereavement (www.cruse.org.uk/)

Parenting

The Relate website has good information about parenting teenagers as well as other websites (www.relate.org.uk/). Relate offers relationship advice and counselling. You can also use Live Chat to talk to a counsellor.

Support Line (www.supportline.org.uk/problems/children-and-young-people-support/) - This is a support line providing a confidential telephone helpline offering emotional support to any individual who is socially isolated, vulnerable, at-risk groups, and victims of any form of abuse. This is primarily a preventative service which aims to support people before they reach the point of crisis.

Young Minds (www.youngminds.org.uk/) - This organisation supports young adults and teenagers with poor mental health and well-being, and offers an avenue of support to people who are struggling.

Redundancy and Furlough

Money Advice Service (www.moneyadviceservice.org.uk) - Offers free guidance on money matters such as benefits, everyday money, family and care, pensions and retirement, savings and work.

Solicitors and Lawyers

A Lawyer's Guide to Well-being and Managing Stress, written by LawCare volunteer, former lawyer, and psychotherapist Angus Lyon, is designed to help lawyers to manage stress. It will help you to understand how to recognise the signs of stress in yourself and others, so that you can take action to manage it before it becomes excessive.

Work Stress

The link below contains public sector information published by the Health and Safety Executive (HSE) and licensed under the Open Government Licence (www.nationalarchives.gov.uk/doc/open-government-licence/version/3/).

Yoga

British Yoga (www.britishyoga.com/) - A website with training and course on yoga as well as spiritual well-being, based in the UK.

American Yoga Foundation (www.americanyogafoundation.org/) - A non-profit organisation for the continued development, practice, and teaching of yoga.